SOCIALIST VISIONS

SOCIALIST
VISIONS

Edited by
Stephen Rosskamm Shalom

SOUTH END PRESS
BOSTON

Library of Congress number 82-061155
ISBN 0-89608-169-9   paper
ISBN 0-89608-170-2   cloth

First printing in USA
Production by South End Press
Cover design by Lydia Sargent

SOUTH END PRESS 302 COLUMBUS AVE
BOSTON MA 02116

AJK9279

TABLE OF CONTENTS

CONTRIBUTORS

MICHAEL ALBERT is the co-author of, among other works, *Marxism and Socialist Theory* and *Socialism Today and Tomorrow*. He is a member of the South End Press collective.

ISAAC D. BALBUS teaches political theory at the University of Illinois at Chicago and is the author of *The Dialectics of Legal Repression: Black Rebels Before the American Criminal Courts* (Russell Sage Foundation), which was co-winner of the 1974 C. Wright Mills Prize of the Society for the Study of Social Problems, as well as *Marxism and Domination: A Neo-Hegelian, Feminist, Psychoanalytic Theory of Sexual, Political, and Technological Liberation* (Princeton, 1982).

MARTIN BIERBAUM is an attorney and planner and director of the Urban Studies Program, Rutgers University, University College, Newark. He has written articles for *Shelterforce*, a national housing publication which he helped found. He is currently working on a study of the impact of the Reagan domestic program on the city of Newark as an associate of the Woodrow Wilson School, Princeton University.

JEREMY BRECHER is the author of *Strike!, Common Sense for Hard Times*, and most recently, *Brass Valley*.

LAIRD CUMMINGS is computer systems manager for a non-profit agency in New York. He is active in the Citizens Party.

HERBERT GINTIS is Professor of Economics at the University of Massachusetts at Amherst. He is co-author with Samuel Bowles of *Schooling in Capitalist America* (Basic Books, 1976), and is presently completing a book on the current economic crisis of advanced capitalism, focussing on the relationship between the state and economy. He is a member of the Union for Radical Political Economics, and book review editor of the *Review of Political Economics*.

ROBERT GOODMAN is an urban planner, an architect, and the author of *The Last Entrepreneurs: America's Regional Wars for Jobs and Dollars* (South End Press) and *After the Planners* (Simon & Schuster). He currently teaches urban planning and architecture at Columbia University.

JOAN GREENBAUM, author of *In the Name of Efficiency* (Temple University Press, 1979), teaches data processing and economics at La Guardia Community College (CUNY). She has been active for many years in the Union of Radical Political Economics. She lives with her children in New York City.

ix

ROBIN HAHNEL teaches economics at American University in Washington, D.C. He is co-author of, among other works, *Marxism and Socialist Theory* and *Socialism Today and Tomorrow.*

MICHAEL HARRINGTON is the author of *Socialism* and numerous other works, He is the chairperson of Democratic Socialists of America.

DOLORES HAYDEN is Professor of Urban Planning at UCLA and the author of *Seven American Utopias: The Architecture of Communitarian Socialism, 1790-1975* (MIT Press) and *The Grand Domestic Revolution: A History of Feminist Designs for American Homes, Neighborhoods, and Cities* (MIT Press).

LOIS RITA HELMBOLD is an intermittently employed college teacher and long-term political activist. She is currently teaching American history and women's studies at Ohio State University. She is working on a book on black and white working class women's methods of surviving the last Depression, while trying to make it through this one herself.

ELLEN HERMAN is a socialist-feminist lesbian activist and a member of the South End Press collective.

AMBER HOLLIBAUGH is a writer now living in New York. She is an editor of *Socialist Review*, a member of the San Francisco Lesbian & Gay History Project, and on the National Coordinating Committee of the American Writers Congress. She is a long time organizer and Commie Dyke.

GLORIA I. JOSEPH is a black revolutionary spirited feminist of West Indian parents and views the world from a black perspective with a socialist base. She is currently a professor in the School of Social Science at Hampshire College, in Amherst, Massachusetts, for part of the school year and spends the remainder in St. Croix, U.S., Virgin Islands, where she is active in The Women's Coalition of St. Croix. She is co-author of *Common Differences: Conflicts in Black and White Feminist Perspectives.*

MANNING MARABLE is Professor of History and Economics at Fisk University and is also the Director of Fisk's Race Relations Institute. He is a vice-chairperson of the Democratic Socialists of America and author of *How Capitalism Underdeveloped Black America* (South End Press) and many other books and articles.

TIFFANY R. PATTERSON is Assistant Professor and Chairperson of the Department of African-American Studies at Luther College in Decorah, Iowa. She is currently completing her doctoral thesis at the University of Minnesota on a comparative history of women and slavery, from the perspective of black revolutionary feminism and socialism.

PAULA ROTHENBERG is a Marxist Feminist who teaches Philosophy and Women's Studies and publishes in both fields. An unwed mother, she lives in New Jersey with her children Alexi and Andrea and their father Greg where she tries to find time to grow vegetables and write fiction.

STEPHEN ROSSKAMM SHALOM is a veteran of Rosa Luxemburg SDS at MIT now teaching Political Science at William Paterson College of New Jersey. He is the author of *The United States and the Philippines: A Study of Neocolonialism* (ISHI, 1981).

CARMEN J. SIRIANNI teaches sociology at Northeastern University in Boston, and is active in Democratic Socialists of America. He is author of *Workers Control and Socialist Democracy: the Soviet Experience* (Verso/NLB), and editor with James Cronin of *Work, Community and Power* (Temple University Press). He is currently working on a comparative study of industrial democracy and workers' participation in the twentieth century, East and West, and editing *Critical Studies in Organization and Bureaucracy* with Frank Fischer for Temple University Press..

WILLIAM K. TABB is Professor of Economics at Queens College of the City University of New York. Bill has a radio program on New York's listener-sponsored WBAI and talks frequently before community, labor, church, and college audiences. His most recent book is *The Long Default: New York and the Urban Fiscal Crisis* (Monthly Review).

STAN WEIR is co-founder, with Robert Miles, of Singlejacket Books in San Pedro, California, which publishes books about work by workers and how-to books for a labor force audience. He is a longtime socialist, blue collar worker, and instructor of grievance and collective bargaining courses for shop stewards.

GWENDOLYN WRIGHT is an architectural and urban historian, the author of *Moralism and the Model Home: Domestic Architecture and Cultural Conflict in Chicago, 1873-1913* (University of Chicago Press) and *Building the Dream: A Social History of Housing in America* (Pantheon). She is currently a fellow of the Stanford Humanities Center.

INTRODUCTION
Stephen Rosskamm Shalom

Lucky for the Left capitalism is so grotesque.

It has not been the clear and compelling vision of socialism that has sustained the United States Left all these years. Rather the Left has developed and grown in response to the horrors of contemporary capitalism: the grueling poverty amid immense wealth, the brutal and persistent racism of both North and South, the ferocious assault upon the inhabitants of Indochina, the subordination of the female half of the population, the oppression of gays, the alienation and powerlessness of most everyone, and the emptiness of a social order whose preeminent value is the dollar. It is these evils that have drawn us to the Left and these evils that have sustained the conviction that there must be something better.

This "something better" we have called socialism, but precious little attention has been devoted to elaborating a notion of just what this actually means. Socialists have turned their intellectual efforts almost exclusively to two other tasks: to providing a critique of the existing social order and to developing strategies for changing it. These are tremendously important tasks; and indeed socialists have delivered a devastating indictment of American society and have explored programs for social change in considerable depth. But in a crucial respect each of these accomplishments remains incomplete, for without a better-defined vision of socialism neither the indictment nor the programs are ultimately compelling.

Socialists have demonstrated the failings of capitalism beyond the slightest doubt only to hear from all too many Americans—who are, after all, essential to any fundamental social transformation—that "yes, things are awful, but could any alternative system be better?" This is a legitimate concern. Conditions are abominable in the United States, but they certainly do not constitute the worst of all possible worlds. It is not true that *anything* would be better, and it is fairly evident to most Americans that quite a few things that have gone under the name of socialism have been worse. And the Left's assurance that socialism does *not* mean endless bureaucracy, forced labor, secret police, cannot fully

1

convince the American people without a clear statement of what socialism *does* mean. Likewise, if the Left's alternative strikes people as wholly unrealistic, their acquiesence in the status quo will be inevitable. In short, only a genuinely inspiring and credible vision of socialism can give meaning to the socialist critique of capitalism.

Strategies for social transformation, too, are incomplete without a socialist vision. The road one takes affects the destination one will reach. The question of how to build a new society depends crucially on what the new society is to be. The relationship between means and ends is no doubt complex, but without an agreed-upon end, there is clearly no basis for selecting one means over another.

The Left has thus sorely neglected the essential task of envisioning socialism. Not that we have lacked works dealing with developments in the Third World or the Second World. The history and analysis of these societies is important, but only of limited value for a vision of socialism for the advanced capitalist nations. There is no question here of "American exceptionalism." The problems and potentialities of modern capitalist societies simply are different enough from those of other societies that the experiences of the latter will not provide solutions for the former. This is not to say that we cannot learn much from the rest of the world. Other societies provide many lessons—both positive and negative—that United States socialists ignore at their peril. These lessons, however, cannot substitute for spelling out in some detail what socialism would be like in the United States or other First World countries.

There have been, of course, previous efforts over many centuries to describe socialism and indeed to set up socialist communities. Looking back at the writings of the "utopian" socialists, one is struck by the breadth of their vision even if one must acknowledge that their idyllic scenes seem dated, incompatible with the economic realities and scale of modern society. Out of the Marxist tradition developed a notion of socialism firmly rooted in the productive potential of capitalism; socialism was a possibility now not just for small islands and remote villages but for large industrial societies. At the same time, however, Marxism narrowed the question of socialism exclusively to economic and sometimes political arrangements. The Left's understanding of the world has advanced considerably over the last few decades and we need a vision of socialism that incorporates these new insights—from the women's movement, from the struggle for black liberation, from the experiences of the New Left—while preserving the best of the socialist heritage.

This volume seeks to initiate a dialogue on the Left aimed at developing a vision of a socialist United States, a vision worthy of the Left's multifaceted understanding of modern day society. In recent years there have been efforts to deal with parts of this question and many of these works are listed in the bibliography at the end of the book. This, however, is the first book devoted exclusively to bringing together a number of views of a vision of socialism, informed by the insights and experiences of the past two decades. Six lead articles, each written especially for this volume, attempt to describe six aspects of a socialist United States: race and nationalism, the family and sex roles, the built environment, politics, economics, and the division of labor. This admittedly artificial and overlapping division is necessary for breaking complex and interrelated issues into manageable pieces, though the authors were free to range over into the other areas as they felt necessary. No effort was made to obtain a uniformity of views in the six articles and, as can be seen, the societies they describe are not fully compatible with one another. Two or three responses follow each lead article and expand upon or criticize the proposed vision of social-ism. And the original authors have been given the opportunity for a brief rejoinder. This format flows naturally from the intent of the book to promote dialogue. The book does not presume to be the last word on the subject; there are no final answers here, only the belief that any answers that do emerge must grow out of the most thorough-going debate.

Any full vision of an American socialism must go beyond this book and provide an account of culture, of "international relations" (if "nations" are to exist at all), of the natural environment, among other topics. These have not been omitted out of any sense that they were less important than the six topics dealt with here; there was simply a limit to what could fit in a single book. Again, the present volume must be viewed as only the beginning of the inquiry.

The authors of the six lead articles were asked to try to describe a socialist United States some twenty years or so after socialism has been established. This time frame means that the authors have ignored the questions of "transition," the period immediately following the institu-tion of socialism. The problems of transition are crucial to any program of social transformation, but as with strategies for change one's view on the transition are logically dependent on what that transition is sup-posed to lead to. So it is not at all inappropriate to devote this volume solely to the consideration of the socialist goal, the standard against which strategies for change and transitional programs must be measured.

The twenty-year time frame also means that the authors are not describing a society thousands of years into the post-socialist future, when humans might be wholly different sorts of beings, with different needs and capacities. By depicting a society at a point sufficiently soon after the establishment of socialism, these essays hope to minimize the force of the frequent charge that socialism might be a fine social arrangement for angels, but not for mere mortals.

*   *   *

In the first essay on politics under socialism, Herbert Gintis advocates a model combining representative and participatory forms. Both are necessary, Gintis contends, for socialist democracy, which requires mechanisms both for satisfying and for developing human needs.

In his response, Isaac Balbus faults Gintis for giving undue emphasis to representation and correspondingly minimizing the value of participation. Paula Rothenberg criticizes Gintis' model from a different point of view, arguing that by stressing the importance of the procedures of democracy he ignores its substantive significance.

In the next lead article Dolores Hayden argues that the built environment is not neutral, that capitalist space does not simply become socialist space when socialists take over the government and economy. Certain spacial arrangements are created by capitalism and tend to reinforce capitalism; a very different built environment is needed to promote socialism and socialist values.

Gwendolyn Wright basically concurs with Hayden's view, maintaining that environmental change, and in particular an environmental pluralism, is necessary (though not sufficient) for any socialist vision. Robert Goodman commends Hayden's discussion for avoiding the extremes of "the 20th century high-tech city" and the small rural community. Hayden's vision, says Goodman, provides an appropriate environment for a participatory socialism as well as having important implications for the program and practice of socialists today. Martin Bierbaum, on the other hand, holds that Hayden concentrates her criticisms of the contemporary capitalist built environment on aesthetic failings and sexual oppression, both of which Bierbaum claims are soluble under a liberal capitalism. For Bierbaum, the more fundamental problem—which can only be solved under socialism—is economic inequality, symbolized by Newark or the South Bronx.

In his article, "The Third Reconstruction: Black Nationalism and Race Relations After the Revolution," Manning Marable argues that only a structure of dual authority can enable a socialist United States to adequately satisfy the needs and aspirations of Afro-Americans. In his view, organs of black self-government must co-exist and share power with the institutions of majority rule.

In her response, Tiffany Patterson suggests that Marable's vision pays insufficient attention to the question of sexism. Moreover, she contends that there is a certain lack of clarity in Marable's treatment of class differences among blacks. William Tabb criticizes Marable from a different perspective, claiming that "The Third Reconstruction" seems unduly pessimistic about race relations under socialism.

Joan Greenbaum and Laird Cummings have written a series of fictional letters which illustrate their vision of the division of labor under socialism. The letters describe a society without many of the divisions characteristic of capitalism, but where considerable decentralization allows a local area to define—within broad national guidelines—its own division of labor.

Jeremy Brecher, in his comment on the Greenbaum-Cummings letters, elaborates on the increased opportunity for choice that socialism affords. Social institutions at all levels will, for the first time in human history, be subject to conscious popular decision. For Stan Weir, the letters provide a takeoff point for arguing that society can be run by a network of on-the-job works councils composed of all who work, whether making cars, doing childcare, or writing poetry, and that only such work groups can prevent bureaucratic or elite rule.

Lois Helmbold and Amber Hollibaugh in the fifth lead essay contend that the family must be viewed dialectically: it is an institution that at one and the same time satisfies important human needs and causes immense pain and suffering. A worthy vision of socialism, they insist, must develop ways to meet the needs now met by the family without the hurt and oppression that families currently generate.

In her comments, Ellen Herman expands on a number of themes discussed by Helmbold and Hollibaugh: the relation between reproduction and sexuality, lifestyles, and the authority of adults over the young and the old. Gloria Joseph argues in her response that the new living arrangements that Helmbold and Hollibaugh see as embryonic of socialism have in fact long existed in the black community. The positive and negative aspects of the family, Joseph contends, are different for black than for white Americans.

In the final lead piece of the book, Michael Albert and Robin Hahnel put forward the case for an economic system that functions by "participatory planning." They reject both central planning and markets as being fundamentally incompatible with socialist values.

Michael Harrington replies that Albert and Hahnel exaggerate the problems of market socialism. And Carmen Sirianni claims that they minimize the difficulties in their own model: the excessive meeting time required, the infringement upon individual consumption choices, and, most significantly, the fact that the model assumes—in Sirianni's view—that people will act contrary to their self-interest.

*   *   *

The need to describe socialism has not struck all socialists as self-evident. In fact, four major objections have been raised to the very idea of trying to depict a socialist future. None of the objections, however, is especially convincing.

The first objection holds it presumptuous for a small group of Leftists to design a future society for millions of Americans. But *proposing* a social vision is not the same as *imposing* that vision. People are free to accept or reject any proposal and it becomes reality only if enough people accept it and are willing to work for it. It is no more undemocratic to propose a conception of socialism than to put forward any other public policy recommendation. Certainly any model of socialism drawn up now will be revised many times, perhaps fundamentally, before a socialist society is actually established. Nothing is inscribed in stone. However, a preliminary model is essential as an approximation of the goal toward which socialists direct their efforts.

A related objection argues that it is impossible for socialists writing today to even imagine what socialism will look like far in the future. It is not just a matter of the many years separating then from now but our inability as individuals brought up under capitalism to comprehend the workings of socialism.

Any position that assumes such absolute limitations on consciousness under capitalism runs into logical difficulties, for ultimately even the belief in the possibility of socialism may be part of the false consciousness generated by capitalism. But in any event it is hard to see any alternative to doing the best job currently possible of constructing a vision of socialism. Of course the future cannot be known and of course new possibilities will infuse the human imagination when capitalism's ideological hegemony is ended. But if socialism does not seem a worthy goal from the vantage point of today, why will anyone commit themselves to bringing it about? And to be a worthy goal, capable of mobilizing large numbers of people, socialism must be more than a few vague notions.

The third objection contends that there are too many urgent, short-term tasks that demand the Left's attention; with nuclear war threatening and the New Right booming, theorizing about future societies is—according to this view—misplaced effort. The proper mix of short–range and long–range political work is a complex matter about which socialists may differ; a variety of tactical priorities are compatible with a commitment to socialism. Surely, however, what minimally makes socialists socialist is that (a) they judge the efficacy of their tactics *at least in part* in terms of the impact on the ultimate goal of socialism and (b) they continually point out that short-term measures will not provide full solutions to the problems of capitalism. And both of these defining characteristics of socialist activity depend upon a fairly clear vision of socialism.

A final objection is that envisioning socialism reflects a millenarian orientation, a religious belief in heaven on earth, and in the perfectability of human society. Such a belief is contrary to the inherent fallibility of human beings and the social arrangments they institute and leads, according to the more extreme formulations of this objection, directly to the Gulag.

Fanaticism is indeed a trait to be avoided and if the objection meant only this, it would be unremarkable. But the objection is pernicious if it posits a necessary link between the attempt to develop a vision of a decent society and fanaticism. Envisaging a socialist America does not entail belief in perfection or that socialism, once established, would be unchanging. A model of socialism represents the best social arrangement socialists can conceive at a particular moment. As experience evolves and thinking advances, so too will the model. At each stage the model will serve as a standard against which society can be measured and toward which the Left can strive. And it will serve too as the foundation upon which all the inevitable refinements in the socialist vision will be built.

If anything is a sign of religious zealotry it is "believing" in socialism without rationally working out what it might mean. The point of this book is precisely to initiate a process of thinking about the meaning of socialism, trying to take it from a dreamy haze to a realistic vision.

In 1968 Richard Nixon told the American people that he had a secret plan to end the war in Vietnam. Vote for him and trust him, he urged, but he could not reveal his secret plan until he was elected. For all too long, the Left has done the same as Nixon—promised a better society but effectively kept the details of that society secret. The time has come—indeed it is long overdue—to begin describing the socialist alternative.

I. POLITICS

Lead Essay	Herbert Gintis
Responses	Isaac D. Balbus
	Paula Rothenberg
Rejoinder	Herbert Gintis

A SOCIALIST DEMOCRACY FOR THE UNITED STATES
Representation and Participation

Herbert Gintis*

INTRODUCTION

A viable socialist movement in the United States must demonstrate the compatibility of its vision of social equality with the American democratic tradition.

It is no accident that Americans equate capitalism with democracy. Nearly all advanced capitalist countries have parliamentary democratic regimes, while, with the exception of Chile, no socialist country has had such a form of government. Moreover, American socialists have often identified with models of democratic centralism—whether in Russia, China, or elsewhere—which at the minimum deny the effective and fundamental formal rights of workers and citizens as extended as a matter of course to members of any liberal democratic society. Whatever they may lack, Americans at least have the right to vote, speak, assemble, read, write, and worship more or less as they please.

This comfortable viewpoint rested undisturbed until recently. The communist parties of Western Europe, under the rubric of Eurocommunism, are increasingly critical of the authoritarianism of the Soviet Union, and correspondingly committed to parliamentary socialism. The intellectual supporters of capitalism, under the auspices

*This analysis stems from work I am jointly undertaking with Samuel Bowles. I alone am responsible for any errors.

11

of such elite political groups as the Trilateral Commission, are increasingly insistent on decrying the "excess of democracy," the "ungovernability" of representative institutions, and the infeasibility of extensive civil liberties. In the U.S. powerful support for a criminal code revision apparently aimed at discouraging effective protest activities is reflective of this trend. And nearly all the capitalist countries in Latin America, Africa, and Asia suffer political regimes at least as authoritarian and repressive as the classical socialist countries—and without the socialists' dedication to meeting the material needs of their citizens. Finally, in the U.S. socialists are becoming more and more aware of the need to develop political goals in line with the working class's historical dedication to political freedom.

Socialism can be conceived neither as the shift from private to social ownership nor from atomistic market production to state planning. These traditional views merely envision a transition from private property (capitalism) to collective property (socialism). We shall suggest by contrast that socialism be viewed as the abolition of property in the means of production, not its mere collectivization. This can be understood only if we view the economy as a political system in which property rights confer political power on owners. The abolition of property rights in the means of production involves vesting access to political participation in the economy directly and equally in all workers, communities, and consumers, on the basis of their rights as citizens in the economic community. More generally, socialism in America must be seen as the deepening of democratic practices in the state, and the extension of democratic practices to the economy and family life. For socialism to come about, Americans must come to see it not as the excision of democracy from the state but its expansion in the state and its intrusion into the economy, where the despotism of the capitalist now reigns supreme, and into the family, where male supremacy and authoritarianism regulate the relations among men, women, and children.

We should make clear from the outset our relation to traditional liberal political commitments. On the one hand we embrace the liberal concern for representative and democratic government, arguing that such government must apply not only in the state, but in the economy, the family, and other sites of participation in social life. On the other hand, we reject the liberal conception of politics as an expression of individual interests, in favor of the view that individuals are themselves produced by the political practices they engage in. Just as work produces not only goods, but also transformed people with transformed capacities and social relations, so politics produces people as well as decisions. This commitment will lead us to propose that socialist political structures must be participatory in order to be substantively representative, since the political choices of individuals and groups have only restricted validity unless made by individuals fully developed through their actual participation in positions of decision-making authority.

Our view, while becoming more popular in recent years, is sufficiently novel to require careful statement and substantiation. First, the word "political" is so frequently identified with the state that it is not even obvious what we mean by the politics of the economy and family. Thus our first task will be to characterize politics in such a way that it becomes clear that it is not restricted to one sphere of social life, but is present at all sites of social activity—the state, the family, the economy, education, the scientific and cultural communities, the media, and the like. Supporters of capitalism will not be enamoured of this formulation, because if one looks at the political structure of capitalist production, it is anything but democratic. Nor will supporters of patriarchy be pleased with applying the concepts of politics to family life, where male dominance is imputed to biology rather than to a political structure.

Second, having a concrete conception of political practices, we must then clearly express what is meant by democratic practices in general. We cannot equate democracy with some simple procedural mechanism, such as "one person one vote." Majority rule is meaningless in family life; and in a factory or office it is absurd to think of workers, consumers, technical and administrative personnel as all having equal voting access to all decisions. Nor can we equate democratic organization with the elimination of authority relations, for such relations will persist in any conceivable society, and indeed are beneficial and liberating when subject to participatory and democratic control. We shall take as axiomatic that individuals, as workers, citizens, and consumers have rights which cannot be violated even by democratic process, and that individuals enter into cooperative endeavors as members of functional groups, with distinct but potentially compatible interests. We will then define the social relations of a site of social activity as democratic when not only formal representative processes are applied to these functional groups, but when the political structure mediates among them so as to promote the healthy development and balanced satisfaction of their mutually contradictory needs.

Third, we will explore what this conception of the expansion and extension of democractic political practices would imply, when applied to specific areas of social life. We shall initially apply our conception to capitalist production, arguing that democratic production is not only more conducive to worker satisfaction and growth, but is also more efficient and provides superior production. This is in direct contrast to traditional economic theory, which holds that through the logic of profit maximization, capitalist production is maximally efficient and worker satisfaction cannot be improved without lowering efficiency, wages, and product quality. We will then apply our conception of democracy to the organization of the family, suggesting that in the first case democratic political practices must include not only equal participation of adult family members in decision-making, but an egalitarian division of labor in household work and child-rearing, and equal access of men and women to participation in the economic system. Lastly, we will discuss the political organization of the state in American socialism. Changes in the state will be formally less dramatic than those which we anticipate in capitalist production and the family. For free speech and assembly, due process, multiple parties, universal suffrage, separation of powers, and equal rights of citizenship are among the most democratic forms in our society. Moreover, they were not "given" to us, but were the product of vigorous struggle on the part of workers and citizens over many years of our history—whence the value Americans place on democratic government, however disenchanted they are by its actual performance in practice. Most of the shortcomings of liberal democracy are not due to its own failings, but that of the rest of society. Nonetheless the U.S. state can hardly be taken as a model, for its systematic frustration of popular initiative and lack of popular responsiveness cannot be blamed entirely upon the capitalist economic structure with which it interacts. The organization of the U.S. state—the structural insulation from public accountability of its executive, judicial, and military activities, its hierarchical and bureaucratic forms—is a problem in its own right. The direct democracy of the New England town meeting or other primary group is, if anything, a less auspicious model, for it offers no solution whatsoever to the problem of a democratic interaction of the multiplicity of primary units which constitute the whole polity.

Why should any vision of democratic socialism be possible in the United States? We will close this paper by suggesting that a socialist movement in America would require no radical break with the cultural and political traditions of our society, but rather the selective intensification and maturation of tendencies that already exist. Workers and citizens, in the U.S. as in most of Europe, have struggled throughout the 20th century for what we call "person rights" over "property rights." Our vision of the political structure of socialism derives from this struggle. The demands of social groups for person rights—the right to vote, the right to organize and assemble, the right to a job, equal rights for women and minorities, the right to control one's body and one's personal relations with others, the right to education, health, and welfare—are direct attacks on capitalist property rights. Socialism in America can be conceived and achieved precisely in these terms: the full expression of rights vested equally in persons in all spheres of life, property rights existing only where they are instrumental to the securing of person rights.

In this brief survey we will not claim to have answered all of the questions we will raise, or even to have adequately anticipated the questions which will occur to our readers. Two problems stand out. First, our concept of substantive democracy may be faulted for an inadequate specification of individual and social needs to which such substantive democracy must be responsive. Second, we do not consider the difficult problem of rational economic coordination between democratically run local production units and a centralized democratically accountable economic planning system. The first problem raises difficult, perhaps insurmountable philosophical issues. The second is more easily handled, though an adequate treatment would require a considerably more technical economic presentation than would be warranted here. We do not apologize for this lack of completeness in our presentation. New social orders are not orchestrated in the mind *first* and then played out. Rather, historical creativity results from the interplay of vision and social practice. In this matter we may be instructed by the history of capitalism and of the idea of capitalism. Adam Smith wrote his celebrated, yet still incomplete vision of capitalist society, *The Wealth of Nations*, in 1776, long after the outlines of a capitalist economy had already taken shape around him.

Thus emboldened let us turn to the problem of socialist politics.

WHAT IS POLITICS?

Webster's New World Dictionary defines politics as "the science and art of government." In colleges and universities, departments of "Political Science" and of "Government" are one and the same. Nothing is more common, then, than to consider "politics" as something that occurs in federal, state, and local government—in the state, for short. Yet for a meaningful approach to the politics of socialism, it is critical not to confuse the two. Politics takes place everywhere: not only in the government, but in the economy, the family, and other spheres of social life.

With this in mind, we shall define a political practice. By a practice on the part of an individual or group we mean a conscious intervention into social reality with the object of preserving or transforming some aspect of that reality. For instance an important aspect of social life is work—appropriating and transforming nature. We define an appropriative practice as a practice whose object is the transformation of natural "inputs" into useful "outputs." Similarly, by a cultural practice we mean the reproduction or transformation of those cultural symbols which regulate the communication of individuals and groups, and help people interpret social reality. By a distributive practice we mean a shift in the allocation of goods and services, political power, and social esteem among groups, within the context of the social relations dominant in society. Finally, we think of a political practice as the conscious project of reproducing or transforming those social relations and organizational forms which regulate social life. This essay is about the organization of political practices in American socialism.

Practices take place in a variety of spheres of social life, which we shall call sites. By a site we mean a sector of society with a set of coherent organizing principles, such as the state, the economy, and the family. It is the social relations of a site which make the political practices of individuals meaningful to one another, coordinate them, and limit them as well. The dialectical nature of political practices is indicated by the fact that politics takes the form of transforming the very structures that give it meaning and coherence.

The two concepts of sites and practices allow us to avoid the identification of sites with practices. According to this commonly assumed identification, political practices take place in the state, appropriative practices occur at the site of capitalist production, and cultural practices occur at such sites as the family, the church, and the educational system. Yet it is clear that all practices occur in some form at all sites. Appropriative practices (the transformation of nature) take place in the state, which employs many public service workers, and in the family in the form of domestic labor. Similarly for cultural and political practices. In the state, political practices take the form of influencing the making, changing, interpreting, and enforcing of laws, the framing of social policy, and the control of the process of delivering state services to citizens. Political practices in the economy include the stabilization or alteration of those "rules of the game" which regulate investment decisions, the control of the production process, and wage determination. Political practices in the family include the change or perpetuation of control of sexual relations and reproduction, the division of labor among family members, and the regulation of members' behavior.

The political character of a society is formed by the totality of its political relations, not just those in the state site. If we look at American capitalism, we observe vast differences in the political organization of its major sites. The electoral and legislative aspects of the state itself are of course formally democratic. Decision-making is vested in individuals elected by the citizenry, which has the authority, if not always the power, to alter the social relations and institutional structures of all spheres of social life. Citizens are formally equal and have formally equal access to the political process. Of course this politically democratic ideal is unrealized in several respects. First, citizens are not normally integrated into the political process beyond the level of periodically casting a ballot. Thus there is no democratic mechanism whereby citizens develop their political skills and information through direct participation in governance. Citizens tend to become passive observers of the political process, even where its performance impacts their direct and most immediate community needs. Second, while there is formally "one person one vote," the political power of the rich tends to be far in excess of their voting power, due to their ability to lobby, to finance elections, and to sway voter opinion through the media. Third, in the context of a capitalist economy, voters have only a limited latitude for effective social policy. The electorate, lacking control of investment and production cannot make substantial changes in income distribution, environmental quality, on unemployment and inflation, unless these changes are compatible with "adequate" corporate profits and a "favorable" business climate. The democratic electorate which oversteps these bounds courts capital flight (export of capital), capital strike (non-investment), and massive unemployment.

The rule of capital within the economy is enforced rather more directly: the modern capitalist enterprise is a despotism of owners and managers. Basic civil liberties, such as freedom of speech, information, and due process are not guaranteed, and rarely exist in more than token form. Limited trade union rights are generally granted; other freedoms of association are not. The authority to make basic decisions concerning investment, new technology, product quality and innovation, and the organization of production, is vested in one or more individuals who owe their position to non-democratic appointment, and are completely outside the control of those whom their decisions affect. The hierarchical structure of authority ensures that the wills of the top echelon managers are transmitted down the hierarchy. Lower level workers at best have a modicum of power to resist, never to formulate, execute, and assess alternatives.

The United States of America, we have been told, is a democracy. Yet a basic institution—work—in which most citizens spend half their waking hours half of the days of their lives, is organized in a manner completely alien to the canons of democracy. Why has this been tolerated? In part, no doubt, because so many of those presenting alternative visions of economic life have not questioned the formally undemocratic organization of production, but rather have stressed the need for a locus of economic decision-making at least as far removed from the direct producers as in the modern corporation—in the centralized state bureaucracy. Another reason for toleration, no doubt, is that we live in a liberal society and liberalism does not conceive of politics as applying to the economy at all. The success of U.S. socialism depends, then, on a successful struggle on the level of culture: people must come to see politics as an aspect of all spheres of life, not just government.

But there is a final reason we have not rebelled more decisively against the undemocratic organization of economic life. It is that the organization of power in the capitalist enterprise has been presented by liberals as a necessary by-product of modern science and technology, that there simply is no more efficient way to organize production. If worker control is more efficient, why do workers not just get together, borrow enough money to start a business, and compete the capitalist firm right out of the market? And if workers prefer democratic production, why do they not simply offer their services at a lower wage to a capitalist willing to allow workers to run the firm? Finally, if worker control is more efficient than capitalist control, why would a profit-maximizing capitalist not introduce it of his own free will? And if democratic production is feasible, why is it not used in the existing socialist countries?

These are formidable arguments on the side of liberal capitalism. Moreover, they are basically political, not economic arguments, and must be effectively countered in any attempt to build a democratic socialist movement in the U.S. For a response we must rely on a basic insight of Marxian theory: the capitalist must control the production process in order to extract profits from the efforts of workers. Why would workers expend their creative efforts on behalf of the capitalist unless constrained by his political power? Numerous studies show the efficiency of worker controlled firms. Such firms could presumably compete with capitalist firms, but they lack one essential ingredient: capital! Moreover, such firms traditionally have been viewed with great hostility by traditional capitalist firms, who collude to destroy them, and by banks, which are under great pressure not to finance worker initiatives. As one banker recently said when asked to finance a worker controlled enterprise, "What are we supposed to do, help the monkeys run the zoo?" Most existing "socialist" societies imitate the capitalist political structure of production because they too are regimes geared to the domination of workers and citizens by a privileged political minority. And there are economically successful examples of substantial worker participation in production decisions—Yugoslavia, for one example, and a host of worker owned firms in the U.S. for another.

Finally, we must scrutinize the political structure of the contemporary family. If the political structure of government in the U.S.

is liberal democratic, and that of the economy is capitalist hierarchal, we may depict the family as patriarchal. By patriarchy we mean a system where political power lies ultimately in the hands of the adult male "heads of household." In a traditional patriarchy, the husband has total control over the women and children in the household, including coercive power, extensive sexual rights over the wife, and control of both her reproduction and the domestic division of labor. While women and children may maintain fundamental civil liberties vis-a-vis the state, their personal autonomy passes over to husband and father. Women then typically move from domination by their fathers, to domination by their husbands, and then perhaps to domination by sons and sons-in-law.

Traditional patriarchy, up to the present century, was securely embodied in law, in which the woman upon marriage passed all of her possessions and personal autonomy to her husband. Such is no longer the case. Beginning with the womens' suffrage movement at the turn of the century, the legal basis of patriarchy has been progressively undermined. At present, the patriarchal political structure of the family rests on two non-legal elements: culture and economics. The cultural basis of patriarchy lies, of course, in the ideology of sexism. Men believe in their right to control the household (they "wear the pants") and are supported by parents, friends, police, and judges. Women have been sufficiently intimidated, that they have often refrained from banding together to defend themselves. The economic basis for patriarchy lies in the unequal position of men and women in the capitalist economy, where men have better and more secure jobs with much higher pay, and where working hours and child care allowing a non-sexist division of household labor are not a viable alternative for most families.

The lack of a firm legal basis for patriarchy in no way weakens its impact. In this respect the patriarchal family is in no different a position than the capitalist enterprise. The dominance of the capitalist is not embodied in law; theoretically, workers could borrow capital funds, hire administrators and technicians, and run a "legitimate" business. In fact, the capitalist has the financial and cultural resources, and this turns into effective *de facto* political power in production. Similarly, it is the financial and cultural resources of men which facilitate their political power over women in the household, and hence reproduce patriarchy.

THE GOALS OF SOCIALIST POLITICAL STRUCTURE

Socialists have always faulted liberal economic theory for its instrumental treatment of economic activity. In liberal economics, the purpose of work is the production of goods, and the purpose of goods is consumption. Thus economic activity is evaluated according to its contribution to its material outcomes, without consideration of the effect of the economic process on people. Socialists, by contrast, have stressed that economics produces not only goods, but also people with more or less highly developed mental, physical, emotional, aesthetic, and moral capacities to relate to one another and enjoy a meaningful life.

A socialist conception of politics for America must draw upon and extend those economic insights. Politics not only produces laws and policies, it also produces loyalties, groups, and meanings. Politics produces not only decisions, but also people with a more or less developed capacity for controlling their lives.

Let us continue the analogy between economics and politics for a moment. We know the problem with capitalism as an economic system is not simply that capitalists consume what rightly belongs to the workers. For we could easily put the capitalists on a luxurious tropical island (or give them Southern California), provide them their consumption (a minute fraction of total output), and run a perfectly decent economy without them. The more serious problem, rather, is that in order to secure their profits they dominate workers, engage in socially irrational production, overpower and exploit peoples around the world, destroy communities, and foster a culture inimical to human equality and personal development.

A similar situation obtains in the case of politics. What is wrong with the political structure of capitalism is not simply that it often produces outcomes neither just nor favorable to the vast majority of citizens. Worse, it produces individuals whose depth of political experience and paucity of relevant information renders them barely capable of controlling their lives and regulating their relations with others to the benefit of all. A socialist political system, then, must produce not only democratic outcomes, but in the process reproduce relations among people conducive to their integrity and growth, and favorable to the perpetuation of a democratic and classless society.

We propose two normative criteria for assessing and transforming the political system. Politics must be both formally and substantively representative. A *formally* representative political structure is one which ensures that those entrusted with political power are chosen by and ultimately subject to the will of those affected by the exercise of power. A *substantively* representative structure is a political system that so fosters the growth of interests and political capacities in individuals that the formally representative system leads to the satisfaction of their needs for esteem and well-being. An organization of political life which leads to representative outcomes, but not to the personal development of participants in it, fails to be substantively representative. A participatory political system is one in which active involvement is not limited to those for whom politics is a profession, but is extended in diverse spheres of decision-making to everybody: doing politics is to be as everyday as going to work.

But can participatory and formally representative politics coexist? With the rise of representative government in the 18th century, liberals have consistently argued the basic incompatibility of these two conceptions of democracy. The ideal of participatory democracy, embodied in such historical examples as the slave supported ancient Greek city-state and the early American New England town, have been seen as incompatible with governance in the large nation-state of modern times. Gradually, the concept of representative government has come to mean the rule of experts, with the passive and sporadic affirmation of the represented through the ballot box. In the liberal tradition democracy came to mean simply a procedure for making decisions in governmental matters (one person one vote, Bill of Rights freedoms) rather than a system of popular power.

Similar arguments have been offered by liberals concerning spheres of social life outside the state, for example the capitalist economy. Given the complex technological nature of modern production, many have asserted that the contemporary economic enterprise can be representative of workers' interests in only the most formal sense, while the necessity for expert administrative and technical decision-making renders the project of participatory politics a romantic dream. Thus Daniel Bell, in his influential *Post-Industrial Society*, identifies the most critical problem of advanced capitalism as the unrealistic desire of citizens and laypersons to control a technical apparatus they cannot possibly hope to understand. And even the most progressive of liberals, John Kenneth Galbraith, advises us that in the modern corporation, complexity necessitates control by a scientifically oriented "technostructure" whose power can be limited from without, but not fundamentally restructured in terms of process.

Yet we believe formal representative and participation are not only compatible goals of political organization: they are mutually supportive. In part this flows from the fact that they refer to distinct and complementary aspects of political practice: representative politics captures the effect of political practices on the stabilization and transformation of the social relations of a site—the rules of the game—while participation captures the effect of political process on

the cognitive, emotional, and interpersonal development of participants. The stability and effective working of representative institutions
require that we form a democratic culture. By this we mean the
broadest possible diffusion of political skills, politically relevant
information, and a source of political effectiveness. An indispensible
means to the creation and survival of a democratic culture is a
participatory political system. Yet citizens will not generally participate in political activities in which their concerns and needs do not
count. Hence the mutually supporting nature of representative and
participatory politics.

The opposition between representation and participation has
always been overdrawn by modern liberalism, which posits an
unbridgeable abyss between technical expertise and social values. This
stance was made popular by the "two cultures" theory of the late C.P.
Snow, who argued that modern science makes experts uncomprehend-
ing of qualitative and cultural values, and non-experts incapable of
assessing technical alternatives. But as the German philosopher
Jürgen Habermas has shown in his brilliant investigation into modern
capitalism, this position cannot be sustained. Science itself is applied
through values and interests which are susceptible to confrontation and
change. Its development depends critically upon creative dialogue
between experts and laypersons affected by their practices. Indeed,
one of the positive by-products of participatory political organization is
the development in both experts and laypersons of social relationships
and personal capacities for creative interaction.

What, then, are the criteria for judging when a political structure
is representative and participatory? Judging the latter, we believe, is
relatively straightforward: the balance between direct and indirect
representation must be flexibly determined within the site in question,
according to the trade–offs individuals make between the benefits of
participation, both personal and social, and other demands made on
their time and energy. For this flexibility not to turn into the
self-perpetuation of an elite of individuals dedicated to a life of politics,
of course, provision must be made for rotation of positions, and equal
access to training in political skills must be ensured.

The criteria of a formally representative political structure are
more controversial. A representative structure is a provisional delegation of authority, and hence a recognition that certain decisions are
most effectively reached through a centralized structure, and certain
individuals are better equipped, by virtue of inclination, training,
personal qualities, or clarity of political vision, to make them. Thus one
criterion of representative politics is precisely that it sustain an
adequate system of authority in society. We must avoid certain
populist and anarchist notions that authority and leadership stand in

inherent opposition to the exercise of popular power. A representative system is a particular structure of authority relations, and is judged in part by the strength and quality of the authority relations to which it gives rise. Even the participatory aspects of the political structure, we must stress, are not a *curb* on the exercise of authority but a redirection towards deliberative bodies of persons whose major career commitments lie outside politics.

The second criterion of a formally representative political structure is that positions of authority be filled according to the wills of the individuals and groups affected by their decisions. This criterion may seem uncontroversial, but it in fact corresponds to only one of the two major contending strands of socialist thought dominant in the twentieth century. According to one strand, the goal of socialism is to represent the "objective" interests of the popular classes, whether the members of these classes express these interests or not. Where the majority of citizens are swayed by ideals and conceptions foreign to socialism, it is the role of the enlightened vanguard to represent the objective interests of workers directly by controlling positions of authority. Another strand with equally deep roots in popular struggle is that the goal of socialism is to allow people to control their own lives. According to this conception, a desirable political structure represents not people's interests, but their wills. It is to this latter strand that we subscribe.

Socialists must thus reject the elitist and manipulative yet venerable notion that workers and citizens, infected with "bourgeois consciousness," must be subjected to the wills of the revolutionary political vanguard. Nothing less than full acceptance of the principle that politics ought to reflect the felt needs of those affected will draw the support of the American people, for whom this principle has always been a source of pride and an object of struggle.

But socialist democracy goes beyond the *expression* of needs to confront the *formation* of needs. In order that interests be adequately represented by personal and group preference, certain preconditions must hold. First, the educational development of the populace must be sufficiently high and sufficiently critical to allow citizens to grapple with the complexities and ambiguities of social life in modern society. Second, freedom of information, speech, press, and association must be complete; for only these conditions will allow individuals and groups to possess the resources to bring interests and preferences into coincidence. Third, the political system must be sufficiently participatory that individuals develop the capacities and concrete knowledge to adequately express and transform their needs and interests. These rights, then, are the touchstone of socialist politics.

These principles run counter to the strand of socialist thought for which socialism embodies the interests but not necessarily the wills of the popular classes. According to this strand, free speech, press, and association are "bourgeois liberties" that mask capitalist rule. Of course, advocates of this view say, these freedoms will reappear in the communist society of the future, but may not be tolerated in a socialist society dedicated to the eradication of capitalist remnants, the construction of the material basis for communism. Socialism, they hold, is a means toward human emancipation, not emancipation itself. As such, personal freedom may be tolerated only insofar as it facilitates the transition to communism.

These arguments must be rejected. Indeed, we believe that one of the major reasons for the spectacular lack of socialist movements in the U.S. is the equation of socialism with the suppression of basic human rights. The overwhelming argument against depredations of civil liberties is that where basic freedoms have been abolished, authoritarian and repressive government has invariably resulted; for those who hold political power normally apply their ability to control thought and association not only against "enemies of the people" but against all contestation of their power.

From the point of view of basic social theory, the idea that socialism is a transitional stage on the way to the classless society must be rejected as a holdover from 19th century utopian thought. If "class" is defined in the narrow sense of ownership of the means of production, it is not difficult to conceive of a classless society. But if we think of the broader picture, in which the division of labor in society induces all sorts of cleavages, inequalities, and conflicting interests, we must admit that no presently conceivable society comes close to fulfilling the utopian ideal. We may expect from American socialism a more equal and more humane society, and a more conducive arena for confronting social inequality, but hardly a yellow brick road toward the ideal community for which all sorts of sacrifices in the form of human freedom can be condoned.

But are not these civil liberties in fact bourgeois in origin and essence? Are they not incurably individualist? And are not socialist values the antithesis of liberal individualism? We think not. Basic civil liberties have been demanded by all oppressed groups in Europe and North America since the rise of the absolute state in post-feudal Europe. They are not bourgeois in origin, though they are closely associated with the bourgeoisie, a subordinate group which has gained dominance in society on the basis of an ideology of which civil liberties have been a weighty element. Nor are they bourgeois in essence. Fascism is an example of capitalism without civil liberties, as is modern authoritarian capitalism in the developing countries. And civil liberties are not, we must stress, individualist, even though they refer to individual liberties. They express in the first instance the power of citizens over a potentially dominant state, and in the second, the ability of groups to organize and express their needs irrespective of their position of dominance and subordinacy, popularity or unpopularity, in society.

Finally, socialist values are not the antithesis of liberal values. Even to pose the question this way is to expose its superficiality. The development of ideas, like society itself, proceeds through the dialectical process of the new transcending the old, while conserving in a new context essential aspects of the displaced system. In particular, we shall suggest below that liberalism holds within it two distinct and potentially contradictory value systems, one vesting rights in persons, and the other in property. These contradictory values did not arise by accident or inadvertance, but through the social struggles which have given modern liberalism its form. Socialist values, among other things, conserve and extend the principles of rights vested in persons, while negating rights vested in property insofar as they conflict with personal rights. Civil liberties are among the personal rights so conserved, extended, and deepened. Negated in socialist values are those liberal tenets incompatible with person rights (such as property rights and patriarchal privilege). Also negated is liberalism's systematic denigration of cooperation and solidarity as basis for social action and well-being.

We have established that a representative political structure roots social outcomes in the wills, desires, and preferences of individuals and groups impacted by these outcomes. It follows that political organization must be democratic in the sense of rule by and for the people. But how may we characterize democratic political structure? The traditionally refractory question is rendered even more so when we wish to apply the concept not just to the state, but to work, the family, education, and other sites of practice as well. We may identify two fundamental issues. First, what is the proper organizational form of a democratic polity? And second, how are differences of opinion and interest among participants adjudicated, whatever the organizational form?

Much light has been shed on the first issue by Robert A. Dahl in his lucid book *After the Revolution*. Dahl identifies several forms of democratic governance. First, *primary democracy*, where the body of the whole meets and decides on the issues in question—as in the New England town meeting. When, in order to conserve time and energy, and to bring expertise to bear on certain problems, the political community designates special groups of overseers and decision-makers, we have *committee democracy*. When in place of primary democracy individuals are elected to hold positions of political power, we have *representative democracy*, in which contact between leaders and led can be strengthened through the use of referenda on specific issues. After analyzing these forms of organization, Dahl rightly concludes that none is inherently superior to the others in all situations. The choice of the proper "mix" of organizational forms must be based on the size of the political community, the nature of the decisions they must make, and the time people are willing to spend in political pursuits.

The issue of the correct manner of adjudicating differences among participants cannot be so readily resolved. The first principle that comes to mind, that of majority rule, is surely insufficient. For on the one hand the majority principle runs into conflict with basic human rights. Is majority rule to determine what I read, what I think, what I eat for lunch, or with whom I am permitted to associate? Clearly not. Are consumers and producers to get representation in proportion to number in deciding how long and hard workers should work, or how they are to organize their production process? Should students, teachers, and parents use the principle of majority rule to decide what is taught, and how?

The problem in each case is that the principle of majority rule does not incorporate the principle that individuals and groups often deserve special rights and incur special obligations by virtue of the particular position they hold vis-a-vis the issue in question. This makes it difficult to formulate a general set of sufficient conditions for democratic participation. A set of minimal conditions can, of course, be framed: freedom of information, expression, and association, due process, tolerance of organized political opposition, respect for legitimate individual and group prerogatives, and otherwise equal treatment of the preferences of all participants in the political process.

To go beyond this set of minimal conditions, we must abandon the common view that politics is a zero-sum game, where the gain of one group is balanced by the losses of others. Political practices involve not only distributive gains and losses, but also the personal development of participants and the transformation of the social relations framing their interaction and cooperation. Differences among individuals and groups must be treated not simply as an occasion for compromise, but as an opportunity for the creative transformation of social relations toward the meeting of the needs of all, as well as an occasion for the transformation of needs towards their ultimate harmonization.

Neither an individualist nor a communitarian political philosophy provides the tools for a substantive characterization of democratic political structure such as that just outlined. For individualist political philosophy, politics is the interaction of atomistic, detached, and self-interested persons acting separately or in coalition towards meeting private interests. According to communitarian political philosophy, individuals are themselves purely the product of the political collectivity within which they operate. The goal of politics, in this view, is the social production of individuals whose needs and desires mesh into a collective and functional harmony—a non-con-flictual "group-mind." Neither of these two approaches is either descriptively accurate not a legitimate goal of political life. Indeed, we may say that each is a one-sided expression of the ultimately *dialectical* relationship between individual and community. The dialectical view holds that communities develop through the contradictions among individuals trying to express their different needs and wills, and conversely, individuals become who they are precisely through their efforts to transform their natural and social environments to meet their individually and group-expressed needs.

If we accept a dialectical view of the individual-community interaction, the inadequacies of both individualist and communitarian political philosophies become clear. The individualist position does not admit that the resolution of a political confrontation may be not only victory, loss, and compromise, but also the reassessment of the needs and preferences of participants. For instance, a goal of women's liberation is not only the attainment of equal rights, but the transforma-tion of the consciousness of both men and women towards healthier and more egalitarian relationships between the sexes. These changes may, under certain conditions, be in the interests of men and women alike. The individualist position also does not admit that individual interest may go beyond *self* interest. Yet we know that in a healthy community people, far from being selfish, often act on behalf of the whole, while deferring to and supporting the legitimate demands of differently situated individuals and groups. Since we are the product of the totality of our social relationships, the vitality and integrity of any group will be compromised by the oppression and mistreatment of any other. In a democratic political system, a precondition for the full expression and satisfaction of the needs of any group must be the reciprocal and conjoint expression and satisfaction of all others.

The problem of communitarian political philosophy, by contrast, is its tendency to minimize the inherent contradictions among individuals and groups due to their distinct material conditions and positions in society. This bias is rooted in the communitarian penchant for viewing the individual as a passive reflection of community values and social relations, while in fact people express their individuality not only through, but also against, and with the goal of transforming the communities that influence their being. The healthy community is not one of well-meaning, like-minded individuals, but of individuals who, through expressing their needs, develop not only themselves, but their community and even those whom they oppose. In a democratic community we welcome those who oppose us not only as deserving in their own right, but as ultimate contributors to the accomplishment of our own projects.

Some substantive preconditions for democratic political organiza-tion in a particular site of social practice, then, might be formulated as follows. First, all procedural norms of formal democracy are observed. Second, conflicts of interest between different groups are recognized as rooted in temporary or ultimate differences in the social positions of these groups. Third, the development of the site itself must be seen as the continual process of resolution and re-resolution of these conflicts, the corresponding development of the consciousness and needs of the concerned groups, and the transformation of the social conditions in which these conflicts are rooted.

The goal of socialist political·structure, then, is the extension of formally and substantively representative political structures to all areas of social life. The proper mix of primary, representative, and committee organization must be chosen according to circumstance, to meet this need.

APPLICATIONS: WORK, FAMILY, AND STATE

Our criteria of socialist democracy can only be justified by their ability to contribute to formulating concrete structures in major sites of social practice. In this section we shall attempt to draw out the implications of these criteria for the spheres of social life in which people spend the bulk of their time and which govern their well-being and personal development: work, the family, and the state.

Many prominent 20th century socialists have placed little em-phasis on the democratization of the workplace. In considering the division of labor in production and the hierarchy of authority relations, they have agreed with their liberal and conservative adversaries that little could be done to avoid these "immutable" facts of advanced industrial society. The pace of work could be humanized, safety and health conditions improved, hours reduced, and pay increased; but the capitalist political structure of work life, the trademark of the modern forces of production, would be taken over unchanged in socialist society.

This stance is doubly regrettable. First, it disarms socialist attacks on the despotism of everyday life under capitalism by excepting a key arena—the workplace—from criticism. Second, the orthodox position promotes a conception of socialism in which workers would lack direct control over the production process, and would thus be deprived of their most powerful weapon against an autocratic state elite: the ability to deprive the state of the material resources it needs to carry out its projects.

The orthodoxy is now being overturned. Yugoslavia has long had a viable system of worker democracy (flawed, however, by the authoritarian nature of the Yugoslav state), and important initiatives in this direction have taken place in such diverse settings as China, Spain, Cuba, and Chile. Even in the U.S., there have been many successful, if limited, forays into the realm of workplace democracy. It has been found in virtually all cases that the democratization of work is quite compatible with modern technology, while more beneficial to the health, well-being, and self-esteem of workers. We suggest, therefore, that the socialist commitment to the democratization of production need not occasion concern that its price would be harder work or a lower level of material comfort.

American socialists must make it clear that in the first instance the issue of workers' control is quite distinct from that of "work humanization" or "job enrichment." Workers' control refers to a reorganization of the political, not the technical structure of the enterprise, and involves workers' power to hire, fire, and advise administrative and technical personnel, as well as organize and reorganize the production process, irrespective of the particular tasks they perform in production. Job enrichment and job rotation, team production and the like may be efffective motivational tools but they do not add up to democratic production, a first condition of which is freedom of information, expression, and association, due process, and universal suffrage in a structure of governance controlled by workers with authority over all major decisions.

Formally speaking, then, the socialist enterprise could be organized as a representative democracy, in which workers periodically elect their managers, supervisors, and technicians, but otherwise leave the structure of production unchanged. This is a constructive first step, but it avoids the criterion of participation, which would indicate a significant shift of decision-making practices away from hierarchical authorities, whether elected or not, and towards work teams, committees, and councils, which directly integrate production and governance. Many experiments in worker control indicate that significant improvements in productivity and worker satisfaction result from such a restructuring of production and decision-making, so we could expect a significant reorientation in the direction of primary and committee democracy in a socialist form. This reorientation would be facilitated by better tailoring the process of job training towards preparing workers more fully for governance as well as production. The success of work democratization, however, must not be gauged by the extent to which centralized authority and coordination are abolished. It must be gauged, rather, by the attainment of that balance between participatory and delegated forms of authority which suits the needs of workers.

But would such a political organization of production satisfy the criterion of substantive democracy? To answer this we must identify the basic groups, with potentially divergent interests, involved in the production process. It is easy to envisage ways in which potentially antagonistic contradictions might arise between groups with distinct vertical statuses. For instance, a powerful administrative cadre could act as a managerial clique, creating a political machine within the enterprise which intimidates all opposition into subservience. Senior and skilled workers could use the threat of withdrawal of services to essentially disenfranchise younger and less skilled workers—for example, by apportioning votes according to accumulated "service" to the firm. These violations of substantive democracy can be minimized only by a carefully constructed economic and legal policy in socialist America. The threat of withdrawal of services by a group of workers with special skills can be minimized only by an educational policy which stressed the overproduction of critical special skills. Such a policy not only promotes social equality by facilitating substantive democracy, but allows for forms of job rotation which reduce vertical differentiation in the enterprise, and increases the opportunities for creative outlets through work for workers in general. The intent of such social policies would not be to eliminate the contradictions among vertically situated groups, but to render them non-antagonistic, in the sense that the political organization of the enterprise itself does not become the means of domination of one group over others.

We have dealt first with the democratization of the politics of work because of the formidable problems it presents: a complex division of labor, large size, sophisticated technology, and the lack of existence of social experience with democratic forms. The political reorganization of family life is in many ways much more easily dealt with. The challenge of transforming patriarchy is not fundamentally in politics, but in culture. Even should people opt for more extended, non-exclusively kinship-related family units in the future, the family will still not require a complex division of labor, technologies will be accessible to all adult members, and primary democracy will be the rule.

The democratization of family life requires in the first instance changes outside the family site. First is the elimination of all legal inequalities between men and women in kinship relations, and protection of the rights of women and children. Second, since patriarchy is reproduced in part by the unequal control of economic resources, democracy in the family requires the elimination of economic inequalities between men and women engaged in production outside the home, and the framing of maternity and paternity leaves, providing day-care facilities, and otherwise so organizing work that an equal division of labor in the household is possible.

These changes alone are probably sufficient to ensure greater economic equality in family life. But would it be sufficient to ensure substantively democratic relations between men and women in the household? Probably not. Even in advanced capitalism patriarchy is fundamentally instituted and reproduced through cultural processes, with increasingly little help from the legal system. As the example of existing socialist countries illustrates, even formal economic equality does not change the basic fact that women obey their husbands, do the child-rearing, and perform the bulk of household work in addition to whatever positions they hold outside the home. The problem seems to be that even full equality outside the family site does not directly confront and creatively transform the cultural values that reproduce the sexual division of labor on which patriarchy is based.

Even if men and women are committed to the abolition of male dominance as one aspect of a general movement toward American socialism, it does not follow that cultural orientations will easily be transformed. Cultural values are not imposed from the outside, but are produced, transformed, and validated by the concrete practices people engage in. The cultural values of patriarchy are the product precisely of the division of labor in the household, in which men are systematically distanced from the chores (and satisfactions) of childbearing and housework. Substantive democracy in the household demands a full equality between men and women in these tasks, not necessarily on a family-by-family basis (socialism must not compromise freely chosen individual differences), but as a social norm and average. Indeed, Nancy Chodorow, in her important book *The Reproduction of Mothering*, has persuasively argued that the core characteristics of male and female personality are generated and reinforced by the sexual division of labor in child-rearing and nurturance. Since there are neither biological, technological, nor moral justifications for the current sexual division of labor, it must be confronted and eliminated in the course of socialist development.

The final application of our principles of socialist politics will focus on the transformation of the liberal democratic state itself—the legislative, executive, and judicial branches of government. Since the liberal democratic state is already formally representative, the major issues facing a restructuring of state politics involve increasing participation and ensuring substantive democracy.

Not all socialists will endorse this formulation. Many have depicted liberal democracy as merely a facade for the class rule of the bourgeoisie, according to the principle that the class controlling the means of production must also control the state apparatus which enforces their economic dominance. Indeed, if this view were correct, a fully participatory and representative economic system, by rendering the working class dominant in production, would automatically lead to its dominance in the state. In fact, however, the proposition that to control one site of social practice (e.g., the economy) *automatically* gives a group control of others (e.g., the state, the family), must be discarded. Workers and citizens have struggled mightily for "bourgeois liberties" over the years, and the formally liberal democratic structure in which these are embedded represents at least minimal protection against domination of either a capitalist or a state elite.

American socialism, then, must be based on extending and deepening the democratic procedures already present in liberal democracy. We must be clear that the liberal democratic state has failed to act in the interests of citizens and workers not so much because of the obstacles to substantive democracy represented by its formal structure, but because of the constraints placed upon it by the capitalist economy and in particular by the control of the investment and growth process by capitalists. Thus it is reasonable to expect that the primary obstacle to transforming formal into substantive democracy in the state is the capitalist economy and its attendant pattern of class power—an obstacle which the democratization of economic life will remove. Yet this alone cannot be expected to give full substance to formal democracy. For U.S. governmental structure presents obstacles to democratic rule which cannot be regarded as simple "effects" of capitalist economic structure. U.S. government is substantively unrepresentative because it is insufficiently participatory. Most citizens play scarcely any political role beyond the passive and periodic act of voting. Citizens become alienated from governmental process in much the same sense that workers become alienated from the work process in capitalism. Lacking the participatory experiences through which citizens develop the capacities to control their political destinies, they are susceptible to manipulation by political regulars. Of course this can be corrected in part by the democratization of state production—worker control for state workers. But this still does not meet the issue of passivity outside the area of the special expertise of the state worker.

Many democratic socialists have suggested a vast increase in referendum democracy to increase participation and a sense of political efficacy on the part of citizens. Referenda are indeed a partial antidote to the lobbying power and other forms of political influence of elites in capitalist society. But socialists ought not to overlook other inherent limitations in contrast to representative, committee, and primary democracy. Unlike primary and committee participation, referenda do not allow differing points of view and distinct interests to be reconciled through creative compromise and transformation of needs. And unlike political parties operating within representative governance, referenda tend to be fragmenting, individualistic, and unmindful of the interests of minorities.

For example, it is quite conceivable that the most substantively democratic outcome of a political process is the application of a "package" of social policies, no one of which is supported by more than a small minority of citizens, but which together (as the program of a party) are supported by a vast majority. Thus separate referenda on increased day care, school aid, benefits to the elderly, or occupational safety may each fail, yet a coalition of the concerned groups may strongly favor the measures taken together. Political parties, then, serve both the creative resolution of conflicting interests among groups and the accurate aggregation of the preferences and desires of groups of citizens with fundamentally harmonious political projects. Referenda can be but ancillary to this process, dramatizing cases of gross differences between citizens and their political representatives, and in which the views of the populace are in fact unclear or inadequately expressed.

The major contribution to be made to an increasingly participatory governmental structure, however, clearly lies in a shift of decision-making power from federal and toward local community government. The history of the U.S. government has been that of reducing the political efficacy of the common citizen by removing the power to decide ever further from the individuals and groups directly concerned, and locating this power in centralized structures more amenable to manipulation by economic and other social elites. Certainly the vision of America as a loosely connected federation of self-governing communities is a romantic notion, but there is a great deal of room for a more rational and participatory configuration of centralized and decentralized decision-making. Communities can become the prime determinants of residential and industrial development, when properly articulated with regional and national planning units. Community control of day care, schools, health care delivery, financial institutions, and other institutions geared to local needs could provide for the participatory interaction of community political organization and the worker–controlled enterprise, within the framework of national guidelines promoting national unity, regional equality, balanced national development, and protecting the rights of minorities.

In sum, the achievement of substantive democracy in the state requires first the maintenance of formal democratic procedures in an extended version of their present form. The locus of legislation should be shifted towards increased power for local communities to increase participation and enhance the likelihood of representative outcomes. What is presently called the "executive branch of government" must be reconceptualized as state production, and hence be subject to the norms of worker control in much the same way as what is currently "private enterprise." As such, the provision of state services must be regulated by committees composed of workers, citizens, and elected representatives.

CONCLUSION

There are no ideal political systems. There are only political systems which more or less fully meet the needs of a given people with given historical and cultural traditions, are more or less capable of reproducing and consolidating themselves internally, and are more or less impervious to external aggression. In short, any reasonable candidate for a political system in a socialist U.S. must, whatever its other virtues, be *accessible*, in the sense that we can get from here to there, and *stable*, in the sense that once achieved it will stand the test of time and the stresses placed upon it by our increasingly uncertain world.

We believe the system we have presented in outline will satisfy these conditions. It is a system predicated neither on infinite love, perfect harmony, nor on the abolition of struggle in society. It will not end human suffering, oppression, or inequality. It is not likely to be a transmission belt to the societies dreamed of by the great utopian thinkers of the past. But it will correct some of the fundamental problems with politics in capitalist society while preserving cherished freedoms. And it will provide an auspicious terrain on which people can continue the age-old struggle for a better society.

Most of all this vision of socialism resonates to the progressive beat of a radical democratic America past and present. It is a vision of an American socialism, echoing the demands of workers, citizens, women, and minorities over the few centuries of our existence as a nation. Indeed, the democratic structures we have suggested are not novel forms requiring a radical cultural reconstruction of social life, but represent the logical culmination of a major strand of the demands of popular groups since the inception of capitalism.

ON THE LIMITS OF A "PRODUCTIVIST" VISION OF SOCIALIST POLITICS
A Response to Herbert Gintis
Isaac D. Balbus

For almost a century and a half socialist political vision has been disastrously narrowed by the Marxist theoretical blinders with which it has been encumbered. The assumption that production (objectification) is *the* medium of human self-genesis necessarily gives rise to the conceptualization of politics as either a means through which the prevailing capitalist mode of production is reproduced or as a means through which the transformation to the socialist mode of production of the future will be achieved, i.e., to a purely *instrumental* concept of politics.[1] The master theoretical assumption of Marxism thus forecloses from the very beginning the elaboration of socialist political *principles*. And, in the absence of these principles, "socialist" political practice will either degenerate into the unprincipled search for the most efficient means to achieve anti-capitalist and/or ostensibly socialist ends (as in the case of Leninism) or be guided by principles that are not specifically socialist but, rather, borrowed from other political-theoretical traditions and thus *ad hoc* in character (as in the case of Eurocommunist appeals to the virtues of "pluralism"). It follows that a commitment to socialist political practice that is neither Leninist nor eclectic—a political practice informed by specifically socialist principles—demands a commitment to a re-thinking of Marxist theoretical assumptions.

Herb Gintis deserves a great deal of credit for recognizing both the necessity for authentically socialist political principles and the necessity for the re-evaluation of Marxist theoretical assumptions that is the pre-condition for their elaboration. I find, however, that his effort to elaborate those principles is unsuccessful, in large part because his re-thinking of these assumptions has not gone far enough. More specifically: his residual commitment to Marxist conceptual categories obliges him to *under*estimate both the necessity and possibility of participatory political arrangements and to *over*estimate the desirability of representative political arrangements. A more satisfactory understanding of the merits and limits of these two political arrangements thus requires a far more critical stance toward Marxist categories than he in fact adopts.

Gintis' argument—insofar as I have been able to understand it—can be condensed into the following propositions:

1. Political practice, which he defines as "the conscious project of reproducing or transforming those social relations and organizational forms which regulate social life," "produces people as well as decisions," i.e., it is a medium for the formation and transformation of human needs rather than a mere mechanism for the implementation of already existing needs that are pre-political in origin. This argument signals Gintis' implicit repudiation of the Marxist assumption that the development of the human species is but the development of its capacity for objectification.

2. It follows that authentically democratic (or socialist) political arrangements must be not only *formally*, but also *substantively* representative.
   a. They must be formally representative, i.e., they must "ensure that those entrusted with political power are chosen by and ultimately subject to the will of those affected by the exercise of power." Political decision-makers must be accountable to the felt needs of their constituents rather than what these decision-makers take to be the "objective" interests of those individuals in order that "socialist" decision-making not degenerate into the domination of the former over the latter;
   b. They must be substantively representative, i.e., they must "so foster the growth of interests and political capacities in individuals that the formally representative system leads to the satisfaction of their needs for esteem and well-being." Since all political arrangements "produce," rather than merely implement, human needs, authentically socialist political arrangements must produce genuinely socialist needs, needs that are "favorable to the perpetuation of a democratic and classless society."

3. It follows that representative political arrangements (freed from the constraints of the capitalist environment within which they presently operate) such as those that prevail in contemporary "liberal democracies" are necessary but insufficient for an authentically democratic-socialist politics, and that they must be complemented by participatory political arrangements.
   a. They are necessary in order to satisfy the criterion of formal representation;
   b. They are insufficient insofar as they cannot alone satisfy the criterion of substantive representation. Representative political

arrangements that faithfully register the preferences of individuals who have not developed "the capacities and concrete knowledge to adequately express and transform their needs and interests" will necessarily fail to be substantively representative. And individuals will only develop these capacities and this knowledge "through their actual participation in positions of decision-making authority," i.e., in the context of participatory political arrangements.

4. The "proper 'mix' of organizational [representative and participatory] forms," i.e., the mix that maximally fosters "the extension of formally and substantively representative political structures to all areas of social life," can not be determined *a priori* but rather "must be based on the size of the political community, the nature of the decisions they must make, and the time people are willing to spend in political pursuits."

5. A more participatory mix, and thus a more substantively representative political system, than the prevailing one in liberal democracies such as the United States requires "a shift of decision-making power from federal and toward local community government." "Decentralized decision-making" is the prerequisite for the widespread, effective participation essential for the "personal development" of the citizenry and thus for a substantively representative political system.

At first glance it would appear that Gintis has set forth an argument that equitably balances the respective claims of representative and participatory democracy. But this is not, in fact, the case. A close reading of his argument reveals that a) he has instead overwhelmingly privileged the claims of representative democracy over those of participatory democracy, and b) that the privilege accorded to the former is nowhere adequately defended and is, in fact, entirely arbitrary.

The priority placed on representative democracy is evident, to begin with, in the fact that *both* of the criteria in the light of which the democratic-socialist character of political arrangements is determined invoke the concept of representation, rather than participation: an authentically democratic-socialist political system must be simultaneously formally and substantively *representative* (proposition #2). But this choice of exclusively representative criteria—on which, as we shall see, his subsequent argument and its conclusions entirely depend—is ungrounded in the overriding assumption about the nature of politics from which he proceeds. It does *not* in fact follow from the assumption that politics is a medium of need formation and not just a mechanism of need implementation (proposition #1) that politics should be evaluated in the light of representative instead of participatory criteria. Indeed, it would appear that exactly the opposite should be the case: if politics is, first and foremost, a realm within which human needs are created rather than merely re-presented, one would think that a commitment to political democracy would entail an overriding commitment not to representative, but rather to participatory criteria. I shall return to this problem below. What should be clear at this point is that the relationship of Gintis' second proposition to his first proposition is simply that of a *non sequitur*.

Consider next his argument on behalf of the principle of formal representation. It consists almost entirely in an effort to persuade us that representatives should be bound by the will, or felt needs, rather than the imputed ("objective") interests, of their constituents. Thus it takes entirely for granted precisely what needs to be demonstrated, namely that representative political arrangements *should* exist, i.e., that political decisions that directly affect the life-chances of individuals should not be made by the affected individuals but rather by those whom they elect to represent them. This may, in fact, be a defensible argument, but nowhere in Gintis' essay does he even attempt to make it. Instead, we are obliged to infer what this argument might look like from what he proposes as the criteria for the determination of the proper mix of representative and participatory political arrangements: "the size of the political community, the nature of the decisions they must make, and the time people are willing to spend on political pursuits."

It seems reasonable to assume, then, that one of his arguments in favor of the inevitability of representative arrangements would be that large-scale political communities demand them; that, as the author of the work on which he relies so heavily (Dahl) has argued, "severe upper limits are set on effective participation in 'democratic' decisions by the sheer number of persons involved."[2] This may be correct, but, if so, it leads as easily to the conclusion that participatory democracy demands small-scale political communities as it does to the conclusion that representative arrangements are inevitable. The latter conclusion would only follow from a demonstration of the inevitability of large-scale political communities. But Gintis' assertion that "the vision of America as a loosely-connected federation of self-governing communities is a romantic notion" hardly constitutes such a demonstration.

Similarly, we are entitled to infer from his reference to the willingness of people to "spend time" on political pursuits that he would argue that the exclusively participatory organization of these pursuits would necessarily demand a far greater expenditure of time than people would (or should) be willing to make, and thus that representative arrangements are indispensable. Once again, this may in fact be the case, but at the very least it needs to be argued. It should be noted that Dahl, who does make this argument at great length on behalf of what he calls the "criterion of economy," explicitly emphasizes that the fundamental assumption on which his argument is based is that individuals are "rational" actors for whom political involvement is a means to purely self-interested ends.[3] Given this assumption, it makes sense to view political participation as a "cost" to be weighed against the benefits of other, non-political activities. But this is not the assumption from which Gintis proceeds; rather, as we have seen, he assumes that political participation is absolutely essential for the "esteem and well-being," the "integrity and growth" of the individual, and thus, by extension, that it should not be considered a mere "cost" that should be "economized." This is not to say that individuals will not set limits to their involvement in even the most intrinsically rewarding political activities— there are, after all, other intrinsically rewarding activities besides politics—but rather simply to suggest that a *socialist* case for the inherent incompatibility between these limits and the demands of full-scale participatory democracy would be considerably more difficult to make than the case that is made by Dahl. And Gintis simply does not make it.

Finally, the implications of his reference to "the nature of the decisions they must make" are less clear, but, in the light of what he says elsewhere in his essay, I think we can take this to mean that he believes that the disposition of at least some political issues is inevitably beyond the competence of the ordinary citizen and should therefore devolve into the hands of their "expert" representatives. Thus he argues that "a representative structure is a provisional delegation of authority, and hence a recognition that certain decisions are most effectively rendered through a centralized structure, and certain individuals are better equipped, by virtue of inclination, training, personal qualities, or clarity of political vision, to make them." But this appeal to what Dahl calls the "criterion of competence" to justify the necessity of representative democracy is vulnerable to the objection that the disparities in political competence that it takes as a given are in fact the *result* of the absence of widespread and effective participation rather than an inherent limit to its extension.[4] In other words, Gintis simply fails to take seriously enough his own argument about the way in which political "capacities and . . . knowledge" are generated through political participation and thus the possibility that an equalization of political participation might well produce an equalization of political competence.

In short, Gintis has not even made, let alone proven, a case for the inevitablity of representative democracy. The case that can be inferred from his related remarks, moreover, is far from compelling. And, I should add, a more compelling case would necessarily entail a serious consideration of what he does not even mention, namely the powerful objections to the possibility/desirability of authentically representative political institutions that have been registered by Rousseau, Michels, and the Anarchists, among others.

Now let us examine his argument on behalf of the principle of substantive representation. As we have seen, the importance that Gintis attaches to this principle signals his awareness that politics is a realm of need-formation and that a socialist politics should therefore contribute to the formation of socialist needs. What must be emphasized at this point is that the (undefended) privilege that he has granted to the criterion of representation obliges him to assign this function of socialist need-formation to the structures of *representative* democracy: "a substantively representative structure is a political system that so fosters the growth of interests and political capacities in individuals that the *formally representative system* [my emphasis] leads to the satisfaction of their needs for esteem and well-being." It is true, as we have also seen, that Gintis goes on to argue that widespread political participation is essential for the "growth of interests and political capacities in individuals" and thus that it is an "indispensable means" to the end of a substantively representative system. But it nevertheless remains a means to an external end, rather than an end in itself: "the proper mix of primary, representative, and committee organization must be chosen according to circumstance to meet this need" of substantive (as well as formal) representation. And, once he has relegated participatory democracy to this instrumental function, he can of course face with equanimity the fact that the "circumstances" to which he alludes—the inevitability of large-scale political communities, complex decisions that "certain individuals are better equipped . . . to make," and significant limits on the time and energy available for "political pursuits"—all militate against its extension. Thus what appears, at first blush, as an argument on behalf of a "balanced" partnership between representative and participatory democracy is in fact an argument that assigns to the latter the role of a decidedly junior partner. And, like most junior partners, its future is, at best, uncertain.

Further reflection reveals that this effort to subordinate participatory democracy to representative democracy through the concept of "substantive representation" is beset by a profound internal contradiction. According to the logic of this concept, participatory democracy is essential for the "growth of interests and . . . capacities," i.e., the development of individuals, without which the formally representative system will be unable to ensure the "satisfaction of their needs for esteem and well-being," i.e., their development. Now, if participatory politics is *already* conducive to the development of individuals, is there any reason to assign this function of enhancing individual development to representative politics, save for the fact that the inevitability and primacy of the latter has been assumed (but not, as we have seen, established) from the very outset? The only possible answer is that political participation is a necessary but insufficient medium for individual development, and that it must be complemented by the distinctive contribution to individual development that representatives alone are able to make.[5] But the assumption that representatives are uniquely able to make a contribution to the development of their constituents that the latter are unable to make for themselves implies that representatives are in a position to know something abut the requisites of individual development of which the individuals themselves are unaware, i.e., it implies knowledge of the "real" needs or "objective" interests of their constituents. Gintis has informed us, however, that "a desirable political structure represents not people's interests, but their wills" because the consequences of "objective" interest representation are inherently "elitist and manipulative." Thus the only argument that can save the idea of a substantively representative, formally representative system from redundancy is one that—by his own indirect admission—makes this idea repressive.[6]

The difficulties that plague the concept of substantive representation are, at bottom, merely the difficulties of a concept of politics that has been distorted by the "mirror of production." As we have seen, Gintis defines politics as "the conscious project of *reproducing* or *transforming* [my emphasis] those social relations and organizational forms which regulate social life." Thus, although his insistence that politics is an important realm of human need–formation indicates his theoretical distance from an orthodox Marxism that consigns need-formation exclusively to the realm of production, he nevertheless retains a *productivist* model of the way in which human needs are formed within the political realm: just as Marx conceptualizes "natural forms" as the objects of the transformative projects of laboring subjects, so Gintis conceptualizes "social relations and organizational forms" as the objects of the transformative (or reproductive) projects of political subjects. This conceptualization, in turn, allows him to assign "developmental" functions to representatives whose decision-making is understood to transform the "social relations and organizational forms" of their constituents. If, in contrast, we were to repudiate his subordination of politics to the model of *making* and conceptualize it instead as collective interaction within which individual development is contingent on a process of mutual recognition—in which the self only develops insofar as it is recognized by another self whose selfhood it likewise recognizes—then we would be obliged to conclude that developmental functions can only be assigned to the process of participation itself. It is, after all, only through participation that mutual recognition can be achieved. But this conclusion leads, of course, to a commitment to the primacy of participatory democracy over representative democracy. To put this another way, Gintis is only able to reconcile his assumption that politics is a realm of need-formation with his commitment to the primacy of representative democracy over participatory democracy at the cost of a productivist model of politics that mystifies rather than clarifies the way in which individual needs are—or should be—formed in collective interaction.[7]

There is yet another way in which his commitment to Marxist categories limits his political vision. I have already referred to his recognition that the possibilities for widespread participatory democracy are predicated on a radical decentralization of decision-making "from federal and toward local community government." What Gintis fails to recognize, however, is that meaningful political decentralization demands an equally radical demographic decentralization—the destruction of the megalopolis and the creation of relatively self-sufficient small-scale communities—that is, in turn, contingent on a profound technological transformation from large-scale, centralized, energy-depleting technologies to small-scale, decentralized, "alternative" technologies. As Ivan Illich has argued, "participatory democracy postulates low energy technology"[8] in particular and alternative technology in general. But Gintis appears to endorse "modern technology" without qualification, and, in any event, any preference for alternative technology that he *might* profess cannot, I argue elsewhere, be reconciled with his underlying Marxist commitment to the "appropriation and transformation of nature," i.e., to a practice that treats non-human nature as a pure object of unlimited human manipulation rather than as a "subject" in its own right whose claims human subjects are obliged to respect.[9] A primary commitment to widespread, meaningful participatory democracy thus demands that we call into question not only the extension of Marx's fundamental category of objectification to the realm of politics but also objectification itself as a mode of interaction between the human and non-human elements of the ecosystem as a whole. It is the failure of Gintis to call this category into question, I would suggest, that ultimately accounts for his failure to make participatory democratic politics anything more than an important adjunct to representative political arrangements.

Finally, Gintis is to be commended for his recognition that a commitment to democracy demands the elimination of patriarchy and the "sexual division of labor in child-rearing and nurturance" in which it is rooted. What he does not seem to understand, however, is that this transformation will undoubtedly eliminate the very "objectification" of nature to which he is also committed. Elsewhere I demonstrate that the symbolization of nature as an object that must be dominated by an ostensibly separate subject is generated in the nuclear form of (what Dinnerstein calls) "mother-monopolized" child-rearing, and that the emergence of authentic forms of shared parenting establishes the necessary unconscious basis for a post-objectifying symbolization of nature and the technologies that are its materialization.[10] The struggle against patriarchy and the form of child-rearing that reproduces it is as essential to the struggle for alternative technology as the struggle for alternative technology is to the struggle for participatory democracy. The removal of Marxist theoretical blinders thus makes possible not only an enhanced appreciation of the necessity of participatory democracy but also, and perhaps for the first time, an understanding of both the psychological and the technological requisites for its eventual realization.

NOTES

1. See my *Marxism and Domination: A NeoHegelian, Feminist, Psychoanalytic Theory of Sexual, Political and Technological Liberation* (Princeton, New Jersey: Princeton University Press, 1982).

2. Robert A. Dahl, *After the Revolution?* (New Haven: Yale University Press, 1970), p. 143.

3. *Ibid.*, pp. 12–13.

4. See Carole Pateman, *Participation and Democratic Theory* (Cambridge: Cambridge University Press, 1970), p. 25.

5. This interpretation is confirmed by Gintis' insistence that the "capitalist economy" is the "primary obstacle to transforming formal into substantive democracy in the state." It follows from this thesis that after the economy has been transformed, and even in the absence of widespread political participation, we should expect representative structures to be far more substantively representative than they are now. This can only mean that there are other means of enhancing substantive representation besides participatory democracy. If, in other words, "most of the shortcomings of liberal democracy are not due to its own failings, but that of the rest of society," then the absence of participatory democracy must be less significant than the presence of capitalist "environmental" factors in making the formally representative system less substantively representative than it otherwise would be.

6. It is, of course, possible to argue that representatives are able uniquely to contribute to the development of their constituents insofar as they alone are in a position to implement the preferences of the latter. But if

this is all that substantive representation means then it is not different from formal representation, in which case the former concept is entirely redundant.

7. In "Communication and Politics: Marxism and the Problem of Liberal Democracy," *Socialist Review* no. 50/51 (March-June 1980), 189–232, Gintis himself argues that the intersubjective dialectic of mutual recognition is constitutive of "self-identity" (208) and that politics is "the paradigm of subject-subject relations." But the umbilical connection between this conception of politics and the primacy of participatory democracy is not explored, and, in the present essay, this conception of politics is inexplicably dropped in favor of the very "subject-object," or productivist, conception of politics that Gintis had earlier deplored.

8. Cited in Stephen Lyons, ed., *Sun! A Handbook for the Solar Decade* (San Francisco, Friends of the Earth, 1978), p. 51.

9. See note 1.

10. *Ibid.*

FORM VERSUS SUBSTANCE IN SOCIALIST DEMOCRACY
Paula Rothenberg

It is, of course, no accident that most Americans fail to identify socialism with freedom. But this is not, as Gintis suggests, primarily because most socialist societies have not been democratic. This explanation, in effect, begs the question by accepting uncritically the ideologically loaded liberal democratic definition of democracy as primarily procedural or formal in nature rather than substantive. This emphasis on procedure and insistence on identifying the most basic rights and liberties with abstract intellectual freedoms has prevented most Americans from recognizing the advances made by socialist societies in extending basic human rights to their populations: namely, the rights to adequate housing, nutrition, medical care, and education, and the right to grow old with dignity free from fear of want.

It is particularly important then that socialists challenge the bourgeois definition of democracy and expose it for what it is, a definition that serves to pacify a population in a society where 20 percent of the population controls 77 percent of the wealth. In lieu of economic democracy, Americans are encouraged to prize freedom of the press (a freedom increasingly few Americans are able to exercise), freedom of speech (how many people have access to a significant public podium), and a host of other political and intellectual freedoms which are robbed of their content by the unequal distribution of wealth and power in America. It is no accident that Americans have been taught to define both freedom and democracy in a way that leaves that unequal distribution of wealth unchallenged and obscures the advances of socialist countries that have made significant strides toward the kind of democratic society that comes with economic justice.

Further, while the acceptance of a narrow, class-biased definition of democracy has been a major obstacle to the growth of an American socialist movement, it is accompanied by other difficulties as well. Among the most serious is the belief held by Americans that socialism is impractical because people will only work if motivated by the prospect of personal gain or threatened by the prospect of personal loss. To the extent that they do identify socialism with some concern for equality of condition and with a rejection of the profit motive, they regard it as hopelessly incompatible with "human nature" as defined (and, we might add, as shaped) by capitalism.

Further, and equally serious, is the secondary definition of freedom foisted upon us by capitalism, the freedom to consume endlessly and mindlessly, and the need to seek our sense of self and self-definition in that process. And finally, the related reality that capitalism has actually created needs and natures in people that can only be fulfilled by capitalism so that in seeking to satisfy their own deeply felt needs they actually replicate them. Once we define the obstacles to socialism in America in this way, we see that the problem that confronts us is not merely encouraging Americans to view socialism as the extension of democracy to various aspects of life, as Gintis defines it. Rather, we are confronted by the need for a sweeping re-definition of democracy and freedom and a re-evaluation of the criteria for determining basic human needs and basic human rights.

The picture of contemporary America that emerges from the Gintis essay is of a society with fundamentally sound and defensible values and structures which has been subverted by capitalism. What we need to do is reclaim those values and structures. He argues, for example, that "most of the shortcomings of liberal democracy are not due to its own failings, but that of the rest of the society" and that " a socialist movement in America would require no radical break with the cultural and political traditions of our society." But this perspective seriously oversimplifies the problems we face by failing either to recognize or properly emphasize the tendencies in American society that will consistently subvert the realization of the very tasks that Gintis rightly posits for American Socialism. Indeed some or all of these tasks may be all but unrealizable within the premises of the political practice he envisions.

The strength of Gintis' discussion of socialist political practice and structures lies in its emphasis on the dialectical relationship between the individual and society and its awareness that "politics produces people as well as decisions." At the heart of his vision of socialist America is the idea first generated within the Women's Movement, that we must extend our notion of politics beyond government to include relations in all aspects of social life. According to his vision, the tasks that confront American socialism then will involve expanding and extending democratic political practice to work, the family, and the state. To this end, Gintis offers us an exciting vision of a society where politics must be both formally and substantively representative as well as participatory. So far, so good. The difficulty arises when he insists that the role of leadership within such a system is to represent not people's interests but their wills. Precisely because politics produces people as well as decisions, the needs expressed by the will of the people within American socialist society may well be expected to express their needs and interests as shaped by hundreds of years of capitalism. Unless we devise a socialist political practice prepared to integrate a strong concern for partipatory democracy with the need to distinguish between the subjective wants and objective interests of the participants, we will find ourselves unable to achieve the goals of a genuine socialist society.

Let us turn now to examine this claim by applying it to Gintis' account of what would be entailed in democratizing work, the family, and the state. Because of limitations of space, no attempt will be made to provide a comprehensive picture of the kinds of problems that may well subvert this so-called extension of democracy to each area; instead, some limited examples of these difficulties will be offered.

WORK

Capitalist politics have created people who tend to identify efficiency with the maintenance of a strict division of labor and the existence of hierarchy and patriarchal authority. Delegations of workers from United States auto plants routinely sent to observe workteam models in factories in other countries usually return home expressing a preference for the existing structure of work in America (and this is duly reported on the front page of the *New York Times*). This preference may well not reflect the real interest of these workers. In fact, the democratization of the work site proposed by Gintis may well need to be carried out against the protest of workers who have been taught to identify their interests with the patriarchal organization of the workplace and the perpetuation of divisions among workers based on race, sex, age, and skill.

The difficulties with this project can be further clarified by turning our attention to the very notion of efficiency itself. Gintis argues that the demand to democratize the workplace has been significantly impeded by the widely held belief that the current organization of capitalist enterprises is the most efficient possible. He chooses to challenge this claim by arguing that democratic organization of work can be equally efficient. But the weak argument he offers— hardly more than an assertion—really is not likely to be persuasive to most workers. Basic to the issue here is the need not merely to extend the idea of democracy to the workplace but to re-define it. An important place to begin is by challenging the definition of efficiency generated within capitalism (and parroted by many workers), since it is this notion of efficiency that undermines the possibility of democracy.

"Efficient for whom?" one might well ask of the current organiza-tion of work in America. The high incidence of job-related accidents and resulting deaths or long-term disability, the extensive reliance of factory workers on alcohol, barbiturates, and other drugs, the shoddy quality of products, etc. testify that capitalist production is not particularly efficient for either the worker or the consumer. What it does do efficiently is maximize the extraction of profit by maximizing the exploitation of the labor force. Unfortunately, however, both workers and consumers have been taught to identify their interests with the definition of efficiency most beneficial to the interests of the capitalist class.

FAMILY

Gintis believes that the family will be easier to reorganize than work because "the challenge of transforming patriarchy is not funda-mentally in politics, but in culture." Although I am not sure why this is likely to make the task easier, I am in agreement with his claim that even creating conditions of full equality outside the family is unlikely to accomplish the democratization of the family, precisely because this "does not directly confront . . . the cultural values that reproduce the sexual division of labor on which patriarchy is based." However, this recognition seems to fly in the face of the earlier claim on the part of the author that American socialism would "require no radical break with the cultural traditions of the society." American culture evidences a profound patriarchal bias. Democratizing the family will require a direct challenge to American culture insofar as it is biased in terms of both patriarchy and heterosexuality. (And the latter bias Gintis ignores entirely.)

By Gintis' own account, socialist development in America must combat patriarchy by bringing about the elimination of the current sexual division of labor within the family. The problem is that this goal may well be incompatible with his insistence that politics must reflect the needs (rather than the interests) of those affected. Many women and men in America experience any challenge to prevailing sex roles as an attack on their fundamental being and will view the elimination of the current sexual division of labor within the home as incompatible with their personal happiness. The patriarchal bias of American culture will be reflected in the experienced needs and expressed wills of both women and men in socialist America. Its eradication may well require a leadership that acts in the interests of women and men by temporarily ignoring their felt needs.

THE STATE

Gintis argues that "the liberal democratic state has failed to act in the interests of citizens and workers . . . because of the constraints placed upon it by the capitalist economy . . ." He regards the fundamental structure of the state as compatible with socialist politics and sees the problem as one of affecting a reorganization that will increase participation. The problem with this portrayal is that it adopts a fundamentally undialectical view of the relationship between the liberal democratic state and the needs of capitalism as if the two were actually separable. But in fact the capitalist state represents the institutionalization of the interest of the ruling class and its evolution has proceeded in step with the evolving needs and interests of the ruling class in order to minimize or suppress class conflict and facilitate capital accumulation. To be sure, certain concessions have been wrung from it in the course of class struggle and that struggle has played a role in shaping its nature. But to acknowledge the role of class struggle does not require that we go to the extreme of portraying the liberal democratic state as if it did not institutionalize the needs and interests of the capitalist class, as if the laws, policies, practices, and procedures that comprise it were somehow neutral in the class struggle only waiting to be grafted onto a different economic system in order to change their character entirely.

Gintis portrays liberalism as encompassing two contradictory value systems, one which vests rights in persons and the other in property, and he argues that socialism must extend person rights, chief among them, civil liberties, which negate property rights and patriarchal privilege. But the protection of property rights and the maintenance of patriarchal privilege are built into the liberal democratic state which arose, precisely, to institutionalize these forms of' privileges. Neither will yield without a struggle and it will be the job of the state under socialism to see to it that these interests are suppressed and eliminated even when and if this runs counter to the expressed will of the people and their commitment to the very civil liberties that liberal democracy has taught them to elevate above all substantive matters.

Where does this critique leave us? Gintis suggests that those who argue against recognizing bourgeois democratic freedoms under socialism play into the hands of those who equate socialism with the suppression of basic human rights and thereby preclude the development of an American socialist movement. He argues that only a socialist vision that emphasizes individual liberties and the promise "that politics ought to reflect the needs of those affected will draw the support of the American people."

The danger in this kind of reasoning is that it allows the definition of freedom and the needs of individuals as defined by capitalism to determine the form and content of our socialist vision. And what of racism, sexism, patriarchal authority, ageism, the freedom to consume mindlessly, to choose among 110 brands of artificially sweetened breakfast cereals? Will a vision of American socialism that denies these deeply felt and warmly cherished rights and privileges appeal to the American people? And if it does not, shall we revise that vision? The dangers are clear.

In conclusion, the strength of the account of politics offered by Gintis is the extent to which the practice he devises is aimed at transforming its participants and the relations among them as well as arriving at decisions, the extent to which his account emphasizes the need to create a democratic culture within which people learn and grow and develop the skills that are required to render their participation in democratic practice meaningful. What is unfortunate is that he stopped short of calling for, not merely an extension of bourgeois democratic values and practices to other spheres of life, but for its re-definition so that genuine freedom and socialism are properly understood as inseparable.

REJOINDER
Herbert Gintis

Isaac Balbus's central point in his discussion of my paper appears to be that I "underestimate both the necessity and possibility of participatory political arrangements and . . . overestimate the desirability of representative political arrangements." Since we clearly conceive of political practices as a medium of need *formation* as much as need *satisfaction*, he considers my position to be at best anomalous. For Balbus holds, with Robert Dahl, that the claims of representative democracy can be defended only on the fundamental assumption that "individuals are 'rational' actors for whom political involvement is a means to purely self-interested ends."

I believe that Balbus is correct in noting that I have taken political participation as instrumental to need-satisfaction and need-development, rather than an end in itself. It is also true that I take representative democracy as an end in itself, along with personal development and satisfaction. I think it possible to argue that *both* participatory and representative forms are derivable from the criteria of personal need-development and satisfaction. But I am not sure, and in an era in which the threat of totalitarianism is pervasive, the positing of liberty and representative democracy as fundamental appears to me to be a costless as well as a politically salutary affirmation.

Hence the basic question is: why have I maintained the fundamental position of representative democracy and the instrumental position of participatory democracy? Balbus is perhaps understandably frustrated at my incomplete argument for this position. Nor will I be able to fully satisfy him in the few pages here allotted to me—Sam Bowles and I will have much more to say on the subject in our forthcoming book *Despotism, Scarcity, and Freedom.*

Let me begin by noting that my use of the term "politics" is *not* limited to activity in the state sector. Rather, it refers to the practice of transforming social institutions in all spheres of social life—including community, family, and economy as well as the state. My position, then, is that it is (a) desirable to trade off between political and non-political practices, and (b) necessary for individuals to limit the spheres in which they actively engage in participatory political practices, and desirable that they have political representation in all spheres, whether or not they participate in more direct ways.

The reason I would give for the desirability of a trade-off between political and other practices on the part of the individual is quite straightforward: politics is not the only form of social practice in which individuals develop and satisfy their needs, and hence each individual must balance off competing forms of activity, of which political activity is only (albeit an important) one. When I am playing tennis, taking care of children, helping a distressed friend, or reading a book, I am not necessarily doing politics. Yet these are valid activities. I certainly agree that a well-balanced person will engage in political practices to a significant extent, and that a healthy society will render individuals capable and desirous of political participation. But the same could be said of many other forms of personal and collective activity. Moreover, individual differences must be respected. Just as some individuals are more religious, more athletic, more workaholic, or more personally helpful than others, some individuals are more political than others. At times I find it somewhat shortsighted of political activists to hold that all individuals in the "good society" should be like themselves, and hence project a vision in which political participation becomes the socialist counterpart of the Protestant Ethic.

Second, it is necessary that individuals limit the spheres in which they participate politically, precisely because "politics is everywhere." Individuals must trade off not only between political and other practices, but among political practices themselves. Balbus ignores this obvious fact. For instance, I participate actively in four or five organizations in a few spheres of my life—my economics department at the University of Massachusetts, the Union of Radical Political Economics, local politics in Cambridge, Mass., and my kid's school. Even in a really democratic society, I doubt that I would desire more participation—though clearly I would have more options (e.g., the local energy commission, the community development bank, the board of my health care delivery service, etc.).

The stress on representative democracy, then, is that individuals have significant control over even those areas in which they do not personally participate, and that those who participate relatively little not be dominated by those who participate a lot—either in general or in a particular sphere. It appears to me quite egregious for political activists to belittle representative forms, when it is quite clear that "participatory democracy" may have the unintended effect of serving as merely another way to dominate people whose interests, expertise, and efforts are directed elsewhere.

The reader will note that my position is quite independent from the question as to whether centralized versus decentralized political institutions are desirable. The above arguments even hold in the case of "a loosely connected federation of self-governing communities," as Balbus's vision appears to favor. As my final point, however, I would like to suggest that this "small is beautiful" position is dogmatic, undesirable, and unrealistic.

By a "dogmatic" position, I mean one which takes a problem for which the correct solution requires a synergistic (dialectical) treatment of a variety of concerns, and dismisses all but one or a few altogether. In the present case, it is clear that both centralized and decentralized mechanisms are desirable, and the real issue is developing a creative combination of the two. For instance, income distribution, personal rights, environmental control, energy policy, economic development, and international relations, among others, require considerable centralized decision-making. While clearly a socialist society could vastly increase political participation even in the centralized aspect of these areas of social policy, to argue that they should be eliminated in the interest of local participation is, quite simply, dogmatic.

Second, a high degree of decentralization would not be desirable even if it were feasible. For the lack of opportunities to deal with national issues breeds a suffocating form of provincialism, and leads to the inability of individuals and groups to identify broadly with others. If politics is the development of people as well as the production of decisions, decision-making that is centralized becomes quite as important as that which is highly decentralized.

Third, a considerable degree of centralization is required by the nature of international economic, political, and military considerations. For one thing, the history of the past several centuries indicates the survival-value of integrated national state apparatuses. For another, a socialist United States will have even greater difficulty in enduring the hostility of foreign totalitarian and capitalist societies than it has now. It would be difficult to locate in history a society which has undergone significant social change that has not had to deal with the enmity and indeed invasion of its international rivals. To ignore this fact is not merely unrealistic. It is self-defeating as well, since the majority of citizens who would otherwise be accepting of a socialist vision are too realistic to look with favor upon the destruction or even significant attenuation of national institutions and identifications.

Let me now turn to the comments of Paula Rothenberg. First, I think it is a fundamental mistake to call the form of democracy we have in the advanced capitalist world "bourgeois." In fact, liberalism never advocated even representative democracy until it became clear that the alternative would be revolution. Consistently throughout history it has been the oppressed who have fought for representative democracy and universal suffrage. The socialist position which denigrates this central element in popular struggles is thus not surprisingly rejected by most workers and citizens.

Second, while I have a good deal of sympathy for Rothenberg's social goals, I tend to find her approach to these issues fundamentally idealist. Let me give two examples. The first is her argument that rather than accepting prevailing notions of socialism and democracy, "we are confronted by the need for a sweeping re-definition of democracy and freedom and a re-evaluation of the criteria for determining basic human needs and basic human rights." This is a fundamentally incorrect and indeed utopian manner, I believe, in which to pose the problem. Just as Engels criticized utopian socialists for conceiving of a complete alternative to the existing society, and then going around trying to convince everyone of the superiority of their alternative, Rothenberg can be faulted for attributing a concrete reality to visions, and viewing the fight for socialism as a transition from one form of consciousness to a completely different one.

In place of this view, I submit that social change occurs through the exploitation of internal contradictions in the existing constellation of cultural forms. I have argued that there are inherent contradictions between capitalism and liberal democracy, and within democratic culture itself. These contradictions have arisen through the very social struggles which have permeated the history of capitalist development. In no way is it accurate to characterize popular political culture as the creation of a ruling class, and imposed upon an unwitting populace. We thus need no "sweeping redefinitions," but rather "internal transformations" of cultural forms, based on a materialist analysis of their internal contradictions. It is this that I have tried to provide.

Another example of idealism is the positing of "objective interests" of people, as opposed to their wills and forms of cultural and political practice, as the guiding criterion of social change. Even if such "objective interests" in fact exist in some ideal realm (the consciousness of the "aware"?), they are quite irrelevant, in and of themselves, to the process of politics. Rather, they are just another excuse for oppressing the masses "in their own interest." But such objective interests, I believe, do not exist. Indeed, if it is true that interests are constituted through political practice, then they do not exist in some ideal realm at all. Of course, it may be argued that such interests are discovered rather than constituted through political practice. But I have already argued extensively that this is not the case.

Rothenberg argues that, since workers are perverted by bourgeois values, their wills cannot be respected in a socialist society. Her vision appears to be that the workers make a revolution in some blind sort of way, and then the "politically conscious" take over and tell everyone what to do, think, and believe. Perhaps this is a bit of an overdrawn characterization on my part, but I think it is essentially correct. I agree that this has happened in the course of history, but when it has occurred, it has represented just one more defeat for the common people. A real movement towards socialism, I suggest, requires that people genuinely oppose economic despotism, racism, sexism, and the like. Socialist activists must have enough faith in the people to support real freedom, democracy, civil rights, political parties, and unlimited personal expression. Otherwise they too will be consigned to the archives of history.

II. THE BUILT ENVIRONMENT

Lead Essay	Dolores Hayden
Responses	Gwendolyn Wright
	Robert Goodman
	Martin Bierbaum
Rejoinder	Dolores Hayden

CAPITALISM, SOCIALISM, AND THE BUILT ENVIRONMENT

Dolores Hayden

Every force evolves a form.
— Shaker proverb, 19th century.

A revolution that does not produce a new space is not
carried to its furthest extent; it fails; it does not change life;
all it does is alter the ideological superstructures, the
institutions, the political apparatus.
Henri Lefebvre, *La production de l'espace*

CAPITALIST SPACE

Drive through any American city, from its commercial areas to its
residential areas, and in thirty minutes you will accumulate
evidence of vast wealth along with environmental decadence. A few tall
buildings downtown tower over parking lots and garages. Perhaps
there will be a park and some apartment houses. Then a tangle of porno
shops, discount stores, fast food places, and gas stations will lead to
freeway ramps, and the freeway will connect miles and miles of
similar, large single family houses on landscaped lots with shopping
malls, industrial parks and the occasional school or church. In the
American city, all the themes, styles, and features of the speculative
builder's prevalent jargon preclude architectural style in the same way
that a string of expletives precludes coherent argument. In addition to
their incoherent aesthetic character, American urban areas suffer from
the presence of air pollution, from excessive traffic noise, and from the

constant blare of outdoor advertising. The despoilation of historically significant sites is common. Boston, Minneapolis, Los Angeles, and Atlanta all fit this pattern: historic differences and regional economic variations are trivial compared to the impact of smog, freeways, cars, utility poles, and commercial strips (Figure 1).

1. Los Angeles, 1980. Cars, utility poles and wires, signs, and a billboard offering cruises to the unspoiled coast of South America: the unifying features of capitalist space in the nowhere city.

Is this capitalist space? Urban historians such as Sam Bass Warner, David Goldfield, Blaine Brownell, and David Gordon have offered systematic definitions of the development of urban space parallel to the economic development of the American capitalist city.[1] They define mercantile, industrial, and monopoly capitalism; they define the marketplace, the factory town, the "no town." With varied periodization, they describe the typical American port city created between 1700 and 1820 as a pedestrian city without much industry. They speak of the typical American industrial city, created between 1820 and 1920, as a city reliant on immigrant labor, characterized by factories, slums, a downtown, and early suburbs. They describe the typical American monopoly-capitalist city, created between 1920 and the present, as a private city dependent on automobiles, sprawling with single family dwellings, commercial strips, and dispersed production sites. In literary terms, one could think of New York in Herman Melville's *Pierre*, Chicago in Upton Sinclair's *The Jungle*, or Los Angeles in Alison Lurie's *The Nowhere City*. It is the nowhere city which represents the current urban spatial expression of American capitalism.

All our cities are becoming nowhere cities. Just as automobiles rolling off an assembly line in Detroit may be red, black, green, or blue, with whitewall or blackwall tires, in convertible or station wagon models, so space produced by the monopoly-capitalist economy is styled to emphasize superficial differences, and to conceal the uniformity below the facade. The roots of both economic homogeneity and aesthetic diversity go back to the 18th century. With Thomas Jefferson's National Survey of 1787 the entire land area of the United States west of the Allegheny mountains was divided into salable space, just as the Commissioners' Plan for New York City in 1811 divided most of Manhattan Island into identical lots to "ease the buying and selling of land." Manfredo Tafuri, the Italian Marxist art historian, has defined American capitalist development as the environment created by the land speculators and builders who moved onto the American rural and urban grids. They were freed from the formal constraints typical of earlier aristocratic town planning by the aesthetic uniformity of the American grid.[2]

The characteristic American eclectic style of building developed with every architectural piece aesthetically unrelated to every other architectural piece. The grid was the perfect setting for architectural ready-mades, that is, building forms such as Greek temples or medieval castles, created at other times and places to reflect power and wealth. These building types retained their facades but were given new interiors and new uses in America. Temples became public buildings such as churches, state houses, and courthouses. Castles became banks or armories. And all of these forms eventually were used for single family houses, fast food places, and gas stations. Physical continuity was provided by the infrastructure of roads, sewers, and utility poles and wires. (The United States consumes more energy resources per person than any other country in the world in support of its gridded landscape and eclectic buildings.) Symbolic continuity was more elusive, but the United States finally achieved a continuity of sorts, an endless sales pitch for mass consumption, promoted by fantasy environments. Businessmen and home owners inhabited a more and more peculiar world by the twentieth century. Polynesian longhouses competed with western corrals to attract restaurant patrons. Norman farmhouses were built side by side with Spanish haciendas to attract home buyers' attention. Office buildings were clad in mirrors or gold-anodized aluminum. Only factories tended to be mundane, large, and boring. Thus the United States developed a homogenous architectural culture of mad eclecticism in its commercial, residential, and corporate building, and many architects and critics have even attempted to legitimize this as "learning from Las Vegas," or "postmodernism."[3]

2. View of Mission Valley, San Diego, California, late 1950s and late
1970s, showing the production of space. From Kevin Lynch,
Managing the Sense of a Region, MIT Press, figure 1.

If many architects and art critics have been shameless prevar-
icators, justifying the aesthetic impact of twentieth-century capitalism
rather than dissecting it, many urban planners have also retreated from
urban problems into technical or financial specialities. Thus, even
among college-educated Americans, even among avowed socialists,
distinctive American spatial and environmental patterns are not
popularly understood as a consequence of American economic development. When Americans describe their environmental crisis, they
mention symptoms: downtown blight, pockets of poverty and crime,
poor public transportation, the high cost of housing, pollution, the
soaring cost of energy. These fragmentary complaints are reflected in
the curriculum of most urban planning schools where public finance,
transportation, housing, and energy are all taught as separate subjects,
as well as in the organization of most local, state, and federal agencies,
where these are treated as separate areas of public policy.

Yet, as urban historians tell us, and Henri Lefebvre, the French
sociologist has argued in his important book, *The Production of Space*,
every mode of production involves the production of built space that
corresponds to that mode in a coherent way.[4] In the United States,
since the early 20th century, the growth of monopoly capitalism has
been based on suburban development, relying on land speculation,
cheap, non-renewable energy, and private transportation (Figure 2).
The aesthetically disconnected pieces are coherent economically.
Thus, to end our environmental crisis, it is necessary to introduce a
vision of another kind of human environment that could be created by
another kind of economy, one based on curtailment of private land
speculation, strict conservation of non-renewable energy resources,
and collective rather than private transportation. Only a new way of
life and work will produce a new and coherent social landscape, and a
new aesthetic.

SOCIALIST SPACE

A clear vision of another kind of environment could be powerful
propaganda for change. Yet even countries which have made great
innovations in terms of popular health programs, mass education, and
political culture have not fully developed and implemented egalitarian
environmental design. The visitor to Peking or Havana confronts
factories, offices, and medium-to-high-rise housing (constructed with
industrialized building systems) which could be in use anywhere in the
world. True, in Peking, the private cars of the U.S. are missing, and in
Havana, the billboards are political, not commercial. In addition,
neighborhood planning for social services and transportation is often

better than in the United States. Yet one finds indigenous building traditions succumbing to a drive for modern technology which produces not distinctive but homogenous results. Indeed, many planners and designers in the Soviet Union, China, Cuba, or Eastern Europe even argue that space is inherently apolitical.

A review of socialist theory concerning design since the early nineteenth century reveals that while the communitarian socialist and anarchist traditions have always emphasized the relationship between ideology and spatial design, this connection has not been explored very thoroughly in the Marxist tradition, at least not until very recently in Western Europe. As a result, communitarian socialists and anarchists have defended model villages or model communes combining agriculture and industry, while state socialists, since the Soviet planners of the 1920s, have tended to favor industrialized building systems, high rise buildings, and large cities separate from agricultural development. Even the Chinese, who have worked to "overcome the contradictions between the city and the countryside," have accepted this approach to urban development in the last few years. But is either the communal village or the precast concrete high rise metropolis the route to socialist space?

THE COMMUNAL VILLAGE

Created before capital began to shape space for production and consumption, pre-industrial villages often appear to be deeply satisfying environments for communal life because they consist of complexes of related buildings, built of local materials, in harmony with local topography and climate. They seem human in scale because they are often structured around symbolic, public spaces for the pedestrian such as the piazza or dancing ground. While the societies which created these villages might have been hierarchical and authoritarian, they were incapable of producing unlivable, incoherent space on the scale of modern societies. This does not make them socialist, but many communitarian socialist and anarchist theorists have tried to devise ways to recapture their sense of wholeness.

The most beautiful towns created in the United States during the nineteenth century, formed with what I have defined as an intentional vernacular[5] architecture, were created by experimental socialist communities such as the American Shakers. Their exquisite design of all objects from tools to furniture, buildings, and village landscapes, reflects a passion for communistic building which is direct, unadorned, and egalitarian (Figure 3). The integration of craft activities and farming, the search for equality between men and women, the desire for perfection in all hand-crafted objects, the cultivation of a symbolic landscape, led the Shakers to create nineteen unique but similar communities between 1774 and 1850. Although they formed a celibate, religious group which can be seen as a strict, limited subculture of six thousand people, they made all of their decisions concerning the built environment in both a democratic and a technically sophisticated way.

3. Center of Shaker village, Hancock, Massachusetts, 1839. The Shakers offered the best example of town building by an American religious communistic society.

For many communitarian socialists of the nineteenth century a return to the environmental harmony of the pre-industrial village was essential to their visions of the socialist future. Even Marx and Engels observed the Shakers carefully, while Charles Fourier, Robert Owen, William Morris, and Ebenezer Howard all shared their environmental ideals to the exclusion of much urban concern at all. Fourier and Owen suggested that individuals combine work in agriculture, industry, and domestic life, and live in groups of about twelve hundred to sixteen hundred people.[6] For William Morris and other members of the Arts and Crafts movement, return to a world of small villages would permit the intensive, personal, artistic labor which industrialization had banished. Hand-carved and hand-painted public buildings were a sign of a happy populace.[7] For Ebenezer Howard, the "cooperative quadrangles" of his "Garden Cities of To-Morrow" encapsulated many of Owen's and Morris's innovations (Figure 4). Yet Howard did suggest federations of satellite towns, which would form metropolitan clusters, and keep some of the advantages of urban concentration for their citizens.[8]

In the twentieth century, this ideal still lives. A contemporary anarchist, Murray Bookchin, speaks of post-scarcity anarchism and identifies miniaturized modern technology as the generating force of a new village landscape.[9] The architect, Christopher Alexander, hopes to generate settlement patterns based on what he calls the "timeless way of building," to form a vernacular architecture which recreates the human-scale spatial patterns of the past, but he has organized their construction according to the systems theory of the twentieth century, utilizing the latest in human engineering and environmental psychology.[10] And the proponent of appropriate technology, E.F. Schum-

4. G. P. Wade, sketch for British Garden City based on pre-industrial village, 1909.

acher, notes that "small is beautiful."[11]

The advocates of the communal village as a model of the human environment often appear to have aesthetics on their side. Folk art and face-to-face democracy are appealing, and yet, throughout the world, young rural people have usually preferred city life to the farm village whenever that choice has appeared. While Charles Fourier attempted to justify the social scale of his ideal communities (phalansteries) by including one male and one female of each of the eight hundred and sixteen personality types in each settlement, his "science of society," promoting social variety and interaction, remained a theoretical abstraction. Life with several hundred people seems very limited if the alternative is life in a city of one million. Although small, for the Shakers, was very beautiful, small is often strict, and at worst, rigid and dull.

THE TECHNOLOGICAL CITY

An alternative to the pre-industrial village has been the idealization of the technological megalopolis where everything is large, clean, and technologically sophisticated. Edward Bellamy's novel, *Looking Backward: 2000-1887*, created a flurry of excitement in 1888 about a fictional socialist city, Boston in the year 2000, equipped with large, magnificent buildings in the eclectic, Beaux-Arts style. Some Christian socialists preferred this novel to any other work of political theory as a popular recruiting device, because it made a socialist future seem so very real to urban dwellers. For Bellamy capitalist technology had provided abundance; abundance had led to the evolution of socialism, a socialism which made a comfortable life available for every worker. Culture and consumption were its key concepts. Citizens frequented concerts, libraries, and great collective dining rooms after a day's work in the Industrial Army. Television provided mass entertainment; pneumatic tubes made possible the delivery of mass-produced goods to every house.[12]

Bellamy was not unlike the architects and planners of the Modern Movement in the 1920s and 1930s in Europe in his idealization of industrial mass production as an aid to the ideal socialist city. Walter Gropius, Bruno Taut, and Le Corbusier all tried to house urban workers in various types of urban housing projects representing modernity. Le Corbusier's ideal City for Three Million People (Figure 5) abandoned Bellamy's Beaux-Arts aesthetic for high-rise buildings of concrete and glass located in a park-like setting, and definitions of machine-age architecture were particularly influential among Soviet designers who attempted to develop plans for futuristic, high-rise

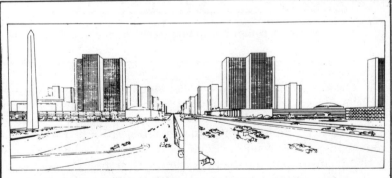

5. Le Corbusier, sketch for Contemporary City, the skyscraper metropolis, 1922.

metropolises in the 1920s.[13] One typical Soviet scheme for workers' housing (Figure 6) showed an assembly line carrying food to modernistic tables in great dining halls with industrial windows.[14] Others used industrialized building components to create small living cells and endless corridors. However, Corbusier's phrase, "A house is a machine for living in," has always been more popular among designers than dwellers. While no one interested in socialism can quarrel with the ideal of modern mass transit systems, scientific sewage disposal, good water supply, or good roads, most people prefer hand-carved wooden doors or hand-made wooden cabinetry to the precast concrete panel and the metal stair when it comes to housing.[15]

6. Sketch for Soviet communal dining room, Barsch and Vladmirov, 1929.

The ideal of the high-rise housing complex and the technological megalopolis contains the misconception that space produced by industrial techniques will be as desirable as machine tools, watches, or cars created by the same process. But urban space is not simply a commodity to be consumed, despite the tendency to treat it that way in both capitalist and state socialist systems. Urban space is a cultural, as well as an economic product. It plays a significant part in the reproduction of society. Dwellings and neighborhoods represent the reconciliation of nature and culture in both a tangible and symbolic way. Built space provides a concrete, physical statement about how a society organizes itself at the scale of everyday life. And its design accounts for a good deal of pleasure or pain, social connectedness or social isolation. If nature is excluded from the neighborhood, as it will be in a high rise, and if human scale is disregarded in favor of the technological culture the high rise represents, then people are uncomfortable.

If the communal village sacrifices social diversity for a sense of wholeness, the technological megalopolis sacrifices humanity entirely. A new flat in a concrete tower block may remove the inhabitants from the old village gossips and provide modern plumbing, but it isolates inhabitants from nature and from public urban spaces. Neither will do. In the 1820s the communitarian socialists made the mistake of believing that if a group could eliminate capitalist space, they could eliminate exploitation and proceed to the classless society. In the 1920s technological socialists argued that space was irrelevant, and that socialists could use capitalist building types and technology. Both were wrong. While the communitarians who gave space a special place were then denounced by Marxists as hopeless utopians, the Marxists who emulated capitalist space were just as quickly denounced by libertarians for building a Brave New World of endless gray high-rise concrete buildings. Any socialist society which wants to do better has to find a middle road, based on a strong understanding of the importance of politics to good design, and good design to politics.

A NEW CODE OF SPACE

The communal village and the high-rise megalopolis, products of nineteenth century theories about the past or the future, tell us less about socialist space, than about socialists' lack of spatial imagination. Henri Lefebvre has stated the task: to create a new vision of socialist space which is an adequate, synthetic vision for organizing by socialists. He says that a new spatial language shared by socialists would:

> . . . first of all, rediscover the unity of all the dissociated elements: the private and the public, intersections and differences within space. It would bring together the terms which have been dispersed by current spatial practice and its ideological justifications: the micro (the architectural scale or level) and the macro (assigned to urban planners, politicians, central planners), the everyday and the urban, the inside and the outside, work and non-work (the festival and fete), the long-lasting and the ephemeral . . . .[16]

Yet what could be the economic, social, and aesthetic basis of a new code of space, eliminating these various hierarchies and segregations? It is not enough to create a new vision; it must be backed by a new social practice.

The social practice most interesting to many young male members of the American left is a participatory democratic socialism, involving as much self-determination as possible in the neighborhood and in the workplace. The social practice most compelling to many women is socialist feminism, especially extending socialist theory to apply to traditional "woman's work" in the household, and at the same time, overcoming the sexual division of labor in society. Certainly in the United States, where there are few distinctions left between work in agribusiness and in heavy industry, the contradictions between the city and the countryside are less striking than between the male labor force and the female labor force. Gender is linked to poverty so closely that any American socialist movement wishing to organize the disadvantaged worker must organize women.

Women's inferior status is often confirmed and reinforced by the spatial patterns of American life, particularly the separation of homes and jobs, the design of dwellings and neighborhoods which require an unpaid homemaker's services in order to be functional, and the reliance on private rather than public transportation. As Eli Zaretsky and other historians have argued, women have experienced the transition from feudal to industrial society as an increasing division between home and work, between public and private space, between unwaged work and waged work, between new definitions of production and consumption.[17] Although women have struggled against their spatial oppression in both socialist and capitalist societies (a struggle I have traced elsewhere[18]), their success has been limited. Feminist organizers have had to deal with an opposition convinced that "a woman's place is in the home," a phrase which underlines the spatial enforcement of the economic and social restrictions women have often had to endure.

In the U.S. in 1919 the Industrial Housing Associates developed corporate strategies to eliminate social activism among white, skilled, male workers in the United States through campaigns for home ownership under the slogan, "Good Homes Make Contented Workers."[19] Home ownership indeed proved to be an effective symbol to justify land speculation, excessive use of private automobiles, excessive purchase of consumer durables, and wasteful use of energy, as well as male chauvinism and racism. As the geographer Richard Walker has shown, since World War II increasing amounts of the U.S. gross national product have been centered around suburban consumption of houses and cars.[20] American male workers are encouraged to perceive the whole world of private status in the home as their real life, and to ignore the public world outside. They have been encouraged to consider themselves as "middle class," as home owners, as patriarchs.

Any form of socialism which deals equitably with women as well as men must involve the reorganization of all socially-necessary labor, not just wage labor. (Even in societies where women are encouraged to undertake factory and office jobs, they usually have a second, unpaid job at home, a situation which the family laws of Cuba and China have not been able to correct in practice, although they state that men must perform a fair share of domestic work.) Socialism must include a plan for the economic and spatial reorganization of homes and neighborhoods, which is aimed at ending some of the separation between public and private space, the macro and micro scales, and work and "non-work" activities, of men and women. It must end the use of large, private domestic spaces as a fantasy world of consumption, by reorganizing their use.

In a socialist-feminist society, spatial organization could begin to eliminate the split between private and public space which supports a sexual division of labor. First, the private sphere would have to be acknowledged as publicly important by the inclusion of public space and paid work within its domain. Second, the public sphere would have to be made to conform to private standards of social respect and human dignity, as a comfortable place without pollution, exploitation, or blight. Or as Frances Willard, the American feminist and Christian socialist, stated her aims to her followers in 1889: women would have to "make the whole world homelike."[21] They would have to bring the world into the home, and the home into the world.

THE NEIGHBORHOOD AS WORKPLACE

What would it take to transform the private sphere? A typical American suburban neighborhood could be reorganized spatially to create two or three times the number of dwelling units found in a block of three-bedroom houses[22] (Figures 7-10). Then housewives' unpaid private household jobs could be transferred to neighborhood producers' cooperatives. These might include:

1. a day care center with landscaped outdoor space providing day care and after-school activities
2. a laundromat providing laundry service
3. a kitchen providing lunches for the day care center, take-out evening meals, and meals-on-wheels for elderly people in the neighborhood
4. a grocery depot connected to a local food cooperative

5. a garage with two vans providing dial-a-ride service and meals-on-wheels

6. a garden (or allotments) where some food can be grown

7. a home help office providing helpers for the elderly, the sick, and employed parents whose children are sick, as well as home repair service

8. a cultural area, with books, records, television, stereo, and movie projector.

The use of all of these collective services should be voluntary; they would exist in addition to private dwelling units and private gardens. These services could offer great economies, however, because of their minimal energy consumption and their saving of domestic labor.

In creating neighborhood producers' cooperatives, it would be important to avoid traditional sex-sterotyping which would result from having only men as drivers, for example, or having only women as food service workers. Every effort should be made to break down separate categories of paid work for women and men, just as efforts should be made to recruit men who accept an equal share of domestic responsibilities as residents. A version of the Cuban Family Code would have to be part of a neighborhood organization's platform.[23] Such a neighborhood organization would have to be wary of creating a two-class society with residents who hold jobs in the larger society making more money than residents in neighborhood producers cooperatives which utilize some of their existing domestic skills. (In China many neighborhood factories and social services do depend on low-paid housewives as workers.)[24]

This proposal for reorganizing residential neighborhoods also indicates directions for transportation, and for public space outside the neighborhood. Personal landownership and personal cars should be replaced by collective land ownership (at the municipal and neighborhood level) and collective transit systems (at the municipal and neighborhood level). These are essential to ensure that speculative overbuilding does not occur, and that a more acceptable level of energy consumption can be maintained. The United States used 41% of the world's private cars in the mid-1970s.[25] A socialist United States would have to cut back drastically, relying on renewable energy sources and on conservation in order to support a non-nuclear energy policy,[26] and a non-imperialist consumption pattern. This would mean not only cutting back on energy consumption within neighborhoods but also cutting back the production of many commodities and creating far greater public controls on all uses of public space.

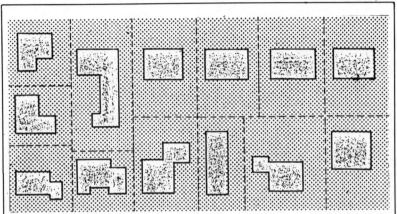

7. Suburban neighborhood, block plan of speculator's development. From D. Hayden, "What Would A Non-Sexist City Be Like?" *Signs: A Journal of Women in Culture and Society*, 5 (1980).

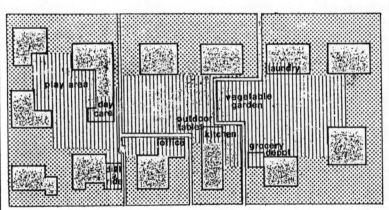

8. Proposed revitalization, same suburban block with new common space and facilities.

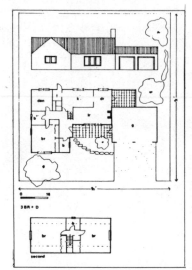

9. Suburban single family house, typical plan, three bedrooms plus den, ca. 1950.

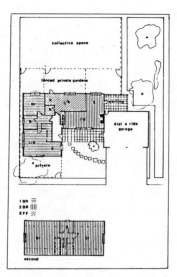

10. Proposed revitalization, same house converted to three units (two bedroom, one bedroom, and efficiency), plus dial-a-ride garage, and collective outdoor space.

THE WORKPLACE AS NEIGHBORHOOD

While the neighborhood must be recognized as a workplace, the workplace must also be seen as a neighborhood in a socialist society. But American industries have not usually been good neighbors. From Pittsburgh's blast furnances in the 19th century, to the Hooker Chemical Company's factory in Niagara Falls in our own times, most companies have dumped waste products on their neighbors whenever they thought they could get away with it. "Model" company towns such as Pullman, Illinois or Hershey, Pennsylvania, have substituted their own type of paternalistic authority for such complete disregard of the environment, but even Hershey is famous for its chocolate smoke.

Just as much a bad neighbor as the factory is the corporate skyscraper, which blocks sunlight, generates winds, and bankrupts municipal budgets. Dark shadows and high winds are only two of the environmental costs of skyscraper office buildings to urban neighborhoods.[27] Skyscrapers also reflect their owners' phallic fantasies and their desire to achieve the psychological domination of space. Because skyscrapers are usually designed to suit major corporations or land speculators, in many cases local communities have fought their construction. In a socialist society, the process of taking over corporate assets could include removing their spatial expression of environmental dominance as well. There would be tremendous symbolic victories to be gained having communities decide whether or not to dismantle a few of these giants: the ARCO towers in Los Angeles, the World Trade Center in New York, the Hancock Building in Chicago, the Transamerica in San Francisco.

External problems are only one half of workplace design. Traditionally workers' comfort in the factory or office has also been affected by their bosses' desire for economic and social control. In any major American corporation, an observer can judge the status of an employee by the amount of square footage and natural light in that person's workspace.[28] Managers have rooms and windows; clerical workers have desks in pools or pens and fluorescent light; cleaning workers have, if they are lucky, a chair in the broom closet. The design of space is used to reward the top brass (even if they are out of town on business all week) and to make it easier to supervise everyone else. Telephone company workspaces, for example, are designed with peepholes for personnel supervisors to observe the workers without their knowledge.[29] Assembly-line workers are subjected to an even more arduous spatial discipline related to both the production process and the supervisor's demands. As assembly lines shaped linear spaces for production (or what J. B. Jackson calls process space), workers were lined up to perform tasks on a moving object, a spatial system guaranteeing that repetitious tasks would replace specialized craft.[30]

New ways of organizing work, involving producers' cooperatives or new forms of workers' control of production, would be likely to produce new patterns of activity. Workers might choose to sit, or stand, or rest; they might group themselves around a single product, rather than let the assembly line roll dozens of products through their ranks. Workers would also need to give top priority to designing for their own health. They would remove noxious substances from their own work areas and eliminate pollution in the surrounding environment as well, as part of a program for the "homelike world."

PUBLIC SPACE: ENDING THE CONSTANT SALES PITCH

American cities in the 20th century have stressed private space more than public space, and often, commercial spaces have altered the character of public space, or have replaced it entirely. Outdoor advertising uses public space to manipulate citizens' thoughts and behavior; department stores, supermarkets, and then shopping malls have replaced public space with space for sales; commercial recreation space has offered children's play of a peculiar nature. All of these uses of space are antithetical to participatory socialism.

Because capitalist space in the United States has stressed disconnected parts, outdoor advertising has been able to become a powerful visual force, reflecting the permissiveness of a government which values advertising or speculative profit, and fails to calculate the external, public costs. It includes skywriting, ads on benches and buses, marquees enticing customers to enter X-rated movies and above all, commercial billboards advertising whiskey, cigarettes, or trips to places unspoiled by billboards. Outdoor advertising has created some of the most expensive and best maintained public visual displays in the U.S., but these displays cater to private profitmaking. Zoning has been a feeble tool used to cluster signs and billboards; in a capitalist society any planner who wished to eliminate them entirely has been considered irrational. Several scandals in the late 1970s revealed billboard owners' corruption of public officials, halting their attempts to regulate outdoor advertising by the promise of favorable placement of political billboards during election campaigns.[31] In a socialist society, however, it should be possible to analyze commercial billboards as public nuisances. They should disappear, to be replaced by public art reflecting the diverse culture of American urban neighborhoods, rather than the long reach of capitalist advertising agencies.

The department store was one of the most significant environmental inventions of nineteenth century capitalism, a space designed for bourgeois families and the upwardly mobile to examine many goods and learn how and where to consume them. Organized to promote customers' wandering in a commodity-filled world, the store's floor plan had no obvious beginning or end, and very little clear circulation. Dresses led to hats or shoes, vacuum cleaners to rugs or dishes, in an endless invitation to consumption. (Many supermarkets have been organized in the same way more recently, placing the necessary items as far apart as possible, to lengthen the shoppers' journeys.) The final stage of the department store's evolution is the shopping mall, whether in a suburban setting or in an urban setting as part of a larger hotel or business complex. In each case a pedestrian area is created with some amenities (perhaps benches, fountains, and plants), but the illusion of "public" space is only to draw customer to the commercial facilities. Indeed the "public" space is often carefully supervised by private police and anyone who does not appear to be a potential customer— young blacks, for example, or elderly shopping-bag ladies—will be kept out of the artificial city the mall's developers are seeking to create.

Like the department store, the amusement park was a nineteenth century creation, the commercial park created for "amusing the million."[32] Its successor is commercial recreation, of the sort offered by Disneyland, Disney World, and various theme parks. These became popular between the 1950s and 1980s because of the lack of public parks and public space in the suburban areas of American cities. However, these commercial parks introduced children to nature, culture, and history in ideologically compromised contexts. Disney's Frontierland celebrates cowboys shooting Indians and Southern planters oppressing slaves in the name of American history. Adventureland caricatures other cultures undergoing imperialist exploitation, such as Dole Pineapple's version of Polynesian culture, the Tiki Palace, or the Bank of America's version of childhood in foreign lands, "It's A Small World." Disneyland's Main Street claims to present small town U.S.A., with commercial spaces beyond every old-fashioned facade, suggesting that the only environmental reality lies in consumption.

In contrast to capitalist recreation, the preservation of many more real historic towns and unusual natural sites offers unlimited possibilities for environmental education linked with social awareness. Both the conservation of ecologically significant sites and the preservation of architecturally distinctive historic districts could provide many public substitutes for capitalist recreation areas based on artificial environments stimulating fantasies of domination and consumption. It would be possible to learn about Native American settlements on the sites where they were located, or to learn about farmers, ranchers, railroads and banking practices, in a manner conducive to better environmental understanding. Surely this is what a socialist society would need to offer a younger generation. There might be playgrounds and even roller coasters in socialist parks, but not good cowboys, bad Indians, and minstrel-singing slaves celebrating plantation life.

PUBLIC LIFE

In the United States, a socialist society would not be able to attempt much new construction. This country is already overbuilt, with more private space per person than anywhere else in the world. The task of creating socialist space in the United States would be a task of reconstruction, involving reorganizing, rezoning, rehabilitating, and equalizing space. Is it possible to achieve theoretical innovation in this context? Perhaps.

The United States, with its skyscrapers, freeways, and suburban houses, has become a model for modern life which is still accepted, for better or worse, in almost every part of the globe. Our wasteful uses of energy, our emphasis on privacy to the point of isolation, are thought of as technical achievements by many designers and planners working with far more limited resources. For Americans to reorganize and restructure their energy use would be to provide a powerful example of learning from past mistakes. For us to come to value the diversity of particular places—neighborhoods or regions—and preserve their environmental features would be a most valuable statement. For the United States to end pollution and maximize community involvement with the care of the built environment, that would be a real achievement. For us to articulate the mediating spaces between private and public domains—porches, sidewalks, green areas—places for people that the car eliminates, that would be progress beyond the tallest skyscraper or the widest freeway.

None of these changes in the built environment can occur without ending land speculation and the use of public space for private gain. But to state a social and environmental vision of the neighborhood as workplace and the workplace as neighborhood may aid those Americans struggling toward a more egalitarian nation. To "make the whole world homelike" Americans must begin to reassert their rights to public space, and give up some of their preoccupation with private space. They can only expect public life to bring social and political rewards when public life takes place somewhere. The nowhere city of the late twentieth century will not give way to community organizing without a struggle. But once recaptured and reorganized, the built environment can be a powerful support for participatory socialism.

NOTES

1. Sam. B. Warner, Jr., *The Urban Wilderness* (New York: Harper and Row, 1972); David Goldfield and Blaine Brownell, *Urban America: From Downtown to No Town* (Boston: Houghton Mifflin, 1979); David Gordon, "Capitalist Development and the History of American Cities," in W. K. Tabb and L. Sawyers, eds., *Marxism and the Metropolis* (New York: Oxford University Press, 1978) pp. 25-63.

2. Manfredo Tafuri, *Architecture and Utopia: Design and Capitalist Development* (Cambridge, Mass.: MIT Press, 1976).

3. Denise Scott Brown, Robert Venturi, and Steven Izenour, *Learning from Las Vegas* (Cambridge, Mass.: MIT Press, 1972); Charles Jencks, *The Language of Post-Modern Architecture* (New York: Rizzoli, 1977); for a critique see Tomas Maldonado, "Las Vegas and the Semiological Abuse," *Design, Nature, and Revolution* (New York: Praeger, 1970) pp. 60-66.

4. Henri Lefebvre, *La production de l'espace* (Paris: Editions Anthropos, 1972). English translation by Allan Kravitz, unpublished.

5. That is, a range of building types created to serve an intentional community. Doloras Hayden, *Seven American Utopias: The Architecture of Communitarian Socialism 1790-1976* (Cambridge, Mass.: MIT Press, 1976).

6. Robert Owen, Report to the *County of Lanark*, and *A New View of Society* (Harmondsworth, England: Penguin Books, 1969); Charles Fourier, *The Utopian Vision of Charles Fouries*, Tr. Jonathan Beecher and Richard Bienvenu, (Boston: Beacon Press, 1971); also see Hayden, *Seven American Utopias*, on "The Architecture of Passional Attraction," in practice.

7. William Morris, *News From Nowhere* (1890, New York: International Publishers, 1968). This novel was written in response to Bellamy's *Looking Backward*.

8. Ebenezer Howard, *Garden Cities of To-Morrow* (1898, Cambridge, Mass.: MIT Press, 1965).

9. Murray Bookchin, *Post-Scarcity Anarchism* Berkeley: Ramparts Press, 1971).

10. Christopher Alexander, et al., *The Timeless Way of Building* (New York: Oxford University Press, 1979).

11. E.F. Schumacher, *Small Is Beautiful: Economics As If People Mattered* (New York: Harper and Row, 1973).

12. Edward Bellamy, *Looking Backward: 2000-1887* (1888, New York: Lancer Books, 1967).

13. Robert Fishman, *Urban Utopias in the Twentieth Century: Ebenezer Howard, Le Corbusier, and Frank Lloyd Wright* (New York: Basic Books,

1977); Anatole Kopp, *Town and Revolution: Soviet Architecture and City Planning, 1917-1935* (New York: George Braziller, 1970).

14. Ian Todd and Michael Wheeler, *Utopia* (New York: Harmony Books, 1978), p. 135.

15. A few new model agricultural villages in Cuba contain attempts to combine technological and artistic approaches to new housing. While industrial building systems are used for the construction of three to four story walk-up apartments for both existing cities and new villages, the concrete panels once erected are not left gray. Instead Cuban graphic artists paint them in several brilliant colors, such as red, yellow, turquoise, or green, creating a play of colored planes enhanced by the strong Caribbean sunlight. Finally tropical landscaping surrounds them, and an indigenous housing type emerges based on industrial components. Yet even the Cubans are tending to favor more severe high-rise housing programs for urban locations, similar to ones developed in the Soviet Union, eastern Europe and recently China.

16. Henri Lefebvre, Tr. Kravitz, pp. 122-123.

17. Eli Zaretsky, *Capitalism, the Family and Personal Life* (New York: Harper Torchbooks, 1976).

18. Dolores Hayden, *The Grand Domestic Revolution: A History of Feminist Designs for American Homes, Neighborhoods, and Cities* (Cambridge, Mass.: MIT Press, 1981).

19. Hayden, *Grand Domestic Revolution*.

20. Richard Walker, "Suburbanization in Process," unpublished draft paper, Dept. of Geography, University of California, Berkeley, 1978.

21. Frances Willard, speech reprinted in *Union Signal*, 1889.

22. This proposal is drawn from Dolores Hayden, "What Would a Non-Sexist City Be Like?" in *Women and the American City*, supplement to volume 5 of *Signs: A Journal of Women in Culture and Society*, (Spring, 1980).

23. "The Cuban Family Code," reprinted in *Center for Cuban Studies Newsletter*, vol. 2, 1975, available from the center, 220 East 23rd St., New York, N.Y.

24. Delia Davin, *Woman-Work: Women and the Party in Revolutionary China* (Oxford, England: Oxford University Press, 1976).

25. Hayden, "Non-Sexist City."

26. Anna Gyorgy and Friends, *No Nukes: Everyone's Guide to Nuclear Power* (Boston: South End Press, 1979).

27. Dolores Hayden, "Skyscraper Seduction, Skyscraper Rape," *Heresies*, 2 (1977), pp. 108-115.

28. Ibid.

29. Elinor Langer, "Inside the New York Telephone Company," in *Women at Work*, ed. William L. O'Neill, (New York: Quadrangle Books, 1972).

30. J. B. Jackson, *American Space* (New York: W. W. Norton, 1977).

31. One of the best critiques of commercial art is John Berger, et al., *Ways of Seeing* (Harmondsworth, England: Penguin, 1975).

32. John F. Kasson, *Amusing the Million: Coney Island at the Turn of the Century* (New York: Hill and Wang, 1978).

ENVIRONMENTAL PLURALISM AND THE SOCIALIST VISIONS
Gwendolyn Wright

Consumerism, waste, the transitory life, and isolation of individuals characterize the cities and suburbs of late 20th century America. Super-highways connect corporate headquarters with industrial parks, separating these work environments from shopping malls and suburban homes. One usually tries to block out this monotonous, regimented landscape, or at least to celebrate only the fragments that are exceptions: parks, architectural monuments, historic districts, or lively urban neighborhoods. But it is exactly their grandiose scale that makes suburbs, business districts, and shopping centers seem so overwhelming. The sense of inescapable order gives the environment of capitalism its impact.

This ordering of space is obviously related to how people live, not only in a metaphoric sense, but also socially. These environments sanction certain kinds of relationships. Both their associations and the limited number of alternatives create a strict control on activities. Hence the difficulties of suburban women raising families and commuting long distances to jobs, or of employees having the opportunity to do anything beyond repeating a routine task: spatial restrictions, as well as other factors, make these situations seem aberrant. One's experiences—and one's aspirations—are based in part on the kinds of environments in which one lives and works. Buildings and land-use plans do not, of course, dicatate management policies or segregation policies; they are not the cause of sex role stereotypes or class inequalities. But certain environments can make it seem futile to break the prevailing patterns. This is part of the power of capitalist space.

Here, as in her other published work, Dolores Hayden analyzes the evolution and the force of capitalist space. She also challenges that vision. Just as high-rise towers and suburban sprawl make capitalist order seem inviolable to many people, so too another vision of the environment can be a foundation for socialism.

The very process of considering how space functions is a step toward change. This tactic has deep roots in the American past. Hayden provocatively demonstrates how, for two centuries, the town

82

plans of communitarians and the cooperative housing schemes of feminists buttressed their determination to effect social change. Similarly, current proposals for reusing the environment of capitalism are an important form of resistance. Rehabilitating inexpensive housing and preserving ethnic neighborhoods; involving workers in the reorganization of their factories and offices; organizing farmers, small industrial producers, or parents into cooperatives: these can be more than piecemeal reforms. Each of these movements improves the quality of people's lives. The change comes about through their own involvement, not through passive consumerism. This "recapturing" of the environment, in Hayden's words, has social and political repercussions. People necessarily ask themselves questions about their conditions, their children's educational possibilities, the kinds of communities they would hope to create. How do residential neighborhoods isolate women and children? How do office buildings intensify hierarchies? What obstacles stand in the way of effecting changes?

Hayden goes beyond a critique of capitalist domination; she also moves beyond appeals for economic restructuring and political representation to consider the ways in which space affects people's daily lives, whether in a socialist setting or in the capitalist world. This is an absolutely essential step toward conceptualizing a socialist future. Changing the environment is not a move of the vanguard; it is not a tactic that will bring about revolutionary change. But by the end of the 20th century, this should no longer be considered a criticism. Issues about the quality of everyday life persist after the most dramatic of political changes. They either assure continuity with the past and a depth of commitment to popular concerns, or they become a source of reactionary resistance. Questions about child-rearing, women's rights, energy conservation, or ethnicity are not secondary. They are key political problems for many people. Socialism in post-industiral societies (in fact, in any society) must recognize that "bourgeois" issues like beauty, imagination, nature, and sex are central to any meaningful vision of a better society. It is this range of issues—each of which has definite environmental dimensions—that is likely to motivate people politically, either encouraging them to organize for change, or stifling their desire to participate in political movements. The core of socialist understanding should be a respect for the problems people care about in their day-to-day lives.

Pluralism is another key factor in this socialist vision of the future. The obliteration of ethnic and regional traditions is one of the consequences of capitalist development which a socialist society would try to reverse, without resorting to quaintness or limited opportunities for minority groups. Socialist space cannot have a singular definition, just as there cannot be absolute standards about correct living arrangements or family relations. Of course, finding a balance between respect for differences and protection of equality is not an easy challenge. Yet socialist planning must take into account varying needs and desires based on age, background, and personal preference. Personal choices cannot be dismissed as capitalist manipulation, or there will be very little support for socialist proposals, no matter how utilitarian or beneficial they seem to their planners. To impose standards for all men and women, as in Russia or Eastern Europe, is a bleak program for the future.

A mix of housing types is one expression of this pluralist social order. Some people will always want to live in cities and others in small towns; some collectively and others alone or in nuclear families. Architectural variation of sizes, layouts, and complexity of housing forms facilitates these choices. The differences would not be related to status, as they are under capitalism. Where one lives would be a matter of choice and convenience; how the building looked would be related to particular tastes and talents, and to the community's ideal of architectural beauty.

Urbanizing the suburbs—bringing in a variety of jobs, services, and types of people—is one very sensible approach toward a kind of land-use planning that encourages socialism. It will create more opportunities for employment and cooperative domestic services. It will encourage reliance on other people, while preserving some of the familiar surroundings of the past. Yet not even the extreme public/private split that characterizes most American suburbs should lead to dogmatic regulations for collectivity. Hayden is fully aware of the need to have local control of such changes—and hence to accept a great range of diverse solutions. Her recognition of the need to preserve private yards and rooms, even when other areas are collectivized, shows an astute respect for the way most Americans will still want to live.

The great attention given to the suburbs is also an important step in conceptualizing a socialist future. For some time, there has been such confusion, such embarassment about the suburban way of life that socialist proposals tended to ignore the issue altogether, focusing instead on tenants in urban and rural areas. Yet millions of men, women, and children do, after all, live in suburban areas and, as Hayden points out, this infrastructure certainly cannot be discarded. Efforts to consider reusing suburban space, like efforts to organize these communities, will involve people of all ages and classes, as a necessary part of a socialist future.

In fact, this involvement was true in the past. It was not only communitarians and radical feminists who tried to use the environment as a means for improving the society in which they lived. Environmental topics have also had a great impact in the mainstream of

American society. Middle-class women and men saw the environment, especially housing, as a key to other reforms. In the process, they asked themselves about the social and economic problems of their time, about their own goals, about their political effectiveness. In the early 19th century, carpenters and artisans discussed how simple, well-made houses could encourage equality. At the turn of the last century, moderate women's clubs and university domestic scientists tried to promote humanitarian factory regulations and better housing for all classes. They encouraged women to organize politically and to educate themselves, arguing that the home and family had become public political issues, even for those people who lived in private homes. Similarly, many of the first public housing activists (especially Catherine Bauer and Edith Elmer Wood) saw decent, state-subsidized housing for the poor as a means for encouraging workers to organize politically and demand other rights.

At the same time, this focus on environmental change has generally tended to erode the underlying goals. The early-twentieth century feminists promoted a model house that was simple, economical, and efficient; but this did not put an end to class differences or to sexual discrimination,. For many American reform groups, the appearance of change seemed sufficient, even if the inequalities that had motivated their actions were still present. Evironmental reform could dull the awareness of social and economic problems, even those it had been designed to address.

This tendency does not mean that environmental reform is inherently an evasion of real social or economic issues. It is a way of involving a wide range of people in issues that matter to them. Housing, working conditions, schools, and transportation networks are inescapable topics in this society. They raise other problems, such as local financial and governmental decision-making, employment possibilities, segregation, and the very quality of daily life. Those connections make such environmental topics inherently political.

It is possible to use the longstanding American fascination with environmental change in a positive, progressive way. One step is to realize that people who are concerned about their homes, families, and neighborhoods are not necessarily reactionary, no more than are people who demand decent jobs outside the home. Among the issues that the "new progressive" movement is using for grass-roots organizing, housing and jobs are indisputably the most prominent, and the most closely related. For many people, housing is more than a commodity, more than a symbol of comfort and stability. Rent control, energy costs, environmental pollution, and redlining are the focus of diverse community-based groups. Elderly people want housing that meets their needs, while suburban women and inner-city minority groups discuss other housing problems. There is no one kind of environmental plan that can address all of these needs. The process of balancing them is part of what it means to have participatory socialism. A diverse range of affordable housing, decent work places, and a non-polluted environment will not create socialism; but it is not possible to have a socialist vision of the future without them.

PARTICIPATORY SOCIALISM AND THE BUILT ENVIRONMENT
Robert Goodman

Dolores Hayden believes socialist designers have missed the boat. They have either accepted the towering inhuman form of the 20th century high-tech city or have proposed its utopian antithesis—the community of small farms, industries and dwellings.

The strength of her argument lies in the rejection of these extremes and her search for humane, pragmatic solutions. Our problems in creating socialist form are not so much the creation of entirely new environments, she says, but taking the overbuilt world we already have, and reusing it according to socialist practice.

In her own search through the murky in-between world of real life design she proposes a series of beginning approaches to support a "participatory socialism." Her reuse scheme for suburban homes expands the possibilities for what is now a socially segregated and privatistic environment. Remodelling some houses to accommodate smaller families would give suburban communities a more varied age and family size population. Using backyards and some parts of existing buildings for more public use would make it easier for families to engage in cooperative activities.

She looks beyond the simple dichotomy of public and private and turns to the "mediating spaces" between public and private ones—such as porches and sidewalks as forms which must be reconceptualized. While the capitalist world tends to make a strong distinction between what is public and what is private, she believes that the more public nature of socialism would allow for a greater richness of use for public spaces, as well as the semi-public, mediating spaces.

Hayden's approach implies an innovative and activist role for designers in moving toward a socialist America. They would pose concrete, "socialist form" alternatives to what exists in both capitalist and socialist societies. Her views take on all the more importance, the more we see that socialism does not inevitably transform design quality. We cannot be content to vaguely promise that better politics will somehow produce better design. Good politics and bad design is still bad design.

The new design approaches to socialist form should be actively criticized, not only among leftist planners and architects, but among all sectors of the progressive movement. Through the creation and criticism of proposals such as Hayden's, a leftist design approach can emerge—much as the concepts of worker self-management, democratic decision-making, anti-corporatism, and anti-centralization have come to represent the social and economic goals of what might be called the decentralist strain of current left politics. As designers we must ask ourselves what kind of workplace environment is sympathetic to worker self-management? What kind of community design best accommodates social and economic decentralization? How would these concepts be applied in existing urban, suburban, and rural situations—and how would they be applied in new situations?

We know, as Hayden points out, that capitalism has shaped the way we use space in this country—be it the information on billboards or the design of the home based on the unpaid labor of the housewife. Given this dilemma, it is not enough to say socialism will free women from housework (in socialist countries it has and it hasn't). What we need to do is to describe the physical environment that would support this freedom. Can we, for example, plan and design food preparation systems into communities which reduce the amount of time needed for women and men in a household to prepare meals—can prepared food be delivered to the home at some mealtimes, or can the family and individuals make more use of restaurant facilities that are within walking distance of their homes?

We have had a dearth of radical analyses which describe why our cities look the way they do. No doubt more studies will be useful in refining this analysis. But if we seriously expect people to be moved towards a radical transformation of society, we must be able to pose concrete ideas of what that transformation could bring about in our everyday lives. How would dwellings change? What kind of recreation and shopping facilities would there be? In short, we must be able to show what will be changed and why the change is for the better.

As designers we are understandably reluctant to be very specific about describing a future environment for which there are few working models from our existing world. How do we know it will work? Will we be dismissed as naive visionaries? Meanwhile the hard line Marxist view tells us we must transform the economic structure of society before we can hope to have the consciousness that will allow us to transform the cultural superstructure of which design is a part.

But do we really know which must come first—cultural change or economic change? And is it really so important to play this chicken and egg game? The Russian experience provides more than enough evidence that socialist economic transformation does not necessarily lead to humane cultural transformation— witness the fate of the Russian futurists in the arts.

Proposing a new environment for socialist America is only one part of the process of transformation. A harder question is what role does design play, if any, in moving us from here to there. This is not the subject of Hayden's piece, but an important next step for designers to consider. Can we creep up on capitalism and subvert it with producer co-ops, community control, and socialist designs?

Did the introduction of public housing move us to a more socialist economic future? The dismal record of the design and management of public housing notwithstanding, public housing did help establish the idea that government should be directly involved in financially supporting the social welfare of its citizens. And in spite of the many failures in design and management, there are many examples of public housing that have worked. Whether we are closer to socialism in America today than we were in the 1920s is hard to say. It is clear, however, that many of our "socialist-type" programs—housing assistance, health care, and social security—are the result of progressive, socialist ideas that have percolated through non-socialist governments.

Hayden has helped us define something she calls "socialist space." It is a design approach that does not automatically spring from the establishment of socialism, nor can the approach itself produce socialism. Her design ideas are rather *sympathetic to* the goals of socialism—more public ownership and use of space, the absence of speculation, the absence of induced consumption through advertising, and the planned and rational use of the country's resources.

The next, and more difficult step in considering socialist space is to examine proposals such as Hayden's in the context of a movement towards socialism in America. If we propose to change existing single family houses in order to provide more public facilities, for example, don't we come up against the American tradition of owning your own? Is the privacy and isolation that Americans find in suburban and rural areas something they would want to part with? Or under what conditions would they part with it? Would they be willing to accept the trade-off of less private space in exchange for more public space?

It is already clear that changing economic conditions have meant fewer Americans are able to reach their dream of owning the traditional single family home. In response to increased housing costs, real estate developers have shifted to cheaper housing types such as mobile homes (which are rarely moved), townhouses, and apartment condominiums. The form of the space has changed, but the individualized home ownership concept has not.

The extent to which designers like Hayden can create and publicize their plans for socialist space helps raise public consciousness about this alternative, and helps promote the politics that make it achievable. A further step for designers would be to align themselves and their ideas with organizations that are involved in progressive social change.

These organizations include left political parties, labor unions, and housing advocacy organizations. Designers might look to the earlier experience of some of the labor unions in New York City which played a crucial role in developing cooperative housing for their members. As an alternative to private ownership, cooperative ownership might be a more comfortable immediate direction for Americans to take than complete public ownership. At a time when many of our major public and private labor unions are considering more socially beneficial ways of using their pension funds, the availability of progressive design alternatives could have an important influence over what actually gets built.

Today, architectural design in America is dominated by aesthetic controversies which pits the school of "modernism" against that of "post-modernism." This is essentially a battle between those who believe in a formalism of simple form—the modernists—against those who strive for more complex forms—the post-modernists. The search for form has brought the modernists to eschew an architecture expressive of the steel, glass, and concrete technology of which it is built, while the post-modernists strive for a more "inclusive" aesthetic embracing both classic motifs such as greek temple columns, as well as the modern ones of steel, glass, and concrete.

But in all of this controversy—in which there is a presumed search for richer architectural meaning—the most meaningful parts of the debate have been omitted. This would involve viewing architectural design primarily as an activity in which physical form is used to give expression to people's desire to have better community places and better workplaces. In the final analysis it doesn't matter whether we lead our atomized lives in modernist houses, post-modernist houses, or split-level colonial houses. What matters is that the form of our present communities reinforces our atomized lives—what matters is that we have not been able to design or build places that support community, that make the workplace more healthy, and that are not wasteful of our natural resources. Hayden's approach, in the tradition of Paul and Percival Goodman's *Communitas* creates an important dialogue in a more hopeful design debate. We would do well to continue it.

A VIEW FROM THE NORTHEAST
Martin Bierbaum

Dolores Hayden decries the current status of the American capitalist built environment. She complains about the incoherent aesthetic character along with air pollution, traffic noise, and outdoor advertising. America's cities are "nowhere cities" composed of "mad eclecticism." She expresses hope that a clear vision of another kind of environment might provide powerful propaganda for change. She calls for a "new code of space."

In this way, Hayden tries to connect herself to a long line of utopian thinkers who have pondered about a more humane and habitable environment. Such thinking, historically, has not been entirely in vain. Despite the desperate and deplorable living conditions in many of America's older cities, utopian thinking has contributed positively to some of the discourse on new town planning and urban redevelopment. Traditionally, utopians have contributed to thinking about the balance between urban and rural conditions, types of housing, and the size of communities. The flaw in utopian thinking is that it usually caricatures a living situation by seizing on just one or two aspects of the social and physical environment. By focusing on so few facets, utopians have made a contribution by highlighting glaring shortcomings of the existing set of conditions, but simultaneously have provided an over-simplified distortion of what might be a desirable future state of affairs.

Hayden's caricature dwells on the aesthetic revulsion to the contemporary built environment and the status of women in latter 20th century Urban America. I feel that her vision fails even as a caricature because she has not focused on the fundamental ills of the ailing American capitalist built environment.

According to Hayden's socialist vision, commercial billboards will disappear. Neighborhoods will be reorganized in more aesthetic-ally pleasing ways. The invidious sexual division of labor will be eliminated. Voluntary collective services will minimize the need for many of the burdens of household work which currently fall dispropor-tionately on women. The differences between the private and public spheres of activity will be minimized which will also lighten the burdens of the sexual division of labor.

Again, my problem with the piece is that I am not at all certain what Hayden's revulsion of aesthetics and concerns about sexual oppression have to do with a capitalist society or how these conditions might be improved under socialism. I suspect that her strong reaction and prescription is a personal one of a woman experiencing southern California. Perhaps as a male living in the northeastern United States, I offer a balancing view.

The milieu that the author seems to desire may already exist in parts of capitalist America. The role of women has undergone substantial changes in the past decade. Certainly day care centers, laundromats, meals-on-wheels, and home gardens are not alien to the American experience. Moreover, the notion that a "woman's place is in the home" seems peculiarly out of date when such a large percentage of the labor force is currently composed of women. Are male suburban homeowners really likely to think of themselves as "patriarchs" when they frequently require a second income derived from their spouse's efforts in order to maintain that "dream house" in the suburbs? Finally, I am dubious about the results of collectivized, institutionalized efforts to replace functions presently performed by primary group relationships. I have already witnessed situations among "progressive" people where "a woman's place is in the home" has been abruptly supplanted by "no one's place is in the home" to the detriment of all involved. People, both men and women, who wish to have children, may have to modify career plans and share responsibility, not abnegate it.

As to Hayden's aesthetic objections, I believe she is reacting to the plastic neon glitter which has characterized much of the sunbelt development in the last decade which is epitomized by southern California. But such "mad eclecticism" is not inherent to capitalism. Instead it is a combination of forces involving private ownership, the lack of comprehensive planning and strong public controls, and also cultural factors. More comprehensive planning and more strict aesthetic controls are possible without social revolution. Private developments such as enclosed shopping malls, retirement villages, and new towns can produce a more uniform and aesthetically pleasing result without socialism.

But more important than any of these individual criticisms, there is a fundamental lack in Hayden's vision. The operative questions with respect to a socialist vision, I believe, are the following:

1. What constitutes a "good community?"
2. How has the American capitalist society failed in providing that community?

3. In what ways might a socialist built environment succeed with respect to that community where the capitalist built system has failed?

Unfortunately, Hayden has not explicitly addressed these critical questions.

What might a "good community" be? In the contemporary context, there is no one "good community." Most of us live in "communities of limited liability" where our ties to the local community are tenuous at best, allowing us to move with changes in life-style, income, occupation, and social adversity. Communities are selected by individuals and households to conform with their changing priorities and personal agendas over the course of a lifetime. I see little inherently wrong with this process given the highly mobile and technologically sophisticated society in which we find ourselves.

People may make their choice with a number of criteria in mind. Individuals may select a community that provides for meaningful personal relationships or they may seek to avoid them. The size of the community may be crucial for some. Some may be desirous of a heterogenous and cosmopolitan milieu repleat with diversity as to age, income, and ethnic and racial groups. Others may find comfort in a single ethnic community, or a retirement village, or a neighborhood focused around child rearing. Some people may wish for a community which makes heavy demands in terms of social and political commitment. To others, such participation and squabbling may prove a tiresome bore.

But a fundamental problem related to all this choosing is posed by the way choices are constrained in modern capitalist America. Choices are not made on the basis of reason, desire, and need alone. Economic calculations must be tied to the preferences outlined above. The aesthetic concerns and elevation of women's rights, I believe, can be addressed within the capitalist context through the expansion of the state's police powers, modifications in the definition of equal protection, and by countering local political fragmentation. Indeed, such changes are already evident.

However, where capitalism seems to fail most miserably is with respect to the limits placed on the distribution of wealth, income, and thereby choice. These opportunities are restricted to too few, and apparently over the course of the next decade they will be restricted to even fewer. The positive vision held out by a socialist alternative must be that social goods and life opportunities will be distributed more fairly on the basis of need and not merely on the basis of income and wealth.

This lack of equitable distribution in the United States has acquired important geographic and physical aspects. Due to the inequalities in income and wealth combined with the relative strength of the private sector, and relative weakness and fragmentation of the public sector, some communities are better able to internalize social benefits while externalizing social costs. Others, usually older central city areas, suffer by the projection of externalized social costs without the ability to glean social benefits. Central city areas in this way become "low income sinks." The social and physical environments thereby created are an unmitigated disaster. The inhabitants of such places are there not by choice but the utter lack of it.

The failure of the American capitalist built environment consists of the degradation and barbarism which characterizes the South Bronx and Newark. The vision of a socialist built environment is not to pander to any particular taste, but to provide an alternative which raises the quality of life in such places to habitable and humane standards. The access to fundamental social services and a supportive physical environment need to be based on human need and not wealth or income. Coincidentally, by addressing the human needs of such areas, the society will enhance the choices available to all, even the relatively affluent, as once again central city living might become attractive once devoid of the desperation attendant to the crime and poverty which now breed there. "The new code of space" must obliterate the chasm which persists between the affluent and the impoverished in capitalist America. The fundamental features of the American capitalist built environment are inextricably entangled with political-economic concerns.

REJOINDER
Dolores Hayden

I'm grateful to Gwendolyn Wright and Robert Goodman for their supportive comments on my article; as architects and writers concerned with the built environment, I think we three are in agreement that space is a social and economic product.

Martin Bierbaum, on the other hand, does not believe that the capitalist built environment is the product of economic and social forces. He seems to believe that most of the spaces capitalism has created are quite satisfactory; the problem, as he sees it, is that the satisfactory spaces are only available to people with money. As far as he is concerned, most of the issues I raise in my essay are cultural issues or consumption issues, and quite irrelevant to the creation of real socialism. To contest this view, I would argue, as Engels did, that "the determining factor in history is, in the final instance, the production and reproduction of immediate life . . . . The social organization under which the people of a particular historical epoch live is determined by both kinds of production." (*The Origin of the Family, Private Property, and the State*, 1884.) My proposals about the socialist reconstruction of the built environment deal with spaces for production and spaces for reproduction; both are essential parts of a socialist transformation.

In addition to this basic theoretical disagreement, or perhaps because of it, Bierbaum parodies my arguments and mistakes my views. I do not argue that our cities are economically incoherent: I make exactly the opposite point, that all American cities are economically shaped by capitalism but aesthetically "styled to conceal the uniformity below the facade." He does not seem to understand how this criticism of space relates to capitalist society: I suggest he review Marxist critiques of the manipulation of workers as consumers of mass-produced commodities; this is the critique I am applying to mass-produced space as a commodity.

Bierbaum also states "I am not at all certain what Hayden's . . . concerns about sexual oppression have to do with a capitalist society or how [they] might be improved under socialism." Well, on this point, I suggest Bierbaum review the work of Bebel, Engels, Lenin, and Heidi Hartmann, before he condemns me as offering the "personal" views of a "woman experiencing southern California," and commits the fatal mistake of condescension: "Perhaps as a male living in the northeastern United States, I offer a balancing view." The poorest workers in American society are women, including minority women, and any socialist program that fails to come to terms with this issue is sure to fail.

Bierbaum also states that since "day care centers, laundromats, meals on wheels, and home gardens are not alien to the American experience," he can't see what all the fuss is about concerning these institutions and women under socialism. His argument seems to have two parts: first, he seems to believe women are already liberated by wage work under capitalism, so I am incorrect to state that "woman's place is in the home," and attempt to restructure reproduction. However, wage work, in itself, cannot liberate women. Under both capitalism and state socialism as we know it, wage work for women is usually low paid, occupationally segregated work, and at the end of the day women have a second shift of unpaid nurturing at home, averaging about 17 to 20 extra hours per week according to recent research in both the U.S. and USSR. Second, Bierbaum seems to believe that existing commercial services have helped relieve women. Currently there is only enough subsidized day care in the U.S for 10 percent of the children of employed mothers; laundromats are actually zoned out of many R-1 neighborhoods, as are daycare centers (and for that matter, abortion clinics have been the target of other zoning battles). I believe that restructuring housing, services, and jobs for women will require a major planning effort to counteract sixty years of capitalist planning to separate "home" and "work" for men.

In thinking of reconstruction under socialism, I believe it is important to use those good existing spatial forms and social forms which are accepted in our culture and improve upon them. I argue that neighborhood day care centers, meal delivery systems for the elderly, and home gardens are just such positive institutions to build on. I am not proposing communal living or "no one's place is in the home"; I am attempting to define collective services to support many different kinds of private households and their needs and desires, in such a way that socialism offers richer options about both privacy and community than are now possible to achieve under capitalism.

Bierbaum prefers enclosed shopping malls, retirement villages, and new towns as spatial exemplars. All of his prototypes have been pioneered by speculative developers; all are sold on a speculative basis;

all are privately policed. The first, shopping malls, are usually open only to affluent shoppers (young blacks, and "shopping bag" ladies, will be hustled out). The second, retirement villages, segregate the affluent elderly. The third, new towns, never include many minority residents or poor residents, nor jobs for low income people other than maids. What sort of socialist world is this? He may think that reassigning these spaces to new groups of people is all that socialist planning and design is about, but I disagree.

Bierbaum also accuses me of overlooking the basic problem of capitalism in the U.S, i.e., unequal wealth, and its environmental expression in the South Bronx and Newark, in favor of paying too much attention to suburbia. I see the two kinds of capitalist environments as intimately related. It was the creation of a national policy of financial support for speculative development in suburbia that drained resources away from old cities and ghetto areas in the first place. And it was the promotion of home ownership for white male workers that encouraged every male home owner to see himself as an owner-speculator concerned with property values in suburban neighborhoods. This is one major reason why Americans have tolerated utterly wretched burnt-out inner city areas in the richest country in the world. Private space replaced public space as a topic of concern.

To organize mass support for a a socialist program, it is essential to offer alternative formulations for the entire American society, not simply the worst piece of it. Some reformers may wish to focus on the ghetto as the clearest symptom of racism, sexism, and economic inequality; I think we need to look at the entire built environment critically to diagnose the overall malaise and prepare a truly radical program for winning the hearts and minds of a majority of citizens.

III. RACE & NATIONALISM

Lead Essay	Manning Marable
Responses	Tiffany R. Patterson
	William K. Tabb
Rejoinder	Manning Marable

THE THIRD RECONSTRUCTION
Black Nationalism and Race Relations After the Revolution

Manning Marable

> In two historic instances Negro Americans have been beneficiaries—as well as the victims—of the national compulsion to level or to blur distinctions. The first leveling ended the legal status of slavery, the second the legal system of segregation. Both abolitions left the beneficiaries still suffering under handicaps inflicted by the system abolished.
>
> C. Vann Woodward,
> *The Strange Career of Jim Crow.*

I

After every significant social revolution, there has been a period of reconciliation, reassessment, and reconstruction.

In the most influential social revolution of the 20th century, the Bolshevik Revolution, the period of civil war and disruption was followed, at least for a half dozen years, by a period of construction and peace. "War Communism" lapsed into the programs of the New Economic Policy (N.E.P.). Described by some proponents as a retreat from "socialist illusions," N.E.P. represented a major advance in the material and cultural life of the peasants and small industrial working class. In such diverse areas as housing, education, and land tenure, N.E.P provided the foundations for what could have evolved as a democratic and culturally vibrant socialist order. Lenin's revolution in cultural relations, as projected in one of his final essays, symbolized the vast changes in popular ideology, consciousness, and culture which are essential in creating a new socialist society.

In the aftermath of the U.S. Civil War, an uneven period of Reconstruction began. Partially because Northern troops were as racist as Southerners, no definite policies evolved relating to "the Negro Question." General William T. Sherman compaigned through Georgia and the Carolinas and issued the famous Order No. 15, which guaranteed blacks the right of pre-emption on former plantation property. Blacks bought or seized thousands of acres of choice farmland, only to give these lands back when President Andrew Johnson insisted on a whites-only land tenure policy. Despite these setbacks, a number of important advances were achieved. The Freedmen's Bureau, a government agency, provided over 21 million rations of food to blacks, and aided in the resettlement of families. Churches and white philanthropic organizations established black colleges, universities, and hospitals. By 1875 over 600,000 black youth were attending Southern schools, when only a decade before it was illegal in most states to teach reading to blacks. Politically, progress was made both in the North and South. By 1873 there were seven black congresspersons, a figure that would not be equalled again until 1967. Many segregation laws, most of which had existed in nonslave states, were voided: in 1865, for instance, Illinois and Indiana repealed laws stating that blacks could not testify in courts; segregated schools in Rhode Island were abolished in 1866. In 1865 Congress repealed an act from 1825 that prohibited Afro-Americans from working as post office employees, and allowed blacks to participate in federal court trials. Jim Crow streetcars were stopped in Washington D.C. in 1865, because of the public protests of abolitionist Sojourner Truth. In general, despite its contradictions, Reconstruction represented a period of greater human freedoms for all Afro-Americans, and raised the possibility of a truly democratic American society.

Yet, most of the benefits from Reconstruction disappeared almost as quickly as they were achieved. Slavery was abolished, but in its place were the sharecropping and crop lien systems of agricultural production, modes of labor in certain respects even more oppressive than enslavement. The total number of black elected officials, which amounted to 670 state representatives, 124 state senators, and 22 congresspersons in the years 1869-1901, dropped to almost nothing. Beginning in 1890, a series of Southern states passed new constitutions which effectively denied all blacks (and a greater number of poor whites) the right of suffrage, in direct violation of the Fourteenth and Fifteenth Amendments. County and town governments adopted a system of convict leasing, in which thousands of unemployed blacks were arrested for "vagrancy" and then hired out to white merchants or businessmen seeking cheap labor. Within a generation after the war, an all-pervasive system of racial segregation was dominant in every aspect of black-white relations. For instance, South Carolina law declared that black and white textile workers could not work together in the same room, use the same entrances, doorways, drinking water buckets and cups, pay windows, or lavatories. Louisiana demanded that its blacks purchase separate tickets at separate pay windows, using separate entrances, to attend all local circuses. In 1909 Mobile, Alabama required all blacks to be off the street by ten p.m. In New Orleans, black and white prostitutes solicited customers in separate districts. As historian C. Vann Woodward has observed, "a Birmingham ordinance got down to the particulars in 1930 by making it 'unlawful for a Negro and a white person to play together or in company with each other' at dominoes or checkers."

The reasons for the reactionary, post-Reconstruction period, which historian Rayford Logan has correctly termed "The Nadir," are varied and complex. The North had no desire to elevate the Negro to the social and cultural status of an equal. In other words, the war was fought "over slavery," but not over the status of the slave. The economic system of involuntary servitude was updated along capitalist lines, in conformity with the demands of Northern industry and the dominant Republican Party. Black aspirations for land tenure, the popular demand for "forty acres and a mule," were largely crushed with the help of the occupying Union army. Black political leaders tended to emerge from the educated, culturally assimilated slave, and freed Negro strata, rather than from the masses of field hands and laborers; as a result, most black Republicans tended to be too conservative in dealing with the former master class. There were of course outstanding exceptions, such as the brilliant Henry M. Turner and Martin Delany. But generally, Reconstruction succumbed to reaction because none of the major parties involved, other than the blacks themselves, had any intention of liberating the Afro-American community from a secondary caste position and from its inferior economic status.

The foundations for the modern Civil Rights Movement, which Woodward refers to as "the Second Reconstruction," are found within the failure and promise of the first. The next conflict was, like the first, over the relationship between black people and the South. One pivotal difference was the fact that this conflict was fought on the terrain of public policy and electoral politics, over cultural and social relations, rather than on the battlefield. This critical distinction within specific phases of social transformation is described in the works of Antonio Gramsci as the difference between a "war of position" and a "war of movement."

Another difference was that the ideological forces of liberation (the combined weight of the NAACP and the Urban League on the political right, SCLC and CORE in the center, and SNCC on the left, plus black nationalist forces and personalities like Malcolm X) were much stronger than were the early black abolitionists (Frederick Douglass, Delany, Henry Highland Garnet), relative to the forces of reaction and racism. As in the first Reconstruction, the U.S. Government, and particularly the ideologically liberal politicians and intellectuals, sought to create reforms for the Afro-American community at the expense of the racial status quo. A series of Federal laws and Supreme Court decisions challenged and eventually destroyed the legitimacy of Jim Crow, much as the Fourteenth Amendment and the Civil Rights Act of 1875 had challenged racial discrimination for a brief time. The Civil Rights Act of 1964 banned Jim Crow in theatres, hotels, restaurants, and all public places. More significantly, the Voting Rights Act of 1965 outlawed discrimination in economic opportunity, all public educational institutions, unions, and housing. Despite the white South's "Massive Resistance," the battle to destroy *de jure* segregation was won by 1970.

Much of the literature on the Second Reconstruction deals with either analyzing the political organizations fighting for integration or the specific public figures which the Movement elevated to greatness. Certainly Martin Luther King, Jr. deserves special note, not so much for his rhetorical eloquence or ability to represent the aspirations of millions of black working people, but for the courage and increasingly progressive political positions he took from 1966-68. Others have commented extensively on the impact of political desegregation upon the makeup of local, state, and federal government. For example in 1964 there were only 103 black elected officials in the United States; by 1970 the total was 1469, and by 1980 the figure exceeded 5000. What really made the Second Reconstruction meaningful, however, were the actual material advances gained by the majority of black industrial workers, farmers, and the petty bourgeois strata during the years 1954-1970.

It was in the general quality of human life—housing, educational advancement, employment, health, and cultural activity—that the benefits of the Second Reconstruction were most profound. Black unemployment rates for married males dropped sharply, from 7.9 percent in 1962 down to 2.5 percent in 1969. Overall unemployment rates for all blacks went from 10.9 percent to 6.4 percent during these same years. Black workers began shifting from lower paying agricultural and unskilled laboring jobs to industrial and skilled laboring jobs. Desegregation and official "equal opportunity" hiring practices meant that thousands of technically qualified blacks could compete on relatively even terms for professional and clerical positions which had been previously "Jim Crowed." As formerly segregated colleges, technical schools, and universities began to admit blacks, several million black youth acquired the academic leverage essential for vocational advancement. These reforms in hiring practices and educational opportunity had a direct impact upon the quality of black housing, black health care, and even infant mortality and fertility rates. Blacks were increasingly able to purchase their own homes, and were now able to afford the physical luxuries (such as indoor plumbing) that most whites had experienced for years. Life expectancies for both black women and men increased as the federal government expanded its social service and welfare programs (i.e. Medicare and Medicaid) to aid the elderly and disabled.

In *The Eighteenth Brumaire*, Marx quotes Hegel as stating that "history repeats itself twice," and then adds, the first time as "tragedy," the second time as "farce." If the First Reconstruction was tragic, then its successor was akin to farce, since so many of the same ingredients which coalesced for reaction came together in the later period. Once again, the impetus for reaction first showed itself within the ranks of the Afro-Americans' allies, the political liberals of both parties. As white middle class constituencies grew alarmed by Watts, Hough, and Chicago's South Side "riots," a demand for law-and-order began to prevail. Just as Delany and DuBois frightened the white postbellum status quo, so too did the Black Panther Party, Malcolm X's Organization for Afro-American Unity, the Republic of New Africa, and the Black Workers' Congress frighten white bourgeois America. "We Shall Overcome" became "What more do *they* want?"; Johnson's domestic liberalism gave way to Nixon and Agnew's "benign neglect" and vicious political repression. The only progressive black alternative to the NAACP–Urban League block of Negro conservatives—the black nationalists—were unable to unite around a common agenda for political work and economic development. The Supreme Court's 1978 decision on Allan Bakke gave rise to concern that the educational reforms for blacks might be undermined legally within a few years. No one, of course, raised the question of a return to Jim Crow; like slavery during the First Reconstruction, the Movement had effectively voided this question from the public arena. What did occur, certainly by the mid and late 1970's, was the partial destruction of most of the material and economic benefits of the Second Reconstruction.

As black political theorist Adolph L. Reed has observed, the destruction of Jim Crow removed "a tremendous oppression from black life. Yet, the dismantlement of the system of racial segregation only removed a fetter blocking the possibility of emancipation." By 1972 or 1973, most of the political outbursts against the system of racial and class exploitation had been depoliticized. In Reed's words, "Black opposition has dissolved into celebration and wish fulfillment. Today's political criticism within the black community—both Marxist-Leninist and nationalist—lacks a base and is unlikely to attract substantial constituencies." Older, integrationist leaders and organizations returned to positions of quasi-hegemony within the Afro-American national community, but they were unable to organize and manipulate black political opinion with anywhere near the authority they had previously. Ironically, the very success of the Second Reconstruction (limited but real) plus the paucity of any kind of critical theory rooted within the historical realities of black society in America helped to undermine the NAACP and Urban League, as well as its leadership elites.

The major distinction between both the First and Second Reconstructions and, for instance, the period of reconstruction after the Russian Civil War of 1918-21, was that the American reformers had no critical theory of social transformation by which they could explain or understand the complexity of the challenges they faced. Amilcar Cabral of Guinea-Bissau provides us with another example. Between 1956 and 1959, Cabral and his associates in the PAIGC developed a theory of social change based upon their knowledge of dialectical and historical materialism—but grounded in the peculiar realities of their country and the social forces which they sought to overthrow. The PAIGC's war for liberation, which culminated in Guinea-Bissau's independence from Portugal in 1973, evolved from both a theory of society and its application in the form of socially progressive institutions.

Returning to the First Reconstruction, we observe no fundamental critique of existing state structures and institutions, no debate over ideologies—only a clear commitment to abolish slavery and guarantee certain civil and social rights at the expense of the racist folkways of the white Bourbon South. The Second Reconstruction generated a great participatory response among the masses of black people, but never became truly a liberation movement with the potential for radically transforming all economic and social relations. The reformist black leaders differed over the goals and tactics of the Movement; the petty bourgeois, radical left wing tended to be isolated from the black working class. As a result, many of the material gains achieved in the 1960s were lost in the 1970s; black political leadership seems more aimless and unchallenging of the capitalist hegemonic social and economic forces than at any point since the rise of Booker T. Washington. "It was historically unfortunate that the American Negro created no social theorists to back up his long line of activist leaders," Harold Cruse wrote. With a critical theory, "the Negro movement conceivably could long ago have aided in reversing the backsliding of the United States toward the moral negation of its great promise as a new nation of nations."

The roots of a Third Reconstruction are found in the inherent inequities of American capitalism, and in the uniquely racist social relations which are inextricably tied to the political economy by tradition, history, and ideological force. The next social revolution in America, then, must involve the utter abolition of racial prejudice in all its institutional forms; to accomplish this, the capitalist means of production must be smashed and uprooted as completely as slavery was before it. The coming revolution against social privilege, the domination of private property over collective interests, and the private ownership of natural public monopolies (e.g. electric power, mass media, heavy industry, transportation) will set the historical stage for the final assault against white racism.

When we begin to ponder the social dimensions of the next American Revolution, the problems both in practical and theoretical terms are nothing short of overwhelming. There is not, at the moment, a body of knowledge which could be described as a Marxian theory of racism which can be directly applied to our understanding of American social reality. Talented and creative Marxist intellectuals have emerged within the black community—from W.E.B. DuBois, Oliver Cromwell Cox, and C.L.R. James to more contemporary writers like James Boggs and Earl Ofari. However, there is no indication that their theoretical work has become the foundation for praxis within the majority tendencies of the Black Movement. Many white Marxist-Leninists regrettably employ rigid theoretical models in approaching black-white relations, ranging from the old Black Belt Nation thesis of the Comintern to the notion of "white skin privilege." No American Marxist consensus has emerged which explains in a practical way the origins of white racism, the interrelationship between race and class in advanced capitalist states, and the role of black nationalism vis-a-vis the emancipation of the white working class. The majority of white American Marxists are hostile, if not downright antagonistic, toward black nationalist movements, theorists, and organizations. On the other side of the color line, black activists who view themselves as both socialists and nationalists reciprocate the feelings of distrust toward white Marxists. The Old Left, from a black nationalist perspective, was patronizing toward black-oriented issues: the New Left of the 1960s had little or no serious dialogue with the advocates of Black Power, while playing it safe ideologically by working with more conservative, integrationist leaders like John Lewis and Julian Bond. Experiences with leftist organizations have left such a bitter taste among many black activists that a sizeable percentage of black nationalists are aggressively anti-Marxist and even anti-Communist in their theoretical work and practice.

Let us assume for a moment that these and other significant

problems of theory and political practice could be resolved. The "war of position," a period of intensive cultural and intellectual struggle, has given way to an overt struggle for state power. The liberation forces have succeeded in controlling the state apparatus. With this critical prerequisite accomplished, the struggle to build a socialist society with a multiracial and culturally diverse community begins.

Given these lofty assumptions, what would be the prospects for black nationalism and the programs for reconstruction after the revolution?

II

Throughout black American history, there have been two distinctly different cultural and political movements that have emerged in the battle against racism and cultural exploitation—integration and black nationalism. Integration is defined here as a worldview which accepts the legitimacy of white civil society's hegemony over black thought, advances a political and economic framework in harmony with the dominant trends within the white-controlled state, conscientiously rejects the alternative standards of behavior and culture established by the black majority, and opposes on principle both *de jure* and *de facto* separation of the races. Black nationalism's goals include the physical separation of the races and the development of autonomous, black-controlled economic, political, and cultural institutions.

A third sub-tendency, often placed within the parameters of black nationalism, is the emigrationist strain of black politics and thought. Unlike most nationalists, emigrationists view themselves as African rather than Afro-American in all critical respects. These blacks do not see any possibility for constructive social, economic, and political relations with whites, and demand the right to be repatriated to the land of their racial and cultural origin, Africa. A socialist revolution would not settle all of these deep, historic divisions among black Americans. The solution to the problem, however, resides in seizing this critical duality of black existence and being, and building upon it. The central contradiction within black society must become, in other words, the central motif for the era of the Third Reconstruction. The historic duality of black life will express itself in a non-racist, socialist society through institutions of *dual authority*. There will co-exist the structures of a multiracial socialist state with the organs of Afro-American self-rule.

The phrase "dual power" or "dual authority" is most clearly identified with certain Marxist theoreticians, most notably Lenin. Writing in his party's newspaper *Pravda* in the midst of the Russian

Revolution, Lenin observed that the collapse of the Tsarist regime had created two governments or states. "Alongside the Provisional Government, the government of the bourgeoisie, another government has arisen, so far weak and incipient, but undoubtedly a government that actually exists and is growing—the Soviets of Workers' and Soldiers' Deputies," Lenin wrote in April, 1917. The basis for the power of the bourgeois state was within the legislature or parliament, the police and armed forces, and the official bureaucracy. "The fundamental characteristics" of the nascent workers' councils or soviets were not "laws previously discussed and enacted by parliament, but the direct initiative of the people from below"; not the traditional state coercive apparatuses but "the direct arming of the whole people"; not the bureaucracy but "the direct rule of the people as a whole." Two authorities existed simultaneously, one representing the oppressor and the other the oppressed. The transfer of authority from one set of social forces to the other would occur when the revolutionaries succeeded in obtaining support from the majority of the working class. "We do not stand for the seizure of power by a minority," Lenin declared. "To become a power the class-conscious workers must win the majority to their side." Thus the culmination of the revolution, the establishment of a socialist state apparatus and public ownership of the central means of production and distribution, would actually obliterate dual power in favor of a sole progressive authority.

In the aftermath of the Bolshevik Revolution, the practical strategy of dual power became elevated to the level of political dogma. Aspiring revolutionaries immediately translated the successful experience of the soviets into the development of political formations within their own countries. Writing in exile, Leon Trotsky explained the evolution of the 1917 revolution and other social upheavals, from the English Civil War to the great French Revolution, from the vantage point of dual sovereignty or power. "The historic preparation of a revolution brings about in the prerevolutionary period," Trotsky wrote in his *History of the Russian Revolution*, "a situation in which the class which is called to realize the new social system, although not yet master of the country, has actually concentrated in its hands a significant share of the state power, while the official apparatus of the government is still in the hands of the old lords. That is the initial dual power in every revolution." The period of equilibrium between the *ancien regime* and the socialist state-yet-to-be was relatively brief. Trotsky admitted that "the phenomenon of the dual power (had) heretofore not (been) sufficiently appreciated," but vigorously denied that it contradicted in any way the classical "Marxian theory of the state, which regards government as an executive committee of the ruling class." The capitalist state could not be overturned unless "a new correlation of forces" was prepared to conduct the transfer of power "only as the result of a trial by battle."

As in so many other instances, the sole representative of Western Marxism who could look beyond the "dual power" lessons of the Russian Revolution was Antonio Gramsci. The workers' councils of 1919 and 1920 in Italy were an attempt on the part of Italian radicals like Gramsci and others to replicate the revolutionary example of the soviets. The councils were to become a means to educate the masses, to build a consensus among workers for socialism, and to establish a kind of alternative sovereignty prior to the collapse of the bourgeois state. The failure of the Italian workers' council movement and the rise of Benito Mussolini forced Gramsci to rethink many of his older theories on the processes of socialist transformation within the unique terrain of advanced Western capitalist societies. Eventually Gramsci concluded that a "war of position" would have to be waged between the progressive vs. capitalist forces over an extended period of time, an uneven struggle fought primarily within the institutions of civil society—that is, the ideological and cultural apparatuses of the state. A kind of dual authority would exist when the moral and political legitimacy of the capitalist state, its hegemony over the subordinate social strata, was overthrown. Only when this occurred could the forces of socialism complete the revolutionary process through a "war of maneuver," the final assault against the coercive apparatuses of the capitalist state. But even in Gramsci's scenario, the phase of dual power is transitory.

In a racist state, the factor of race is not an accidental phenomenon, an added element to the ideological apparatuses (or "superstructure") which provides unique character or historic presence. Rather, the existence of racism as an underlying force within public policy and all social relations connotes the necessity for the postcapitalist state to provide structural guarantees to the nonwhite population for its safety and survival. Dual power or dual sovereignty between the black nation and the postcapitalist, predominately white society must exist in order to protect blacks from the inevitable attacks of racist whites as well as to construct social/political institutions which will erase any privileges that whites formerly received simply for being white. This dual power would exist as long as white racism was perceived in any form as a part of public policy decisions and within the general pattern of racial relations. Unlike the soviet model or Gramsci's workers' councils, it would not be a creation of capitalist society, but a product of the seizure of state power and the transition from capitalism to socialism. It would not be a product of the majority (workers) but the creation of a distinct but critically important minority (blacks).

Officials of the multiracial socialist political system will be chosen by all citizens in regular elections. All blacks would have the right to vote in these general elections and legislators elected from the black national community would serve within the new socialist state apparatus with white, Hispanic, and other Third World colleagues. Blacks—with certain exceptions given later in this paper—would pay taxes to the central government and would be subject to its laws. It would be expected that perhaps 12 to 16 percent of the socialist legislators, administrators, and key politicians would be Afro-Americans.

The central government will be responsible for providing all citizens with the essentials of a decent, humane life: free and readily available health care facilities, jobs, free education from the preschool to postdoctoral levels, and clean, comfortable housing. Concurrently there will exist institutions through which blacks can guarantee their self-determination as a national minority, and participate in the administration of human services for black people. These will be national, regional, and local bodies and will be based on two organizations which will have played the central or determining roles in the prior transition to socialism.

The first of these organizations will be the Black Nationalist Party. (I will, for the present, give hypothetical names to these and other organizations, governmental agencies and bureaus; the functions and roles of such formations are the essential concern, rather than the specific names.) The Black Nationalist Party would be somewhat like a constituent assembly or a democratic, mass-based legislature of the majority of black Americans. Diverse in class orientation, the Nationalist Party would include large numbers of radicalized black intellectuals and petty bourgeois groups, thousands of students, working people, and the unemployed. During the struggle for revolution, the Nationalist Party would have moved gradually from being a predominantly petty-bourgeois, "parliamentary-style party" toward a genuine coalition party led primarily by black workers. Much of the activity of the Nationalist Party would occur within black civil society, outside the arena of production. Nationalist Party members and leaders would initiate new "Freedom Schools" in black churches and mosques; sponsor food, clothing, and producer cooperatives; direct independent artistic and cultural forums within black communities. As in most constituent assemblies, Nationalist Party members would probably disagree over many theoretical issues, but would find a general consensus on the significant issues that needed to be addressed.

The second organization that would have been crucial in the socialist transformation and upon which the institutions of black self-determination might be constructed would be leagues of black workers, the most revolutionary and militant forces within Afro-American society. In structure and in outlook they would closely parallel Gramsci's model for the Italian workers' councils in 1919. Unlike the trade unions, which were distinctly the social products of capitalist economic production, these leagues of revolutionary black workers would represent the push toward socialist economics. They would be far more class-conscious, theoretically and programmatically, than either the old trade unions or the great majority of members and cadre in the Nationalist Party. Its tactics and policies would be nationalist but explicitly Marxist as well; discipline would be far greater, and the central organization of the leagues would exert a greater influence over its members. In Gramsci's view, "this new type of organization, as it develops, grows and enriches itself with functions organized hierarchically, forms the scaffolding of the socialist state."

Under American conditions, it is probable that Gramsci's assessment would have to be modified: both the Nationalist Party and the black workers' leagues would play a joint role in the transition from capitalism to socialism. For one thing, both organizations would have a similar structure. Both would draw their strength from the black working class, although the Nationalist Party would in all probability have a substantial petty bourgeois following and leadership. As the class struggle deepened during the Third Reconstruction period, contradictions would be manifested within both groups. The leagues or councils would have a strong tendency towards economism and might underestimate the need for some elements of private enterprise for a brief period of time. In both forces, blacks who advocated integration and a restoration of the civil societal relations between blacks and whites during the pre-revolutionary period would present a real danger. Form this vantage point, it would seem most likely that the new black socialist state apparatus would be the product of both political groups and constituencies. Yet, such a new state would have to be constructed in a manner that would permit those millions of integrationist-oriented blacks the right to align themselves with the new, white socialist state and new cultural institutions. Black groups and communities with a longstanding identification with integrationist goals would gravitate sharply toward full participation within the multiracial state apparatus; black nationalists would have little difficulty or hesitancy in opting for the separatist institutions.

The construction of the new black socialist state apparatus would begin at a national level. A national convention of black activists, drawn equally from the Black Workers' Councils and the Black Nationalist Party, would be convened. From this gathering, a National Assembly of Afro-American People would be established. This would be the central legislative body for blacks in the post-revolutionary society. The National Assembly would also include social forces outside of the two major organizations: black student organizations, black trade unionists, independent black consumer and producer cooperatives, neighborhood associations, progressive black religious organizations, and black feminist organizations or collectives. The National Assembly would be unicameral. It would elect representatives to serve on an Executive Council (Exco), which would be the executive branch of government. Both bodies would conform to certain specific criteria. At least 20 percent of all representatives should be black youth and adults under the age of thirty. At least 50 percent should be members of a black workers' league or revolutionary council or have some direct political and personal link to the working class. At least 50 percent of both bodies must consist of black women. All the participants, of course, would be black.

The first task of the National Assembly of Afro-American People would be to initiate regional assemblies or congresses. Again, participants should be selected in equal numbers from the Black Workers' Leagues and the Black Nationalist Party. The criteria for membership according to race, class, sex, and age would be enforced. Subsequently, or perhaps simultaneously, local and city-wide assemblies or congresses would be introduced. A reciprocal relationship would exist between the local, regional, and national legislative bodies. Local assemblies would have the authority to suggest legislation to the national body, interpret and implement edicts of the national body, and nominate local members to serve on regional and national levels. National representatives would be selected in proportion to the size of the black population within a specific region or local constituency. A form of recall or referendum might be introduced whereby regional and local assemblies could challenge the legislation of the National Assembly or replace representatives who were not voting in the best interests of regional and local blacks. Only the National Assembly and Regional Assemblies would have the constitutional power to levy taxes, and Regional Assemblies would be limited to taxing only privately owned property (automobiles, land, buildings, etc.) within a given district. All legislators and their staffs would receive annual salaries not exceeding the median wage level for a black industrial worker, computed annually. There would be a strictly enforced term of office during which all elected officials and bureaucrats could serve within the state apparatus.

Funding for the new black state apparatus would be derived from four primary sources. First, the multiracial, central socialist state would guarantee in its new constitution the right of the National Assembly of Afro-American People to control a fixed percentage of federal taxes collected annually. Such a figure would be based on the percentage of blacks to whites nationally, in proportion to the total amount of federal revenues for a given year. Second, the multiracial but white-dominated socialist state would guaranteed the right of the National Assembly to expropriate any private property within any given area in which a majority of residents were nonwhite. Third, the National Assembly would levy taxes on all black producer cooperatives, and collect rents or fees from any property owned by the Assembly. Fourth, for an indefinite period of years the National Assembly would receive a special fiscal subsidy from the socialist government for reparations—payment for the historic exploitation and oppression of black Americans. Regional and local assemblies would submit annual budgets for approval by the National Assembly's Executive Council. A committee of legislators from the National Assembly would coordinate all budgets and set fiscal priorities for the black community.

The central government would have limited input into this budgetary process in order to ensure harmony between the financial policies of the National Assembly and the larger society. If disagreements between the two bodies cannot be resolved, however, the National Assembly would retain final authority, for control over one's budget is a vital prerequisite for group self-determination. The National Assembly and its regional and local components would have certain powers of government and administration, but would not be entirely or distinctly separate from the multiracial government. There are no provisions here, for instance, for an Afro-American judiciary. The socialist Supreme Court would interpret legislation passed by both the central government and the National Assembly. Programs and policies would be worked out in concert and there would be much coordination between the two sets of political institutions. However, the National Assembly would have the right—if such became necessary—to insist upon and initiate a complete and uncompromising break from the central socialist state. The socialist constitution would have to guarantee the right of total territorial separation for any and all black Americans. Similarly, other ethnic minorities such as the Hispanics in the American southwest and Native Americans from Alaska to Florida would have the legal right to territorial separation. Only with this ultimate resort can minority rights be securely defended. The threat of physical separation will serve as a counterweight against the continuance of racist ideology and practices.

Many of the functions of the National Assembly would be carried out by bureaus and agencies which would address the economic, social, and cultural interests and needs of the Afro-American community. One of the more important bureaus that would have to be established would be the National Anti-Racist Bureau. (Here again, the function rather than the name is the central concern.) Charged with insuring the constitutional right to live in a "decreasingly racist society," the Bureau would have offices in every major city and town in the nation. It would function primarily as a kind of Special Prosecutor—investigating and filing charges against individuals, organizations, institutions, businesses, and any governmental bodies.

The penalties for racist behavior could range from voluntary re-education to life imprisonment. "Racist behavior" would include the public provocative use of racially derogatory symbols and language; continued patterns of black employee discrimination in job advancement, evaluation for promotion, pay increases, etc. and economic policies of price fixing within private business or producer cooperatives which take advantage of black consumers; the lack of black representation in state or local government or private business in relation to the proportion of blacks within the area, constituency, or market.

The socialist central government and National Assembly would provide a comprehensive agenda for the restructuring of American educational and cultural institutions. Regarding the education of the black community, the basic agency involved in this work would be the National Center for Black Education (NCBE). The NCBE, in coordination with the National Center for Hispanic Education and other related agencies, would provide the basic guidelines for the operation, curricula, management, and budgets for all nonwhite educational institutions. This would include all public and private schools, colleges, trade schools, and universities with more than fifty percent black student enrollment or whose physical plant was located within a majority black community (e.g. Columbia University in New York City). NCBD would have at least five major divisions: Elementary and High School Education; Collegiate Education; Adult Education; Parochial School Education; and Research and Development. All education, except parochial, would be absolutely free of costs; tuition, books, transportation to and from school, clothing, and annual student salary would be paid for by the government, or by the government and the recipient's (or recipient's parents')—employer. NCBE would appoint all superintendents of major black public schools, supervisory personnel, college presidents and key administrative staff; qualifications would be technical excellence, professional ability, and a political commitment to the goals of NCBE and the socialist revolution. Religious colleges, theological seminaries, and private schools would have the right to operate without NCBE intervention, but they would receive no financial assistance of any kind, and parents and/or students must assume all tuition fees and related costs. All operating budgets of both black public and private institutions must be submitted to NCBE for scrutiny.

The National Center for Black Education would also take a special interest in the activities of historic black-majority colleges and universities (e.g. Tuskegee Institute, Hampton Institute, Atlanta University). Each college would be administered directly by NCBE administrators; faculty or staff opposing the goals of the revolution would be dismissed, or more usually demoted from administrative or policy-making posts. All administrators and faculty chairpersons would be subject directly to NCBE evaluation, on both professional and political grounds. Academic scholarships and campus employment would be used to attract the most enthusiastic and gifted caliber of black student. NCBE would underwrite a major cultural and academic expansion on every campus; each college would have up-to-date scientific equipment, a radio station, an undergraduate library, art gallery, theatrical facilities for major cultural events, and an historical museum documenting the legacy of each black institution. Schools would not prohibit white attendance, but would strive to maintain an atmosphere conducive to black culture and social life. All black university graduates would receive special consideration for government-related jobs. All colleges would develop a policy of indirect participation and involvement in the political, cultural, and economic life of the local and regional black communities.

In the cultural sphere, black life would revolve around the Africana Cultural Institute (ACI). ACI's chief goal and responsibility would be the preservation and encouragement of Afro-American culture, traditions, and history. ACI would have at least three major subdivisions: Arts, both performing and creative; Humanities, which includes political philosophy, languages, ethics, history, and traditional religions; and the National Archive for Africana Culture. In the arts, ACI would sponsor dance companies; jazz, blues, spiritual, gospel, and contemporary popular black music composition, recordings, distribution of recordings, and live presentations in black communities; film production and distribution of black artists and black cultural events; subsidies for black painters and sculptors. In the humanities, ACI would provide direct grants to black college faculty engaged in research. ACI would publish academic research in Afro-American literary criticism, literature, philosophy, religion, history, and other areas of the humanities. Existing black humanities journals would be subsidized directly and left under existing management, whenever possible. In scope ACI would assume many if not all the activities done currently by the National Endowment for the Humanities, except that the direction of policy making would be in black hands, and the funding would be many times greater. The

National Archive for Africana Culture would initiate 1930s–style "WPA" projects: tape recordings of musicians and older black artists; interviews with the major and minor figures in African, Afro-Carribbean, and Afro-U.S. culture. The National Archive would purchase, catalogue, and display the papers of every major historical figure in Afro-American history. The complete works of influential black intellectuals, from DuBois and Garvey to Julius Nyerere and Imamu Amiri Baraka, would be published and distributed at a nominal cost to the public. The National Archive's staff would also provide geneological research for any Afro-American family upon request, without charge.

Economic activities within the black community would be planned by two bodies, the National Center for Black Economic Development (NCBED), which would be the joint administrative body for the National Assembly and the central socialist government, and the Black Workers' Councils.

The NCBED would be staffed solely by black workers, either from the Workers' League movement or from the Black Nationalist Party. This would be the only agency of dual power within the new bureaucracy that would be comprised entirely of black workers. The entire scope of activity initiated by the NCBED would be dedicated toward the realization of at least eight basic principles: the abolition of profit as the central criterion for determining investment; the abolition of structural unemployment; the progressive but gradual abolition of all centers of private economic production, moving toward either state or cooperative ownership; a gradual decline in the use of material incentives to reward productivity, and the increased use of moral and political incentives; the abolition of all discrimination in the workplace based on sex, race, ethnic, and personal sexual preference criteria; the progressive abolition of income distinctions based upon the character of work; the initiation of the thirty-hour work week as a standard throughout the country; and the development of workers' councils.

Black economic reconstruction would be complicated by many intricate and long-standing problems. First the overwhelming majority of Afro-American workers are currently employed in industry, manufacturing service, or unskilled related jobs. When clerical workers and lower level civil servants are included in this group, this amounts to about 90 percent of all adult black workers. Many of these workers will have been unemployed because of factory layoffs, deliberate disruption of the economy, and political unrest for many weeks or months. Between 20 to 25 percent of all black people are permanently unemployed and/or have never held steady jobs. About 40 percent of all black youths are unemployed. Simultaneously, black producer and consumer cooperatives will be operating in many urban areas but at various levels of efficiency and profitablity. The crisis of authority and law enforcement will also create temporary but widespread shortages in food and other essentials, deepening the public panic for immediate employment, an adequate food supply, and public order. Hundreds of thousands of black families, the supporters of the revolution, will expect the new government to launch massive construction programs for public housing, creating jobs in ghetto areas as well as improvement in living conditions. Other revolutionaries within the black community will call for the complete separation of all black economic institutions: factories run by black workers would operate primarily according to the interests of the local black community, not the state. The black entrepreneurial strata—owners and operators of small ghetto commercial food, clothing, and hair-dressing establishments—might attempt to use their important economic position within the community to threaten, halt, or at least frustrate government efforts to expand its controls over private enterprise.

We should approach all those economic problems within the black community with two distinct goals: short term stability and long term socialism. Unless every black person who desires a good job gains employment shortly after the revolution, it will be increasingly hard for socialists to argue that a socialist economy creates full employment. The immediate goal of the new black economic policy would be to provide full employment by any means necessary and as quickly as possible. This might mean that the National Assembly and central government would have to support certain aspects of "Black Capitalism" on a temporary basis. For example, the governments might provide subsidies for black-owned and operated small businesses (with gross annual incomes under $250,000 in 1980 dollars) with strict price controls and labor relations guidelines. Government grants would be available to black consumer and producer coops. White-owned businesses within majority black communities would be expropriated or purchased and given to the direction of black employees and the local community, with government assistance. A public works program for building and park restoration, garbage control, and political education could employ thousands of chronically unemployed black youth. Gradually, as the major manufacturing and industrial firms are nationalized and full employment is obtained, a greater degree of socialism within the black economic sphere will become possible. One potential alternative can be termed "communization." Major businesses or factories whose physical plants were located within the black community would be directed by a black workers' council, democratically elected. Each council would also include appointed representatives from the immediate black neighborhood. The council would be responsible for all decisions affecting the production of goods, hiring policy, and so forth. A National Assembly staff representative would be a liaison person between the council, community organizations, and both governments.

Another major dilemma facing the black community after the revolution would be the quality and character of black housing. The majority of black families do not own their own homes. The construction of many residential buildings occupied by Afro-Americans is poor; in rural areas most houses still lack complete plumbing facilities. Here again, both socialist governments will be expected to provide the means for adequate housing, and perhaps even the possibility of some form of home ownership, for virtually all black people. The governments must state clearly that decent housing is a human right, that every black American will reside in clean, comfortable dwellings within a short period of time, and that this will be achieved by any means necessary. A policy of housing expropriation and resettlement would be initiated in which properties owned by enemies of the state would be allocated to the poor, the unemployed, and the physically handicapped as quickly and as fairly as humanly possible. All absentee-owned apartment buildings or single family residences within any predominantly black neighborhood would become property of the National Assembly, without reimbursement, and systematically turned over to community organizations, local black nationalist political organizations, workers' councils, or the tenants for management. Both governments might provide short term loans or grants to minority contractors and builders, with specific instructions for restoring existing properties and building new homes for black families at minimal cost. Community co-ops and workers' councils would apply for federal grants for building homes and residential apartments owned directly by workers. On a long term basis, both governments would initiate a national home construction program and home loan policy. All home mortgages would be voided; all black families could apply directly to the dual governments for grants for energy conversion to solar power, home restoration, and expansion, with minimal or no charges.

The greatest and potentially most difficult problem facing both socialist governments' relations with the black community would be "the land question." The central tenet of black nationalism has always been the historic right of the Afro-American people to self-determination. As principal leaders and cadre in the successful revolution, black nationalists would have a right to expect the immediate option of black territorial autonomy and some form of self-rule. The new socialist Constitution would declare that all separate ethnic and cultural groups possess the right to a national homeland within the United States territory proper; separate or dual governments within a city or single state; and the right to repatriation to a country of one's choosing at government expense. The basic assumption here is that blacks who desire to integrate with whites could continue to do so; blacks wishing some distinct physical separation are provided the material to do so.

The major federal agency supervising these problems of resettlement would be the New Lands Administration (NLA). In carrying out the provisions of the Constitution, the NLA's work would fall under at least four major divisions: an Historic Claims Commission (HCC); an Urban Claims Commission (UCC); a Repatriation division; and an Autonomous Settlement Division (ASD).

The Historic Claims Commission's primary task is to help black Americans establish communities or individual farms within the territories of the original Southern slave states, including Maryland, Kentucky, Missouri, Texas, and Oklahoma. HCC would provide: transportation, housing and resettlement of Northern or West Coast black families wishing to return to previously-owned properties or to any new property within the region, and agricultural and technical assistance in marketing and producing farm goods. The HCC would sponsor the construction of special rural cooperative towns, which could be termed "Ujamaa Vijijini"—Familyhood or Socialist villages in Swahili. The central socialist government and the National Assembly would either purchase or expropriate a tract of land suitable for rural economic development. Preferably, tracts would be established in areas geographically, socially, and culturally suitable for black family resettlement. Upon the application of a black cooperative, workers' council, neighborhood association, or collective numbering more than, say, one hundred individuals, the HCC would provide technical assistance and financial stipends to facilitate relocation. HCC would build homes for each family, and provide up to 300 acres of agricultural land per person. Persons wishing to find nonfarm employment would be assisted. All physical property would be owned jointly by HCC and the black collective living in the Ujamaa Vijijini. All agricultural or manufactured products would be owned by the collective. Residents would elect commissioners to direct the economic and political life of the community. The commissioners would be paid by the HCC. All economic losses sustained by the Ujamaa Vijijini would be absorbed by the HCC budget.

The Urban Claims Commission would give black city residents grants or interest-free loans to purchase and refurbish parks, vacant lots, and other property for agricultural and related uses. UCC would provide grants to black workers' councils and trade unions for the purchase of urban property for workers' families or for the community.

The major political responsibility of UCC would be the establishment of Semi-Autonomous Black Districts, political entities which would be created at the expression of sections of the black nationalist population.

The criteria for the Semi-Autonomous Black Districts would be as follows: all districts must contain a minimal residential population of 10,000, at least 40 percent of whom must be of Afro-American descent. Separate black communities within a city or an immediate geographical area could qualify as a single, Semi-Autonomous District (e.g., Watts and Compton in Los Angeles; Harlem and Bedford–Stuyvesant in New York City). At least 10 percent of the voting residents would have to sign a petition submitted to the National Assembly for the creation of the Semi-Autonomous District. The National Assembly would conduct and supervise a plebiscite on the question. With 50 percent or more approval, the mechanisms for the creation of the district would begin. The district would elect representatives to both the Regional and National Assemblies, and would create its own Local Assembly. Special District Commissioners would also be elected to supervise normal municipal activities, such as garbage collection, education, street maintenance, and so forth.

All residents (black and white) in the Semi-Autonomous Districts would pay only one-half of the allotted personal income tax to the central government. Special district taxes would be levied on private property and nonfood items, at the discretion of the district commissioners and UCC. White residents would retain all constitutional rights under both the central socialist government and the National Assembly. Whites could run for public office, and participate in the daily life of the district. Residents of the district will retain representation in the central government, if they desire; the central socialist government is required to provide all special services and administrative assistance to the districts. The Semi-Autonomous Districts would have special authority over several key governmental and economic areas. First, district commissioners would control the local police organizaton, replacing any officers or patrol personnel who were not desired. All educational institutions within the area would become the property of the district government, which would be run in cooperation with the NCBE. All private property would be subject to expropriation by the district commissioners, subject to the approval of the UCC. Finally, any laws passed by the central socialist government which did not express the best interests of the district's electorate, would be subject to nullification by a majority vote in a plebiscite. This right of nullification would be subject to the approval by the chief administrator of the UCC and the Exco of the National Assembly. It would be my assessment that the majority of Afro-Americans would reside in Semi-Autonomous Districts within fifteen or twenty years after the socialist revolution.

The Repatriation Division of the NLA would be concerned with those Afro-Americans who wished to return to any African or Carribbean nation of maternal or paternal ancestry. The Repatriation Division would provide direct grants and loans to black families, workers' councils, community organizations, and trade unions for permanent settlement; any costs for learning an African language prior to settlement, for transportation, and for housing would be provided upon request. The Repatriation Division would also sponsor, in cooperation with NCBE, one to five year academic scholarships and travel fellowships for temporary work in Africa, for black high school students, college students, and adults. All black university students, young black workers in industry and politically active youth would be encouraged to spend at least two years in an African country, either in a university or performing a special service skill.

The Autonomous Settlement Division of the NLA would be the largest bureau and most difficult to coordinate successfully. Many nationalists would advocate a complete and total break between black people as a group and whites within the central socialist state; others would call for a series of autonomous black city-states within the existing government; emigrationists would want the government to negotiate the resettlement of several millions of Afro-Americans back to an African country or countries. The goal of the Autonomous Settlement Division would be to find a consensus among nationalist positions on the land question, and to implement a stage-by-stage program which would be in the best long-term interests of Afro-Americans. If the policy collective of the Autonomous Settlement Division concluded that a separate state for blacks within the United States was realistic and desirable, then all related government agencies would channel their activities towards the realization of such a state.

Autonomous Black Districts, a "nation within a nation," would have to conform to certain physical requirements. A minimum of 250,000 residents, within any given territorial space, would be eligible. Districts would have a black population of at least 50 percent. As with the Semi-Autonomous Districts, the National Assembly would supervise the initial plebescite. At least 15 percent of the voting residents would have to petition for the plebescite; at least two-thirds of the residents would have to approve the referendum. With an affirmative vote the district would end its direct political relationship with the central government. All personal income taxes payable to the central government would stop; all representatives would be instantly recalled. District commissioners would be elected to supervise the transfer of state power to the district. For a limited period of time, the National Assembly would provide fiscal and technical assistance to the district, and the central socialist government would pay a substantial reparations subsidy directly to the district government. Sections of land would be transferred from the central government to the district, to insure adequate physical space for population growth. After the period of transition, the Autonomous Black District would declare itself a sovereign nation. The District would retain fraternal ties with the National Assembly, but it would be an autonomous entity in every respect—economically and politically. The terms of the separation agreement would expressly prohibit military or economic intervention by the central socialist government. Whites remaining in the Autonomous Black District could be subject to disenfranchisement and involuntary removal from the new nation. It would be the responsibility of the central socialist government to resettle these whites and to provide some compensation for lost personal properties.

The theory of dual authority is rooted in the premise that socialism and national self-determination are compatible goals. A black nationalist does not have to reject dialectical materialism and the body of Marxist literature as the basis for critical theory, simply because some Marxists object to nationalism of any form as being a "bourgeois deviation." It is highly probable that a great many white socialists (and quite a few black Marxist-Leninists) will oppose a separate state apparatus for a few blacks in the post-revolutionary society. Opponents would insist that racism would be abolished simply by legislative fiat; that the unequal position of black workers within the means of production would be eliminated; that blacks' reasons for a separate-but-equal state or economic structure would disappear.

This is exactly the kind of perspective which reinforces the hegemony of white authority, privilege, and power. Since white Americans as a group are largely devoid of an original, legitimate and autonomous American culture, they logically deduce that blacks must also be a clean "cultural slate." Because some white leftists have abandoned racism in their personal or individual relations (in most, but not all respects), they assume that once seizing the state apparatus that they could legislate race distinctions out of existence. This highly irrational viewpoint is based on the economic determinist notion that racism is purely a product of the forces of material production. This reduces the problem of race to the "superstructural" level, where with other similar kinds of questions (like sexism) it would be dealt with "after the revolution" without difficulty. The creation of a separate and Semi-Autonomous state apparatus such as the National Assembly would frustrate whites' attempts to put blacks in the back of the (socialist) bus. Dual authority means that the contradiction which divides the cultural and social life of the black nation could be resolved both on the side of nationalism and integration. Dual power means that blacks as a nation would already possess the infra-structure and economic resources necessary for a territorial or physical break from white-dominated socialism. Blacks would have an alternative political institution, directly responsible to the major black forces of liberation, the Nationalist Party and the Workers' Councils. The inevitable reaction against black progress which followed both the First and Second Reconstructions would be sufficient reason to anticipate the possible attempt by the new socialist state to reverse some or all of the gains of black progressives.

III

We return to the present. Capitalism forms the basis for all cultural life, social relations, and economic production. White racism afflicts the entire constellation of human relations and thought within capitalist America. The progressive forces are bickering and divided amongst themselves over theory, strategy, and tactics. No socialist revolution intrudes upon the immediate political horizon, not to mention a Third Reconstruction.

Any discussion about the prospects for black America must be informed by the realization that white racism predates capitalism. Nationalization of the basic industries, banks, and financial institutions and seizing state power (via the ballot and the bullet) will not automatically erase 350 years of white racist supremacy, ethnocentrism, and hatred. Socialism will not create a new cultural democracy, but it should provide the material foundations for a really vibrant and egalitarian relationship across the color line. Special concessions will have to be made for the legacy of slavery and the unfinished revolution in civil rights in the 1960s. White revolutionaries must prove to the black community that it is possible for them to reject the years of racist education, socialization, and ideology, and commit the new society toward the goal of cultural democracy. If they waver or falter in the slightest, the only viable political alternative for the masses of black working people will be to develop their own separate state entity, completely rejecting whites as co–workers, supporters, or allies.

Some final points: some critics might question these projected liberation institutions on the grounds that they do not effectively deal with other important contradictions, such as the division between women and men or the dilemma of socialist bureaucracies. These are vital issues that can only be explored tentatively here.

The need to struggle against sexism within the black community would be a major position supported by both the Black Nationalist Party and the Black Workers' Leagues. The National, Regional, and Local Assemblies would have a minimum of 50 percent black female participation. Before and after the revolution, the struggle against the oppression and degradation of black sisters would be a primary and fundamental interest of all institutions within the liberation movement.

The greatest problem in the post-revolutionary period will be the failure to deepen the class struggle. The class struggle could move from the conflict within the factories between workers and capitalists to a potential struggle between socialist bureaucrats and the masses. The scenario might occur this way. After an intense period of social unrest, major relocations of millions of individuals and the seizure of private properties amounting to billions of dollars, a lull in the revolutionary movement would occur. An ever-deepening degree of conservatism in political and civil society would be manifested in the thoughts and activities of the revolutionary forces. Such a turn of events would be natural, even predictable, if history is an accurate guide. As the crisis of Soviet socialism gave birth to the excesses of Stalinism, a similar process could evolve here.

Gradually, a great number of individuals within the state apparatus might revert to the practices and policies inherited from the former capitalist bureaucracy. Party cadre might be elevated to positions within the government on the basis of their technical expertise rather than their commitment to socialism or black equality. Leaders of trade unions and workers' councils might become unwilling to abandon their positions of authority to return to their factories and have other workers replace them. Men growing to maturity in an overtly sexist society might find it difficult to accept the quota of 50 percent of all government positions going to women. Government posts would have a limited financial appeal, but in other ways the compensation would be extremely attractive—from having a secretarial staff to special rights for government-owned automobiles, houses, and consumer goods. These forces toward conservatism could crystalize into a bureaucratic caste or stratum, with an economic, social, and even psychological need to remain in posts of responsibility. Unless the socialist governments passed strict rules setting time limits on tenure in office, and encouraged to the broadest possible extent mass participation within these new agencies, the spirit of protest would be sacrificed upon the altar of bureaucracy and order.

The critique above may seem to assume throughout that a socialist revolution would be an inherently good thing for all Afro-American people, and that the success of the Black Movement depends upon the successful completion of the socialist transformation. But, there is *no guarantee* that socialism would *ever* end white racism, as it is encountered on a day-to-day basis by individual Afro-Americans. It is probable that a socialist revolution would create many new problems for black people. But it is also my firm conviction that any black liberation movement that does not call for, at some point, the end of capitalist production and the redistribution of wealth and property along more democratic lines is *no liberation movement at all*. We may applaud the previous black movements for fostering a series of meaningful and valuable social reforms, but within the contextual framework of capitalism it is utterly impossible for black people to achieve any measure of collective security, freedom, and power. History, economics, and common sense tell us this. Socialism will only provide greater political space, and richer cultural and material foundations for the preservation and development of black working people. It won't solve the problem of white ethnocentrism overnight, in twenty years, or perhaps within a century.

We cannot hope for the revolution and the Third Reconstruction within our current century. Socialism is not "on the agenda" in our country, but the battle in civil society for socialist or capitalist ideological hegemony wages daily. As we prepare ourselves and others for the next American civil war, we might consider what we would do with state power if it were truly ours. This is a speculative but hopeful contribution toward the foundations of that socialist society—the new cultural democracy.

SOURCES

James and Grace Lee Boggs, *Revolution and Evolution in the Twentieth Century* (New York: Monthly Review Press, 1973).

Martin Clark, *Antonio Gramsci and the Revolution that Failed* (New Haven and London: Yale University Press, 1977).

Harold Cruse, *The Crisis of the Negro Intellectual* (New York: William Morrow and Company, 1967).

Antonio Gramsci, *Prison Notebooks* (New York: International Publishers, 1973).

Irving Howe, ed., *Essential Works of Socialism* (New Haven and London: Yale University Press, 1976).

David L. Lewis, *King: A Critical Biography* (Baltimore, Maryland: Pelican Books, 1970).

August Meier and Elliot Rudwick, *From Plantation to Ghetto*, Third Edition (New York: Hill and Wang, 1976).

Roger L. Ransom and Richard Sutch, *One Kind of Freedom: The Economic Consequences of Emancipation* (Cambridge: Cambridge University Press, 1977).

Adolph L. Reed, "Black Particularity Reconsidered," *Telos* (Spring, 1979), pp. 71-93.

Robert C. Tucker, ed., *The Lenin Anthology* (New York: W.W. Norton, 1975).

U.S. Bureau of the Census, Department of Commerce, *The Social and Economic Status of the Black Population in the United States: An Historical View, 1790-1978* (Washington, D.C.: Government Printing Office, 1979).

C. Vann Woodward, *The Strange Career of Jim Crow*, Third Revised Edition (New York: Oxford University Press, 1974).

SEX AND CLASS IN MARABLE'S THIRD RECONSTRUCTION
Tiffany R. Patterson

The issues raised by Manning Marable in his discussion of the Third Reconstruction are critical to the success of any socialist revolution in America. At the core of Marable's thesis is the idea that the historical development of racism in this country is unique and deeply rooted in the fabric of American society. This analysis leads to the conclusion that "there is no guarantee that socialism would ever end white racism, as it is encountered on a day-to-day basis by individual Afro-Americans." Yet it is equally clear that "within the contextual framework of capitalism, it is utterly impossible for black people to achieve any measure of collective security, freedom, and power." Socialism, Marable suggests, will remove the material and institutional basis of racism but will not solve automatically the problem of white ethnocentricism. To address this reality, Marable proposes that in post-revolutionary society, a system of dual authority would have to be built into the new socialist structure.

Under this system of dual authority, black people would exercise direct control over their own political and cultural institutions which would be separate from the main government structure. The responsibility for providing all citizens with the minimum requirements for a decent life—jobs, health care, education, housing, etc.—would remain with the central government. However, in order to guarantee their self-determination as a national minority, black people would establish their own institutions at the national, regional, and local levels. These structures would be spearheaded by two organizations formed during the transition to socialism, the Black Nationalist Party and the Black Workers' Leagues.

Through the leadership of these two organizations, a National Assembly of Afro-American people would be developed as the legislative arm with representation built in for all segments of the black community. Regional and local assemblies would also be developed. A series of committees addressing such issues as racism, education, black economic development, etc. and several bureaus to carry out the functions of the assembly would also be established.

Funding for this structure would be provided by the control of a certain percentage of the federal taxes proportionate to the black population, the expropriation of any private property within a given area where black people dominate, the levying of taxes on black producer cooperatives, the right to collect any rent or fees on property owned by the Assembly, and a fixed fiscal subsidy from the government. This last source of revenue would be built into the constitution for an indefinite number of years as compensation for several hundred years of racist and economic exploitation.

Finally, the socialist government would have to guarantee the right of total territorial separation for any and all black Americans as well as other national minorities. This possibility would serve as political leverage against continued racist practices and ideas.

The model proposed by Marable is provocative and exciting and is clearly supported by the history of racism in American society. The concept of dual authority may very well be the key to the ability of socialism to end racism. Skepticism toward socialism as the answer to the racial dilemma in this society has been voiced by a considerable number of black thinkers from both the left and right. Marable's theoretical speculations on this subject are critical if dialogue among socialists over how to create a racist-free society is to be liberated from the mechanistic musings and the romantic humanism so characteristic of earlier discussions within the Marxist arena.

I would like to make explicit two assumptions about the transition to socialism that underlie Marable's model and draw attention to one weakness in his model.

Implicit in his discussion is the assumption that during the period of socialist transformation, black and white workers will be able to rise above the barrier of race to the extent that the latter will not violently oppose the concept of dual authority. Racism has been remarkably successful in dividing black and white workers as well as other segments of the society. It has also been very successful in dividing the political left as well. Marable bases his model on the assumption that this struggle will be resolved. But how it is resolved could shape in very critical ways what kind of society will exist in the post-revolutionary period. If, for instance, during the period of socialist transformation, racism diminishes to the extent that black and white workers are able to challenge the capitalist forces as a cohesive unit, then the consciousness which will develop among both groups may very well lend considerable support to the idea of dual authority. This support could ease the establishment of such a model.

On the other hand, if black and white workers carried out the struggle against capitalism as disparate units, antagonistic toward each other but unified in their opposition to the capitalist system, then once the period of transition was over, the smoldering racism would once again surface. In this event, the attempt to establish dual authority would require a bitter struggle which might, ironically, give support to the reactionary forces within the black community.

This possibility leads to a second point regarding the assumptions underlying the model. There appears to be an implicit premise that the power of the petty bourgeois middle-class leadership of the black community would be sufficiently weakened during the period of transition as to be insignificant. But this would be dependent upon the outcome of the struggle between black and white workers. If the workers are able to conquer the demon of racism and develop that critical revolutionary consciousness necessary to understand the necessity of a dual system, then the power of the petty bourgeoisie will be further weakened.

But race and racism in this society have a way of unifying black people and preventing them from expelling the enemies within as they seek to protect themselves from the enemy without. The opposition of white workers would allow the petty bourgeoisie to solidify their power by calling for racial unity and making it more difficult for the masses of black people to cut their ties with the black middle class. The black petty bourgeoisie will not relinquish its power easily nor can we ignore the petty bourgeois tendencies among black workers. The success or failure of dual authority or a dual system will depend upon a variety of factors and no one factor will necessarily be determinate. But certainly how the struggle for socialism is accomplished will play a critical role in the type of society that is eventually established.

The weakness in Marable's discussion is his assumption that equal representation of all groups—women, youth, the elderly, workers, etc.—will be sufficient to address the particular concerns of each of those groups. While this may be true for most groups, given the nature of sexism in American society it is not sufficient for the problems of women.

Sexism is an integral feature of the patriarchal-capitalist system. Black women have been victimized as women and as blacks. However, all too often, their oppression as women has been hidden under their oppression as blacks. As a consequence, there is a considerable amount of denial within the black community over the sexual oppression of women. Equal representation will not be sufficient to address this particular problem.

The removal of sexism generally from the society will require that the roles and positions of women be addressed directly under a new socialist government. In addition to promoting an anti-sexist ideology, the government will be required to establish programs that will concretely address the oppression of women. Socialist governments such as Cuba, Grenada, and Mozambique all have recognized the necessity of dealing with the concerns of women as a special and separate issue. Within a dual system, the problems of women will have to be viewed as a category unto itself. Therefore, Marable's model should include committees on sexism and a Bureau of Women's Affairs in addition to the proposed equal representation of women at all levels of the system. Only in this way will women be able to exercise self-determination and to eradicate sexism from the black community in particular and the whole society in general.

The concerns raised above do not invalidate Marable's model in general. They merely point out issues for further examination. Though the model is highly speculative—necessarily so, given that we cannot predict with any accuracy the outcome of the struggle for socialism in America—it is nevertheless an excellent place to begin the discussion of how socialism will end racism. The ideas presented by Marable are based on the recognition that socialism is not sufficient to end racism and we must begin to consider what else is necessary for socialism to work in a multi-racial society with the particular history of the United States. As a contribution to this dialogue, Marable has presented valuable theoretical considerations that must be further debated and developed by all Marxist thinkers.

NATIONALISM AND PESSIMISM
William K. Tabb

A revolution gives priority to dreams. The moment of victory is a moment of pure chaos—like the chaos of nature, the hidden structure of the forest, the unconscious. Beautiful new imagery rises into view. The usual resistance has been blown up with mortars. . . .

But soon the liberators must put their liberated dreams in a drawer. They must recognize their utopianism as an efficient intoxicant, distracting the masses from tackling the tasks of the present. Before we can have what no men ever had—thus sticking our necks into a new noose—we must have what all men ought to have. We want decent housing and medical care, increased educational levels, a secure and peaceful society with honest goals, an open and forthright public debate, lively cultural expression, respect for one another and our own various races, a place to go dancing on Saturday night and of course, free baseball games. . . .

It is the next generation—the ones we are making literate, the ones who are born with Marx, the ones who will have a socialist movement without excuses, with power—that will define what I've been seeking.

An Unauthorized Autobiography of Fidel Castro; A Totally Free Man by John Krich (Creative Arts, Berkeley, 1981).

Economists are not known for their sense of humor. Indeed the profession lays claim to only one joke and it lacks salience for anyone who has not had a course or two of the dismal science. The joke is, however, worth telling because it is germane to the task at hand.

Three men are cast ashore on a desert island, a chemist, a mathematician, and an economist. A can of beans washes up on shore, alas the only remains of the ship. The survivors struggle with the problem of how to open the can. The chemist says, "We'll build a fire; the heat will expand the metal and the can will burst open." The mathematician says, "I will calculate the trajectory probabilities so we can catch the beans." The economist has sat silently. "What do you have to contribute to solving our problem?" they ask him. "Simple," he replies. "Assume a can opener."

Unless you have sat through lectures and read learned articles which make unrealistic assumptions necessary for the deterministic models which preoccupy economists, this joke may appear rather pallid. But we economists think it's just the cat's meow.

All this is to say that I have strong reservations about a project which begins, "Assume the revolution is over; what would socialism look like?" After all, your revolution may not be my revolution, and one which relies on white male scientific socialists may leave us in a different place than an internationalist-feminist one, where logically the after would look quite different. Moreover, there is no day after in that sense. Winning power and establishing a societal context for self-actualization are two different things. The way "we" take power, white man, may preclude certain day-after social relations, if you follow my drift.

Because revolution in economically backward countries lacking democratic institutions—Czarist Russia and Imperial China—did not immediately and, what is of greater concern, have not to this day satisfactorily overcome racism and the oppression of certain nationality groups, many of us suspect that there would have to be a continuing special attention to racism in a revolutionary U.S. of A. (and to sexism and classism as well). Such a fear presumes a revolution that just happens, leaving us much as we are today with our existing attitudes and capacities. As one who apparently shares this fear, Manning Marable projects institutional structures to address problems that should have been resolved by the revolutionary process itself.

I believe, however, that "The Revolution" would be more than the Third Reconstruction. It would involve a transformation not only of race relations but potentially of all human relations. Twenty years after the Revolution I would hope for the end of imposed scarcity, the rational allocation of resources to meet basic needs, the redesign of work, and mass participation in decision making. I hold these hopes because of my view of the trajectory our revolution would take. Many political tactics appropriate to struggle within capitalism would no longer fit a coherent strategy for social transformation. In this light much of what Manning Marable has to say about institution building, accountability, and criteria for resource allocation belongs more properly to the movement-building period we are now in and to the early stages of transition than to socialist society proper. The latter should have solved the blatant forms of systemic inequality that his design is erected to eradicate.

The revolutionary process is one in which all progressive segments of society are won over to a common program. This unity would—in my revolution—include a commitment to full employment at safe and healthy jobs in a worker-dominated environment subject to social production priorities democratically decided. Therefore, racism as a weapon of ruling class control would have been discredited, in the struggle for power, through an analysis of how racism and the division of labor disorganized the working class, dividing it in ways that historically perpetuated capitalist thinking and social relations; a revolutionary movement would learn to be both anti-racist and anti-capitalist.

If the above is central to what becomes in point of fact the actual revolutionary process, it would not be necessary for the National Assembly "to support certain aspects of 'Black Capitalism,' " even "on a temporary basis," as Marable suggests. On the other hand if the revolution was a sudden seizure of power by an insurrectionist workers' movement pushed beyond economism by a sudden and cataclysmic depression—then some form of dual power, a continuation of basic reformist tactics (a more far-reaching New Deal) might be necessary. This I think is Marable's point.

The form that transitional institutions take will depend on the nature of the Revolution. In the best of all possible revolutions a mass movement would have to have existed for some time and won power not simply through collapse and default by the ruling class but through a slow process of winning over the people to the movement and its goals. Following this sort of transition, the "war communism" institutions and governing assumptions Marable puts forward would, I hope, be both unnecessary and viewed as undesirable.

To take an example close to home (my home at least), Marable writes: "Each [historic black-majority] college would be administered directly by NCBE [the National Center for Black Education] administrators; faculty or staff opposing the goals of the revolution would be dismissed or more usually demoted from administrative or policy-making posts. All administrators and faculty chairpersons would be subject directly to NCBE evaluation, on both professional and political grounds."

Following the revolutionary scenario, I assume that there is another way to look at the question. It would be to ask: How can we assure an educational process that promotes skill development and social commitment? Or we could ask: What role are predominantly black colleges going to play in the revolutionary process and will their transformation in the crucible of struggle suggest new concepts of what education is about?

Asked this way the matter appears in a different light. Now the growing revolutionary consciousness and commitment is part of a de-colonializing of the mind. This cultural revolution would be integral to the post-revolutionary period (assuming that revolution is the point of seizure of state power taking place within a continuing revolutionizing of social and productive relations in the society).

So, if there are still department chairpersons after the big R, they will be the comrades who have earned the respect that is indicated by their position of leadership. If the school community lacks judgment, perhaps a visiting NCBE site committee, after extensive discussion with individuals and through public evaluation sessions, might act as a catalyst for reassessment. I would hope that they would not think to come in, hand around loyalty tests, and take it on themselves to dismiss and demote, and then move on to Salem U. to spend a few days repeating their cleansing ritual.

I have similar hopes for economic institutions: that we would not need separate black taxing units or production entities defined by racial separateness. The historic debate on self-rule should take on new meaning in a socialist world. Once an internationalist outlook replaces national chauvinism, everybody can have home rule in a non-antagonistic sense. Diversity has new meaning because of the lapse of big power dominance and foreign (i.e. trans-national capitalist) control. One Ujamaa Vijijini would be another's Ejito community. All would be established on the basis of present needs and utopian inspiration; some would try and recapture the mythic past, others, use myths to build new futures. Historic claims and resettlement would have to be drastically tempered and undertaken in the context of limits imposed by just allocation. (Otherwise Russell Means would have all the rest of us, black and white, deported.) Such continuing cultural differences would be a pluralistic not an antagonistic contradiction.

In a society of virulent racism black unity is essential. In a truly post-revolutionary society, differences among blacks will be more evident. In New York City today there are thousands of black Haitians, Jamaicans, and others from elsewhere in the Caribbean and from Africa who have arrived last year and ten years ago—as well as Afro-Americans who have been here for 300 years. Are they all to be lumped together as "Black"? Are they to be governed by Marable's black institutions of dual power? If black integrationists reject separatism, what is to be their relation to "black" institutions of dual power? I think Marable's structures belong more to the control needs of the pre-revolution than to a desirable vision of the socialist state.

As a basic alternative I would prefer allocation through institutions of pluralism and local control combined with universalist entitlement programs. For example, good housing would be a priority as part of the basic needs commitment of the socialist government. Adequate levels of food, shelter, health, and education would be a first priority not only for blacks but for everybody. Because they are disproportionately poorly housed, blacks would gain disproportionately more from such a universal entitlement approach. Because everyone would have adequate income under a full employment-comfortable retirement incomes policy, everyone could afford the upkeep on his or her home. Cooperatives or municipal housing (something on the order of British Council Housing) would not pay much attention to the race of tenants except to insure that any vestiges of racial discrimination were satisfactorily overcome. Because all families could apply for loans or grants for solar conversion it would be unnecessary for a separate program to help families who happen to be black to convert to solar.

It is here that I hope that we can do better than Marable's implictly more pessimistic view of the type of revolution that we might expect. Are we talking about institution building in a society where those in the socialist leadership who are white are militantly anti-racist and the vast majority of black people have a longstanding identification with integrationist goals? Are we contemplating a society in which the exploitation that now underlies racial oppression and bigotry would be gone; in which workers, black and white, would be molded by a common working class reality in the context of juridical equality, equal access to schools, housing and so on; in which community would be freely chosen and not exclusive of other community identities? If so, it would appear that there is an extreme workerism in Marable's designs. Black male trade unionists may not be better feminists than their white brothers. The point is that workerism, even if it is black workerism, denies the richness of life experience among people who, while they are blacks and workers, may also be female, gay, churchgoing, integrationist, professional—and along with any or all of these—militant socialist.

Marable sees the continuing need after the Big R for a Black Nationalist Party which would have moved from being "predominantly petty bourgeois" to "a genuine coalition led primarily by black workers." Its purpose in part is seen as imitating what are essentially counter-institutions: freedom schools in black churches and mosques, sponsoring food, clothing, and producers coops. But we would ask: Why wouldn't the public school in the black community be a freedom school? Why wouldn't all food and clothing be available from worker-consumer cooperatives? And would blacks need their own exclusive networks separate from those which produce and distribute food and other consumer goods for other citizens?

Marable proposes Leagues of Black Workers which he counterposes to the trade unions. Yet what is described is a group that would function as communists have always seen themselves functioning within working class organizations. This new type of organization is really the party organization at the point of production. If black and white workers are employed in the same workplace, what role will whites play in relation to those black workers' leagues? Can we discuss the latter without mention of their interaction with whites who are likely to be a majority in many workplaces? It is surely the case that black caucuses have been an important vehicle for black workers in their struggle against racism in the workplace. Undoubtedly black leadership will be important to a revitalized workers' movement that must play an important role in any radical restructuring of society. But the interesting questions concern how a counterpart white militant leadership can be developed and finally how black-white unity can be forged. Such unity would have to give primacy to the struggle against racism if it were a socialist movement. It would discuss how racism—and sexism—are used to divide workers and how these divisions allow for intensification of exploitation and structure alienation at work.

But let me end on a more pessimistic note. There is evidence that Marable's more cautious vision could be truer to the mark than my own. More than a quarter of a century has passed since Brown vs. the Board of Education dealt a decisive blow to the political and legal institutions of "separate but equal." And it took 85 years from the 14th Amendment guaranteeing equal protection under law to reach Brown. Today we have Reaganauts dismantling enforcement of the hard-won rights of blacks: testing the water on repeal of the Voting Rights Act of 1964 by making its renewal a contested issue, appointing right-wing incompetents to a weakened Equal Employment Opportunity Commission, and trying out tax exemption for segregated schools. It is a long hard road and white allies in the struggle are not always dependable.

We are products of our social heritage and racism is deeply ingrained in American culture. Parallel organizing efforts are essential for the foreseeable future. That we cannot do better at getting beyond such guarded, wary, and hesitant steps toward unity is a measure of how far the revolutionary movement has to go in the United States.

I have argued that our view of the revolutionary process guides our judgment of what a socialist future would look like. Further, in conceptualizing a better world, we bring baggage from which those who have struggled and won a new society will have to a greater degree freed themselves.

Like Manning Marable we are all creating institutions for the transition, building conceptualizations useful in today's struggle, knowing that our rules will be considered and modified by the coming generations of blacks and whites, yellows and browns, reds and Reds who also make the Revolution.

RESPONSE AND SELF-CRITIQUE
Manning Marable

The task of projecting a social revolution cannot stand outside the terrain of one's own history. The first draft of the "Third Reconstruction" was completed in the summer of 1979. My primary political tasks at that time were journalistic in character. I was serving as communications coordinator for the National Black Political Assembly, an unstable coalition of black reformers, Democrats, and revolutionary black nationalists. I was also engaged in writing a weekly newspaper column on contemporary black politics for four dozen publications. Ideologically, I could have been described best as a "left nationalist"— an advocate of black cultural, educational, and social institution-building; consumer and producer cooperatives; the nationalization of major industry; and a planned economy. Theoretically, I was heavily influenced by the works of W.E.B. DuBois between 1933-1945, the one phase in DuBois's long and productive career when he came closest to a radical black nationalist posture. I have grave misgivings concerning the viability of political work with the majority of white political formations; and my understanding of burning political issues which were largely undiscussed within black nationalist organizations (such as patriarchy, the problem of nuclear energy, etc.) was at best elementary. This was the social/political/cultural matrix upon which this essay was conceived.

In retrospect, it would be intellectually dishonest to alter my original argument fundamentally, because at the time it was written, it opened up a new series of theoretical questions for me, and indirectly, for other black nationalists within my immediate circle. Nationalists as a group have been organized usually around questions of superstructure, or civil society—education, aesthetics, culture, social relations, political parties—but have been grievously lacking in any theoretical understanding of economic problems. The essay reveals a general shortcoming within all black nationalist ideology, an inability to present a reasonable and workable model for commodity production, land tenure, and the distribution of goods and services along democratic lines. The seizure of state power by socialists does not mean that the economic organization of society will be socialist after a generation. China under the leadership of Deng and company provides a classic illustration of a socialist society moving backward in history towards capitalism. This is not to suggest that a socialist America would want to nationalize every corner delicatessen, or expropriate "mom and pop" groceries. The goal of economic reorganization, however, must be equated not with full employment, but with worker self management, at all points of production. By reducing the duration of the normal work week to 24 hours, (e.g., in shifts of 4 workdays at 6 hours per day), the goal of full employment would be achieved almost overnight. More decisively, this would permit millions of workers to participate in the democratic reorganization and direction of the economy and the administration of the state apparatus. A reduction in the workday would also eliminate the necessity to depend upon petty capital to provide employment for black and white workers who are outside the labor force. A national priority to provide financial support for locally initiated consumer cooperatives would create alternatives to service-oriented petty capital; within several decades, private entrepreneurship should be a relic of the past, not unlike feudalism or slavery.

The evolution of my own political praxis in the 1980s has caused me to reassess other problems inherent in socialist reconstruction. With greater confidence, I now acknowledge that the majority of black people would be better served if separate black taxing units did not exist—for the simple reasons that this apparatus would be exceedingly difficult to carry out democratically, and that it would add to the levels of state bureaucracy. Black integrationists who had no ideological or social commitment to the preservation of a uniquely black cultural identity must be free to select their own lifestyles and neighborhoods without fear of being repressed by a nationalist-oriented state ombudsman. My commitment to socialist-feminism, which in 1979 was only cognitive and not essentially integral within my own worldview, permits me to recognize the validity of Patterson's criticisms concerning sexism. More than any other political tendency within black America, nationalists have historically articulated theories which serve to perpetuate the exploitation of women, and the suppression of the rights of lesbians. Socialist men, black and white, generally have not taken a principled position in favor of uprooting patriarchy. A socialist American will have to go well beyond the goal of the fifty percent representation for women at all levels of the state apparatus to insure that sexism in the workplace and in all social relations is vigorously combatted.

The only area of disagreement I have with Patterson is her unjustified preoccupation with the "power of the black petty bourgeoisie." The black elite derives its influence today from its strategic position as a buffer stratum which translates the prerogatives of the state and capitalism within the black community. Stripped of that historic function, the bulk of the petty bourgeoisie would virtually be powerless. If the socialist state actively solicits the contributions of black workers, and if all administrative functions are controlled by revolutionary forces, then any educational and cultural advantages that the black elite may have over black workers will be neutralized.

On the other hand, Tabb disagrees with the basic thesis of the essay—the theory of dual power after the revolution. The real root of discussion here lies in our divergent interpretations on the role of the state. Generally, Marxists equate the state with an apparatus to enforce the collective will of the ruling class over other social groups. For Trotsky, "dual power" meant the evolution of an alternative state which would provide the basis for proletarian democracy and workers' rule. Council communists viewed workers' "soviets" as the embryo from which a new political order would develop. My concern, writing then chiefly as a black nationalist, was that even under such conditions, no structural guarantee could be forthcoming from white workers which would make it unnecessary for separate black agencies to exist. Most of the socialists I knew were anti-racist in their personal relations with blacks and Latinos. But the majority of white workers were so deeply racist that, in my judgement, the black masses could not afford to place their lives and destinies in their hands even after the exploitative capitalists were banished from power. Another state, simultaneously within and outside the primary socialist apparatus, was necessary to provide an institutional check on the residual racist practices and tendencies of the majority of white, anti-capitalist forces.

Tabb characterizes the various institutional structures of dual power as revealing a disturbingly pessimistic view of whites' abilities to overcome their own racism. Let us redraft this issue as bluntly as possible: why are whites unreliable allies? I would not be the first black activist to ask this question. Regrettably, yet understandably, many black nationalists have a ready answer: *all* whites benefit from racism, either economically or culturally. My research since the late seventies convinces me that 1) the white bourgeoisie benefits decisively from racist propaganda, primarily because it divides workers; 2) the white middle stratum and working classes benefit from racism in relative, but not in absolute terms. In other words, every gain of the Civil Rights Movement indirectly benefitted the material interests of the majority of whites, yet white workers are still rewarded in the capitalist labor market simply by being nonblack. The super-exploitation of national minorities produces surplus value which in part artificially elevates the wages of whites at *some* historical periods. Yet overall, racism allows the capitalists to perpetuate the exploitation of white workers, in such a manner that whites are collectively worse off than if racism in socioeconomic relations did not exist. Racism gives many whites a false sense of security under capitalism, and obscures the essential dynamics of their own brutal suppression.

All successful socialist revolutions that have occurred to date have had at least one basic factor in common: the majority of the population was won over to the immediate program of the revolutionaries, but in no way could the mass of anti-capitalist forces, considered as individuals, be considered truly Marxist in their personal praxis. Revolutions are generally won by rallying a decisive bloc of the populace against the status quo, the previously existing order of things. Let us review briefly, for example, the history of the Soviet Union in regard to sexism. In 1917-1918, the Bolshevik government advanced one of the most progressive and anti-sexist agendas with respect to the rights of women ever achieved. The majority of Bolshevik males, from Lenin to the local party cadre, promoted policies which seriously damaged Russian patriarchy. The "Honest Leninist" male, counseled Marxist ideologue A. V. Lunacharsky, would "rock the cradle so that his wife could go out to a meeting or study." However, an outward political commitment to oppose sexism did not mean that the majority of males within the society were not still deeply sexist. With the defeats of Trotsky and Bukharin, and the rise of Stalin, patriarchal relations returned with a vengeance. Hundreds of vocal feminists were murdered by the late 1920s; "girls were also beaten and punished severely simply for attending the meetings of the women's clubs."[1] The historical parallels regarding the race question in the U.S. should be obvious. White workers and Marxists may temporarily (and perhaps genuinely) advance a militant program of anti-racism in the process of seizing state power. Racist white workers will find it beneficial, in terms of their own narrow material interests, to unite with black and Chicano workers in transforming the workplace. But the majority of white workers will continue to be affected psychologically, socially, and culturally by white supremacy for many years after monopoly capitalism ends. Revolting against capitalism does not directly translate as revolting against racism, particularly when many whites perceive themselves as unaffected by it. These "pessimistic" remarks, as Tabb would say, do not mean that racism cannot ever be destroyed. My point here is that most Marxists become economic determinists whenever the issue of race is discussed. As the primary victims of racism, blacks cannot afford to fall into this theoretical trap.

A socialist America will contain millions of white workers who will embrace an anti-capitalist program, yet who will nevertheless act out their deeply ingrained racist practices within civil relations. It is even questionable whether revolutionary whites, when pressed to make difficult decisions under enormous pressures, will side with the interests of oppressed national minorities against any sizable oppositon from white workers.[2] Tabb's implication that the war of position against capital will transform racist white workers into racial and cultural egalitarians does not square with the history of previous social revolutions. The burden of American history is the legacy of race and class, and the intricate intermarriage between white supremacy and monopoly capitalism. To insist, as some dogmatic Marxists often do, that the transfer of the ownership of the means of production to the working class will create the material conditions for immediate biracial cooperation and social harmony, is to greatly underestimate the power of an idea: racism. Unless blacks, Chicanos, Puerto Ricans, and others have some measure of dual power after the revolution, the possibility of a cultural democracy, and the very existence of socialism itself may be lost.

There remains one historical question that Tabb fails to address. Blacks *are*, and are *not*, Americans. Unlike the waves of European immigrants who obtained passage here, searching for religious freedom or economic prosperity, we came against our collective will. Historically, blacks have every reason to distrust America and to hate everything it stands for. Some blacks under socialism would seek to develop semi-autonomous or completely independent territories within this nation's boundaries. Others would want to be transported to a majority non-white Third World country. White socialists may disagree politically with the various agendas that emerge from the black working class. But they must recognize that blacks historically have a legitimate right to assert their own self-determination. The specific institutional forms suggested in the "Third Reconstruction" are speculative, to be sure. Yet they are a statement of the material realities of U.S. history. Personally, I became a Marxist because I am convinced that black people cannot obtain freedom or self-determination under capitalism. I can sympathize with the struggles of non-blacks (e.g., the current struggle for socialist democracy in Poland), but my decisive commitment remains to defending the interests of poor and working class blacks. The real source of disagreement between Tabb and myself appears at first glance to be supestructural—that is, ethnicity and racial relations under socialism—but it is actually an organic product of the material processes of race and class in mostly white America. Socialism must be international, yet all revolutions are profoundly national, and assume the shape of that nation's cultural/ economic/political dynamics. If white socialists today cannot recognize the legitimate fears that many blacks and Latinos share that the prospective socialist nirvana will be achieved for "whites only," what will unfold when socialism is actually won?

The burden of proof rests with white Marxists, not with black workers and activists. It is not enough for Tabb to insist that "we are talking about institution building in a society where those in the socialist leadership who are white are militantly anti-racist." We remember the racist betrayals of populists like Tom Watson and the early 20th century white suffragists. Racism circumscribes our collective history. Black people must judge socialism not by the promises of its white proponents, but on the basis of whether it will create real freedom.

NOTES

1. Sheila Rowbotham, *Women, Resistance and Revolution: A History of Women and Revolution in the Modern World* (New York: Vintage, 1972), pp. 147-161.

2. Along these lines, a short list of examples of the inevitable cultural chauvinism inherent within socialist construction and/or practice includes: the repressive posture of Stalinist Russia towards Jews, Ukrainians, and Asiatics; the French Communist Party's racist polemics against Northern African guest workers in France in the 1970s and 1980s; the hostilities between English-speaking blacks in eastern Nicaragua with the Sandinista government; Vietnam's battles with its "Overseas Chinese" population.

IV. THE DIVISION OF LABOR

Lead Essay   Joan Greenbaum
& Laird Cummings

Responses   Jeremy Brecher
Stan Weir

Rejoinder   Greenbaum
& Cummings

LOOKING FORWARD
Letters From Luke, Jane & Runya
Twenty Years After the Revolution Begins

Joan Greenbaum and Laird Cummings

Luke
Seattle, N.S. +20
Feb. 20

Dear Jane,

Do you remember? Those exciting, exhausting months just before the Revolution. You and Jason Fuller and I used to sit around for hours talking about the kind of society we wanted to build, the way we wanted to live our lives. And then you and I met again briefly some years after that at a meeting. There were so many meetings I have forgotten exactly when that was.

Yes, it is your old comrade Luke writing you out of the blue. I ran across Jason last week here in Seattle and he gave me your address. It was terrific seeing him again, and we spent the evening together talking about how our lives today compare with what we had imagined then. Anyway, it's out of the excitement we shared that I am writing you, both to re-establish contact and to ask you to contribute to a project Jason and I dreamed up. You know that Jason works for the Library of the Revolution. Well, he thinks that he can persuade the Library Council to support research for a book comparing revolutionary dreams with reality. Maybe, if we can get a chain of letters going, we can write the book ourselves.

So, what I am asking is that you try to describe your community and your life, with particular emphasis on how labor is divided in the home, on the job, and in the community. I am not interested in surveying how various communities have solved particular problems, like how to get the garbage collected, but more generally in how people live their lives and manage their activities. I know that this request is a tall order, so it is only fair that I try to tell you something of my life first.

Twenty years ago, before the Revolution began, much of Seattle's economy was either dependent on military production at Boeing or on a growing financial and commercial sector. A lot of economic planning and reallocation has taken place on a regional level with the aim of economic self-sufficiency balanced with ecological cooperation. One of the results has been the development of a lot of light industry like the furniture commune I work in. Actually, it is the re-development of the light industry which existed in the area before it came to be dominated by the aero-space industry before the Revolution. The heavy industrial sector was converted right after the Revolution to producing energy-efficient mass transit, and now supplies most of the Northwest with solar-powered monorail, tram, and shuttlecar systems. The combined industrial strength of the region is able to support a high rate of social labor such as the community-based clinics and mobile health teams like the one Emma works in.

You probably never met Emma, but you must remember my talking about her and our then year-old baby Alex when we saw each other last (which would make that 15 years ago, right?). Emma has worked for the Regional Health Network since it was set up, and currently is organizing and giving a series of seminars on new practices in midwifery to mobile health worker recruits. Alex is now sixteen and is spending the year with a work group building a new rail system along the coast. He loves the work, and is planning to join one of the new environmental groups which will be organized next summer.

Emma and I live in a large apartment complex built on Mercer Island before the Revolution. There are about 500 households in the complex, which consists primarily of two and three bedroom units. We have added a number of new buildings to the complex for collective functions, including a new dining hall. Last year we decided to set up a dining commune which serves the entire community. Everyone works one four hour shift each week, sharing and rotating all the various tasks as equally as possible. The new system works very well, and has made the dining commons the center of community social life.

Most of the people who live in the complex work in the nearby industrial district where the furniture commune is located, and all other essential services are available in the complex. For the most part, people need to travel only for leisure and community-wide activities. With the lower demand, our mass transit systems effectively provide most of our needs.

Our residential complex has its own schools. Up to the age of three, child care is available for all children primarily through community centers, but with provisions for home care as well. Children between four and eight have four hours a day of school, and another four hours of supervised play groups and after-school activities, in which parents generally participate. Nine to twelve year olds spend six hours a day in school, again here in the complex, and then three hours helping or playing in the activity centers at their parents' workplaces. I spend half a day each week in the activity center at the furniture commune. The aim of these centers is to begin to relate what the children are learning in school to the outside world; it also gives us all a chance to be with our kids in the afternoons once in a while. Thirteen to fifteen year olds spend four hours a day in classes and three hours on work assignments with a collective or community work group. At sixteen, everyone spends a year in community service, after which they have a year totally without obligations in which they can decide what they want to do.

I have mentioned the furniture commune several times now. You may remember that I always wanted to work with my hands, and that I had been working with a collective of cabinet-makers since the Revolution. That collective merged ten years ago with a furniture factory to establish our current commune. Our commune is now one of the three major furniture producers for the entire region. We mass-produce institutional furniture, but nearly half of our total production is in hand-crafted cabinetry, mostly for individual use. We have tried to combine the strengths of the different kinds of production, adding quality work to mass production, and adding some assembly line techniques and automation to the routine functions in cabinet making. Everyone in the commune spends one third of their time in mass production work, one third in craft production, and the last third in administrative chores.

The commune is organized into production teams (mass production and craft) and administrative teams. The mass production teams are responsible for specific product lines; I am working with a team that makes kitchen cabinets for the new prefabricated housing being built for agricultural collectives in the western part of the state. The craft team I work with produces a variety of pieces, either by special order or from our own design. We share tools and skills and help each other out a lot. The administrative teams provide support for the production teams and the commune members. I work on the supply team which is responsible for obtaining all resources required by the commune, from new "capital" to size 8 screws. Sharing all the different kinds of jobs which have to get done, we try to feel equally committed to carrying out the commune's Production Plan, and I think this probably helps account for the commune's success. Nothing is ever left undone because someone feels it is not her or his job to do it. The commune has done very well, so well that it has exceeded regional production quotas in each of the last four years.

Seattle is a very exciting place to be this year. We are in the middle of the Tenth Year Review of our Economic Plan, and there is debate and discussion everywhere. The exceptional productivity of our commune has been a topic of debate on several levels. In community discussions of production goals, we have often been used as an example of the proper path to follow in achieving higher productivity. Our commune adopted a policy five years ago of automating all the dangerous, unpleasant, and boring jobs that we could. Most of the tasks selected for automation were either in the administrative or mass production areas. Our productivity in these tasks has certainly increased overall, freeing more workers for craft work or making it possible to reduce the total time worked. The policy seems to have worked well enough in the commune, but I am skeptical about wider applications. We may now spend fewer hours a week doing unpleasant work, but some of the time we still spend on mass production or administrative work is even less pleasant than it used to be. I'm not sure that fewer hours relating to machines is better than more hours relating to people. Besides, I don't think our productivity can be traced to technology alone. Our organization, our division of labor, our spirit, these features of our lives are more important than technology.

Our work plan follows the national standard of a 30 hour work week for everyone 18 to 60 and 15 hours for people over 60. In addition, everyone has six hours of community service each week, on assignments which rotate yearly. This year, my assignment is really kind of fun; I am a caretaker of a small park in our neighborhood one day a week. Last year one of the teenage work groups helped build some housing in the park for our mini-zoo which now boasts 17 monkeys, including 3 babies. Next Spring, the younger children are planning to plant a garden in another part of the park. People really use the park, so it is rewarding to work there.

Our working hours and conditions are set by the collective, following the national guidelines on division of labor pretty closely. I spread my work time over five six-hour days, half of one of which I spend with the kids in the commune's activity center (now that Alex is grown I have to keep my hand in), and one and a half of which I spend on supply team chores. The rest of the week I spend doing design and production work. That really isn't as much time as I would like to spend, and I often put in some extra time in the shop when I am working on an exciting project.

I think that a lot of our high productivity is due to organizing our jobs in ways that maximize our usefulness as human beings and producers, making use of all our talents and energies. Or at least we try to. But it isn't always clear what that way is. We are currently having a serious struggle in the commune over our Production Plan and about how to respond to the increased productivity. Some members want to shift the division of work from craft production to the more efficient mass production in order to expand distribution and income. The rest of the members are pretty evenly divided between wanting the opposite, to shift more work to craft production, and wanting to contribute more time to community service assignments and to furlough allowances. I favor the last policy. As the labor force grows and productivity rises, Socialism can come into its full promise, turning more and more labor time to social improvement and to collective purposes, and at the same time increasing the time available for individual creativity. But only to the degree that we can learn to manage ourselves.

The furniture collective has had a fairly successful experience with self-management in the last ten years, both in economic results and in process. Most policy decisions are made by the Policy Council, which consists of elected representatives of the production and administrative teams. On questions where there is substantial disagreement, and on major issues like the commune's Production Plan, only the Workers' Assembly can make final decisions. At times like the present, with the big struggle over the Production Plan, no decision is likely until some form of compromise can be reached. Officially, major decisions require at least a two-thirds majority. The policies set by the Assembly and Policy Council are carried out by the coordinating committees of the work teams, which see to the organization of tasks, arrangement of work schedules, and planning. Workers spend three months on these committees every two years. These coordinating committees do enough of the routine administrative work so that we have been able to keep the number of workers assigned full-time to administrative chores under 5%. Some day we hope to be able to eliminate even these remaining technical and administrative "roles," and we have steadily reduced their number as the coordinating committees have gained experience, but vestiges of the old division of labor do linger on.

The practice of management in the collective is not quite as democratic as the plan, and I spend a lot of time on a committee established by the Workers' Assembly to propose improvements. We have collective organization, majority control, high participation in self-management, good communication, but we have all these less perfectly than we would like. Making decisions by two-thirds majorities is way short of full consensus, but we haven't found structures that make that possible on a large scale. Some smaller production teams have achieved consensus decision-making for the last few years, but wider applications have not worked. There are quite a few workers who seem to have no interest in serving on the Policy Council and who, when it is their turn to serve on the coordinating committee for their team, do not really get involved. I know a few people, however, a few older workers, who surprised themselves by really getting involved in their coordination work, and then went on to run for the Policy Council. I think they weren't confident that they, individually, could contribute to self-management. The younger workers seem to have no such problems. They think they have all the answers, and indeed they have many, but it seems too easy for them. I am very proud of what our revolution has created for our children's generation, but at times I am a little jealous too. Their youth was so much freer and more fulfilling than mine was. And sometimes their confidence in themselves makes it difficult for them to see how others look at things.

Within our management structure there has been another problem recently: that of too much power being wielded by coordinating committees, particularly in the larger production teams. Even though membership on the committees rotates constantly, by the very nature of the committees' responsibility to get things done, they sometimes violate democratic principles. Last month, for example, the coordinating committee of one of the mass production teams tried to extend work schedules for most of the workers to make up for an error in planning. The team refused. After much debate, and anger, the coordinating committee accepted their mistakes. The committee members decided to work on a Saturday to make up the lost production. When they came in, the whole team showed up as well. The committee's error was in assuming too much responsibility as well as power. Collective discipline is a restraint but not domination. Fully democratic, non-authoritarian management is very difficult to achieve, however; in the end it remains Management and involves some degree of domination. A large part of the problem is that it is still difficult to conceptualize management without domination. We have come a long way, but must struggle to improve.

I hope that I haven't made life here sound like all work and meetings and debates. It really isn't like that at all. Work and self-management do take a lot of time, of course, but there is plenty of time left over. More importantly, these activities are fulfilling enough in themselves that we have a lot of energy left over to devote to our individual lives. I have been putting in several evenings a week on a project that excites me a great deal. I have been meeting for a year with a group sponsored by the Association of Workers' Assemblies that is collecting materials for an exhibit on the history of labor in our community. We have found some really wonderful material. There is a rich history of attempts at worker self-management in Seattle, dating back to the General Strike of 1919. The comparisons between their attempts and our efforts today are fascinating. In fact, I have become so interested in this research that I am planning to use my next sabbatical to go back to school to study history. Everyone here gets one year in five off from their regular work assignments, though not from community service obligations. Many people use these sabbaticals for additional education or special projects, often leading to changes in occupation. Much of our most creative cultural work is done by people on sabbatical from other occupations. I am due for a year's leave starting in the Fall.

Jane, although I have been writing this letter for hours now, it seems like I have hardly begun to tell you about our life here. But I have to close. Tomorrow I am on duty for the breakfast shift in the dining hall and have to be up early.

I hope I have been able to communicate some of my enthusiasm for the project Jason and I have been talking about, and that you will try to describe how work is organized in your community for our book of letters. And I would love to stay in touch with you again. Do write soon and tell us about your life.

> In struggle, your old friend
> Luke

> Jane
> Clairmont, N.J.
> N.S.+20
> March 15

Dear Luke,

I was so pleased to get your letter, I can't tell you how it made my day! I think the last time we met was fifteen years ago at those awful bureaucratic meetings in Chicago when everybody was arguing about how to decentralize. In some ways it seems like a lifetime ago, and yet your letter helped me put into perspective how far we have gone and, oh yes, how far we will always have to go. I will try to tell you a little about my life and the workings of my community, although it does seem so difficult to begin. You asked me specifically about our forms of division of labor so I will focus on that.

I live in a household of five adults, four children, and two adolescents. I guess in the days before the revolution we would have thought of the adolescents as "kids," but since they are working members of society they seem to look at themselves differently, and I must say that seems more constructive than our terrible teen years. I am thirty-seven now so more than half of my life has been forged within our working definitions of a socialist society. How I marvel at my six and ten year olds who have never known another way of thinking! Just the other day Zoe, the ten year old, asked me a question about how "in the old days" technicians could have said that they would not get politically involved. She was writing a paper on transitions in scientific thinking and it was beyond her experience to imagine that a person could have considered "scientific" education separate and distinct from any other part of life.

Having grown up in a somewhat traditional nuclear family, I find our household unit both liberating and at times extremely difficult. I am part of a couple with a man named Michael. He is a parent of two of my children and we seem to have a warm understanding about our goals and plans. Right now we have just begun a new five year agreement with each other and two of the other adults in the house. I find it important to use these agreements as a means to stabilize things; perhaps it is my "old" way of thinking, but I enjoy the knowledge of this kind of security. Within our household, children (under age thirteen) are the direct responsibility of their parent or parents although it is the responsibility of the household to see that our ideas are carried out. Michael and I do more day-to-day child care for our children than we do for the others, but it is the job of the household to share the load. I think I'm pretty good at being a parent about two hours a day; beyond that I get to feel put-upon so my child-care load is usually in two hour slots. Michael can deal with kids much more consistently than I without getting that closed-in feeling so his house work load is usually longer. I am trying to get better at child care, but I think I still get stymied by the image of my mother having sole responsibility for our welfare when we were young. Could you even contemplate what it must have felt like to have been a "mother" and be on call all those hours every day, constantly responsible?

Maybe I should tell you something about this town and the kinds of work we do so that you could better understand our community division of labor as well as that within our household. Clairmont used to be a suburb or bedroom community to New York. I guess many men, and in later years some women, spent several hours a day traveling to and from their jobs in the city. One of our first community decisions was to try to list and then develop as many jobs as we could within the immediate area. In actual fact, this turned out to be a lot easier than we had initially thought. Over the last five years, the overwhelming majority of jobs for residents of the town are within walking or bicycling range. Of course there are people who live here and work other places, but for those who choose not to divide their work life from other parts of their life, it is now quite possible.

In the years immediately before the revolution, this area had begun to be a base for white collar jobs concentrated around the computer field. Since there was some knowledge about this within the community, we decided to expand on it and began to develop shops for manufacturing and assembling computer components as well as including data entry services ("keypunching") and expanding the computer programming shops we already had. As you know, most of the work in the computer field, particularly the data entry end and the assembly work, is quite routine and hopelessly boring. I think that we have effectively used the national guidelines for rotating tasks, sharing decision-making and shortening working hours to make these jobs more acceptable. Currently we are trying to automate some of the more boring jobs and to go on and develop other new community functions. For the interim period, since fifty percent of the community workbase is involved in routine computer jobs, we have shortened the hours of the most repetitive work (like data entry) and have been fairly successful in rotating these positions around the work force. At one point we had tried to pass off this "shit work" on adolescents, but they rightfully rebelled and now only do their share of it. Like many communities we use the same rotation scheme for other necessary but not terribly interesting jobs like garbage collection, street cleaning, and transport driving. I think our town also has been fairly successful at developing within the community resources and jobs that we consider especially important. We decided, for example, to focus on training teachers, and while we don't have the resources for formal education, once the teachers are trained at schools outside the region we do a lot of on-the-job training. In a similar vein we consider early child care to be very important. Many households choose to keep children at home until four, but in addition to home care our goal is to have small child care centers every two blocks so in those winter months we don't have to take the little ones far.

We have recently adopted a new method of applying the national work-time guidelines to the question of child care. Under the guidelines taking care of children—your own or those of others—counts toward your 36-hour work assignment, while other household chores don't count but are to be shared equitably. The problem we faced was that because of old habits many men got so involved in their outside jobs that they didn't opt for time with their children. At first we thought this something for the parents to decide on their own, but this seemed to lead to a situation that was unfair to the youngsters. So now we insist that both parents of a child under thirteen must spend six hours of their work time with the child.

I should comment for a moment on the allocation of labor time because our application is a little different from some areas. We use the national standard of a 36-hour week which we balance between low-skilled tasks, skilled or what used to be called career tasks, and community work and planning time for each adult. Adolescents and people wanting to return to school get their skilled time (about ten hours a week) to use for formal education. We rotate the low-skilled tasks on a yearly basis and give people the option to continue in their skilled work or return to school or training programs for a new "occupation." We are now able to offer retraining options to people at five year intervals and, although we don't have the same flexibility you have with your sabbatical plan, we are really pleased with this. We hope that in the future we needn't be so rigid about the retraining or skill switching, but for right now we still need these constraints for planning purposes. It wasn't until a few years ago that the economic base of our region stabilized enough to make room for this retraining option. Before that time, like most poorer areas we worked the full work week.

In your letter you talked about decision-making and I'm really pleased to report that I think we've made the greatest leaps in our ability to deal with this. When I last saw you we were in those endless meetings: debating, discussion, and never quite reaching meaningful consensus. It looked like the endless meeting dilemma would squelch the idea of sharing social planning. The initial training programs that the national government set up were of some help to us in learning how to use our meeting time effectively. Remember the suggestions from the early women's groups? Our training used these and the national guidelines to focus on listening, understanding each other, concentrating on single issues, and rotating speakers. As you mentioned, it's as though a whole new type of people has been born! Having placed our priorities on group process we have really learned to use the meeting place as a method to get things done and have become quite clear about separating those issues that need further discussion from those that we can act on. I used to dread going to a planning meeting, but now, several times a week I participate in our division's housing committee and I also work with the county-wide coordinating committee.

I remember my mother always talking about the painful separation between the head and the hand. By that she was referring to the problem that some people were to do the thinking and others the work.

I guess that until we learned that we could all participate in decision-making in a non-chaotic way we just weren't able to envision mending the head and the hand back together. Remember the argument that said we could never achieve socialism because some people just didn't want to get involved? How naive we were to think that every decision had to involve everyone. True, I am sometimes frustrated by the decisions I didn't take part in, but I can ask to work with that planning group or I can voice my opinion to a member of that group. There are times when I enjoy being a leader and decision-maker, and other times when I really want to take a back seat.

I have been rambling on about the community and have just realized that I haven't told you what I've been doing. First, in terms of social labor time I have been performing my low-skilled work by assembling computer components. I don't suppose that it's any better or worse than any factory type of job and I have been able to arrange it so that I get this task over with in two days rather than doing it a few hours each day. I think that we've done well at re-designing the plant so that the natural lighting, plants, and carpets make it more pleasant and quiet. Within the shop we rotate the most boring jobs and have agreed to meet over lunch break to discuss and plan for improved shop design and a more comfortable work flow. While it is a low-skilled job, we have all been trained to understand the technology that we are working with. The training period is five days, and we are asked to make a one year commitment to our shop.

I must say that I really like the people I work with. There are forty of us (unlike some areas we have chosen to use existing space and concentrate in a number of small shops) and since it is near my house, I get to see a number of them after work. I recall something from our school years about an argument being made for "economies of scale," but for the life of me I can't imagine how that would apply to assembly work. Not only are the small shops more comfortable, but they also give us the option of being able to switch to new products quite easily because we don't have all that much tied up in plant or equipment. I bet that that old argument was mostly a cover for controlling workers!

My skilled time and my meeting time overlap somewhat by my own design. For the last few years I have been working in the housing area. I started simply by listing houses and apartments and speaking with people who wanted to live in them. Actually, this was considered a fairly unskilled job, but I had a great deal of interest in it so it was important to me. I am also beginning to learn about home repair, carpentry, plumbing, and other skills related to housing. At some point I think that I would like to study more about architecture and the mechanics of building construction. It is hard for me to imagine that when I was in high school the housing field consisted of hundreds if not thousands of different job titles from architect to real estate agent. Clearly all of these do not interest me (and I must admit I am a lousy carpenter) but the task of helping people find and maintain decent housing is one that I really enjoy.

My planning time is also devoted to housing plans and priorities. Like other areas, our first housing goal was racial balance. This has almost been accomplished now and while people within the community get first choice on housing, people moving into the community have a little more choice these days. On a day-to-day basis there are actually very few decisions our planning group needs to make. As labor-time incomes are the same for all adults, people can choose their housing on the basis of what they want and the number of people in their household. We live in a large older house, but the trend these days seems to be toward the newer apartment units where households can get suites with private rooms linked to collective kitchens and maintenance areas. There is a lot to be said for those and the design is beginning to be quite interesting, although not as attractive as the ones I've seen out there on the West Coast where you are. Because we made the decision to allocate our resources toward maintaining our existing housing stock, little of our resources go toward building new housing units and thus the waiting list for the collective units is long.

We have managed to convert a number of the old banks and insurance offices into private office space so that those of us in the older houses can have a place to get away to and close the door on household cares. I'm writing this letter now in my "office" which I share with a woman from the assembly plant. It's interesting to remember as children how terrified we were of the images of crowded quarters and lack of choice that we thought were associated with socialism. But choice clearly does not have to depend on income as we then thought. The planning group makes the basic decisions on how to use space (particularly some of the older mansions) and is called on to help arbitrate a situation when more than one household wants the same house or apartment. These types of dilemmas are declining because we have learned to use the space we have in better ways.

I guess that I had better close and say that I eagerly await hearing from you again. In some ways I think it important that we don't lose sight of the fact that our generation has the capacity to see things through two sets of glasses. True, we often slow the younger ones down with our fears and warnings about capitalism and patriarchy, but I think our knowledge and warnings are necessary. It's about time we got busy and started writing about the world we knew and the one we have helped shape. I've written to my mother and urged her to describe her "lives" to our children. Maybe this letter, like yours, can help put what seems like ancient history in perspective for them and for us.

Toward the continual revolution,
Jane

Runya
Littletree, Georgia
May 18, N S + 20

Dear Jane,

It's nice to get a letter from my daughter once in a while, even if it is asking me to do something. Actually I am glad for the opportunity to sit down and try to put some of my thoughts and memories on paper. I'll begin by describing some of the immediate pre-revolutionary ideas so that you and the children can get a perspective on how false the basic assumptions of our society were.

First and foremost was the notion that "human nature would never change." Those who accepted the status quo (no matter how grudgingly) clung to this frayed piece of ideology as though they were hanging on to a life raft. They were taught to believe that the way things were, was the way they had always been and would always be. Having been trained in aggression and competition they saw only this and would argue that even if you changed the economic and social system people would remain competitive and aggressive. This training held as a firm barrier against arguments for change and served to color our impressions of the world around us. I will use your example of the division of labor as a way of explaining how this ideology prevented people from seeing problems for what they were.

I'm sure your children would have found the pre-revolutionary work world a strange and terrifying place. Societal division of labor was assumed to be so complex as to require hundreds of thousands of job titles and categories, each requiring its own peculiar specialties. Adolescents were expected to "choose" a specialty and study towards it. Once locked into it, their knowledge and skill in other areas quickly diminished, often leaving them high and dry when the need for that skill disappeared. While it was becoming quite common for people to change "careers" several times during their working lives (as old occupations were automated, rationalized, or moved to other places) this career change phenomena was not easy to accomplish in the face of the labor market.

The labor market was a most extraordinary thing. A main tenet of capitalism, you remember, was the belief that the market or exchange mechanism governed and in fact balanced the supply and demand for all things. This concept was extended to the human sphere where people were asked to sell their labor power as if it were a commodity within the market system. Labor power, the commodity the worker was expected to sell, was divided from the actual labor or work one did on the job. Selling one's labor power within this market required a good degree of competition and, of course, reinforced the idea that people were basically competitive. Imagine trying to compete within a labor market where people were differentiated according to their minute specialty area! As the number of jobs grew smaller, the competition intensified. Your father, like so many men of his age, was brutalized by this process. I do wish he could have lived to see the changes.

But the labor market was further complicated by other divisions that were created and reinforced both economically and socially. There was the concept of a "reserve army of unemployed" which acted as a buffer or source of ready workers. It was made up of people who were not generally employed, but needing wages, could be drawn into the labor market. And for most of the Twentieth century women were the mainstay of this reserve pool! We were trained to stay at home, raise families, and tend house, but were called into the labor market when the demands of capital dictated. I don't know if you remember this, but this treatment of women, known as the sexual division of labor, was considered "natural."

Still other divisions existed to make activity within the market painfully competitive and forcefully aggressive. Joining division by gender was an overwhelming separation by race. In this country, non-white races were made to feel inferior and were treated as such within the labor market. Even in the 1960s and '70s when liberal ideology took root, the effects of liberal thought were minimal in the arena of labor market competition. These kinds of divisions were fundamental for a system that needed to maintain rule by dividing and conquering. It had the effect of setting would-be workers against each other in the battle for economic survival.

Divisions within the labor market were but a prelude and a weeding out process to divisions within the labor process itself. The labor process, or the way in which work was done, was based on the principle that mental labor was separate and distinct from physical labor. Seeing societal division of labor as requiring thousands of specialized job functions, people were trained to expect these same divisions within the detailed division of labor on the job. The labor process was really a rash of rationalized procedures and minutely divided tasks. Divisions within the workplace reflected those in the larger society: workers were entrenched in a hierarchy, categorized by gender, race, level of education, family background, and a then measurable entity (although I don't remember how) called "intelligence." Workplaces were themselves divided from home places and other aspects of workers' lives.

Workers who scrambled higher in the hierarchy were allowed mental or decision-making tasks, while those who hung on to the lower rungs of the ladder were only allowed to do repetitive or physical tasks. As capitalism .attempted to remove creativity and decision-making. from workers and place this knowledge and control within the realm of capital, the majority of jobs became more boring and routine. Management often wondered why workers seemed so dull and uninspired, but given the mindless tasks people were asked to do on the job it's a wonder that we functioned at all. And as knowledge and skill were abstracted, these jobs were able to be automated. In the battle for jobs this clearly pitted workers not only against other workers, but divided workers from technology, creating a fear of capital-controlled technology.

This whole process was made to appear natural and inevitable. Because it was necessary to divide labor within society (we all can't do everything) we were led to believe that we had to divide labor *within* the workplace and even *within* the individual, even to the extent of separating the head from the hand as you point out (it really gives me pride to see that you remember some of the things I taught you). In this way social division of labor was used as an excuse for the detailed division of labor. We were taught that this detailed division was efficient. Since capitalism was based on accumulations of capital and this accumulation required ever increasing spirals of accumulation, this form of efficiency was considered necessary to get more labor out of workers *and* to control the way in which their labor was applied.

I know that when you were a child I used to rant and rave about the dangers of capitalism and I guess that the passage of time has done little to quiet my anger. Essentially, it was a system of minority rule, for it was the few who could accumulate enough capital to control the many. In late capitalism the control mechanisms were no longer blatant; rather they depended on people internalizing the need for control and thereby controlling themselves. It was in this way that patriarchy and racism were used to subordinate entire groups of people, and in suppressing large groups at a time this made it easier for a tiny minority to rule.

When people tried to change this system they were labeled idealists or utopians—dreamers who may have pretty ideas but no way to implement them. This tactic was used particularly against women. We were told that if division of labor without subordination were possible it would have been done. Many would point an accusing finger at the Soviet Union, China, or other existing "socialist" countries and say that these were living examples of how innate and inbred were the notions which led to hierarchical, bureaucratic systems. And back we came to the starting place for these arguments—the belief that human nature was basically competitive (almost as if we were genetically forced to pit individual against individual). If our dreams didn't get us our genes surely would!

For many of us the false assumptions were worn thin by the realization that our lives were so fragmented that there just had to be other ways to live. And indeed there were, for when we stopped to look at our day-to-day activities—the ones we actually controlled—we could see that we didn't organize ourselves divisively. In workplaces, for example, it was clear that at the bottom of the hierarchy, the ways workers related to one another were nothing like the ways that capital prescribed. Community groups, women's groups, workplace coffee klatches, informal groups within the military: all of these were like beacons pointing to the fact that what we took to be the division of labor was not the only form it had to take!

In retrospect, I think it was our own *belief* that the division of labor could take another form that led us to try to rid ourselves of the subordination and fragmentation piled upon us. I'm sure others will give you other interpretations, but in my eyes it wasn't until we started to have trust in ourselves and our ideas that we were able to concretely change things. We had to see for ourselves that division of labor in society and the detailed division of labor we were pressed into, were not of the same tree. Recognizing that some division of labor was necessary we have been able to weed out both the causes and effects of it that are the most detrimental to the individual.

But changing beliefs and outlawing the more divisive aspects of labor division are only part of the revolutionary process. As you and your children know, the educational foundation of society has had to be stripped and rebuilt. Capitalism and patriarchy were systems of control—control of one group by another. The socialism we have been building needs cooperation and flexibility to grow. For me, a fundamental difference is the fact that when I was your children's age, I was brought up in a system that taught me to be competitive and fight for control. It is so exciting to see how involved today's children are in cooperative activities and how flexible they are about changing tasks, jobs, and even ideas. I do believe that your children shed unworkable or faulty ideas the way I used to change clothes!

Well, all of this writing only makes me want to see you and the children. I am planning to take six weeks of vacation this year and hope that I can arrange to come up there for a week and have the kids come down here for some of the time. Thirty years ago, if anyone was to tell me that I would choose to work on a collective farm in Georgia I would have thought that they were crazy. But you know that I love it.

By the way, I've finally decided to exercise some of my retirement options. This year I will be cutting back to a 15-hour week. Yes, Jane, your mother at sixty-two is finally learning to slow down! It's not that I'm tired, but rather that I think I have begun to learn to lessen my own need for control. Being "needed" has been so important to me that I think that I was scared to take the time off, but I have finally figured out that the farm will run without me.

In your last letter you mentioned that your block association was starting a collective garden. I do think it's a good idea that even you Northerners learn and share in farming skills, but really, Jane, the amount that you will be able to produce will be so trivial I think it's ridiculous. I think you carry the notion of sharing knowledge and skills too far. Anyway, I'll take a look at it when I visit this summer. Also, it wouldn't be a bad idea if you called your mother more often.

Love,
In struggle and love,
Runya

SOCIALISM IS WHAT YOU MAKE IT
A Response to "Looking Forward"
Jeremy Brecher*

There was something very moving to me about these letters. Something about the way they show a socialist society as a world people make—living, learning, developing their values, and creating solutions to the problems they face. This process itself is what constitutes the alternative to capitalism and to a top-down, bureaucratic socialism. And it seems so possible: dealt with concretely, the problems of building socialism are not so different from the things people already do in their lives.

One consequence of seeing socialism as what we make it, rather than as something that can be derived from a set of pre-established principles, is that a socialist society remains an arena of choice and conflict. All the things which might seem desirable to one or another individual or group cannot be done simultaneously. And so choice and conflict over whether to stress craft production or automation, or whether individuals should be able to trade off their childcare responsibilities, will persist. These are not only conflicts over means to agreed ends, or over differing interests, but also over values, over what constitutes the common good. The virtue of a socialist society—as we can see in these letters—is not that it eliminates social conflict, but that it allows that conflict to take a form that encourages the free development and fulfillment of the needs and values of all members of the community.

For this reason, I would like to address my comments to the *dimensions of choice* these letters suggest a socialist society would face: the questions that people in such a society will be called upon to answer. The answers to these questions cannot be derived from the notion of socialism itself; they will have to grow out of the learning experiences and evolving values of those who answer them. Nor will the answers that seem most desirable in reply to one question necessarily be

*I would like to thank Jill Cutler, Michael Ferber, Marty Bresnick, and Peter Rachleff for their comments on an earlier draft of this piece.

compatible with those that seem best in answer to another question; mutual compromise and creative coordination or synthesis of different values and practices will be central to making a socialist society work.

SOME BROAD CONSIDERATIONS

Social Boundaries

One of the best features of these letters is the way they show the transformation of the boundaries between the spheres of social life we think of in terms of "the economy," "the family," "the household," "the community," "the workplace," "the individual," and the like. These boundaries do not completely disappear; there is still, for example, a boundary between the home and the workplace. But the boundaries themselves have become subject to shaping by conscious community decisions. For example, in one workplace, a decision is made that childcare will be done in part within the workplace, rather than entirely in the home or school. In another case, it is decided that society as a whole should play a role in determining the division of labor within the household by insisting that fathers bear a share of responsibility for the care of their children. On the other hand, communal households are in general allowed to determine their own internal division of labor as they see fit, provided it meets certain (unspecified) criteria of fairness.

Not all determinations of the boundary between public and private spheres will be easy. For example, who will have bottom-line responsibility for care of children? And how will such responsibility relate to the control of conception?

The change in the nature of boundaries between social spheres has several aspects. First, the boundaries themselves become the object of social decision-making; they are not (as now within capitalist society) the unintended results of decisions being made within particular spheres. Second, social decision-making cuts across these boundaries, so that for instance what in current society would be an "economic" decision of whether to build houses or apartments is not separated from the "social" decision of whether people want to live in nuclear families or larger communal groups. What is produced is not a question separate from how it is produced. "Economic," "political," and "social" planning are all aspects of the single question: how do we want to live? Third, while boundaries are no longer absolute, they remain as an aspect of decentralization, a way in which particular individuals and groups can regulate their own activity within guidelines set by the broader society but without its continual direction or interference.

Time

The society described in these letters is marked by a series of temporal cycles. These include such things as the daily and weekly work cycles, the 10-year cycle in which the Seattle community reviews and revises its economic plan, the five–year period for which Jane and the man she lives with make a personal contract, and the individual (and generational) life cycle in which individuals are born, grow up, and ultimately grow old.

These cycles are very important in the way continuity and change are organized in the society described. Since all possibilities cannot be realized at once, decisions must be made and carried out over a period of time. To have every decision constantly subject to reversal would make life chaotic: if people decided to create bus systems, built the necessary factories and roads, and reorganized urban life around the expected traffic flows, and then suddenly decided to have subways instead, they would be in trouble. Yet it is essential that even the most basic decisions be reversible in some way. The 10-year review of the Seattle economy and the 5-year domestic agreement provide a way that continuity can be maintained over time, interdependent activities can be coordinated, and yet decisions can be reconsidered and reversed periodically. The ability to reverse past decisions is the soul of socialist freedom, the only way to escape the "dead hand of the past."

Of course, time-cycles are of different lengths, and this can cause problems. Children mature and may not choose to fit into an economic plan they had no voice in establishing. Community, domestic, and workplace cycles may not entirely coincide. But that merely illustrates why the management of a socialist society is in part a problem of coordination.

Space

The reorganization of space has been an important part of the social reconstruction described in these letters. This has taken several forms. As an aspect of economic decentralization, regions have become increasingly autonomous, with invisible economic boundaries dividing them from each other. This results in far less movement of people and materials across these boundaries: New Jerseyites no longer commute in massive number to New York City; Seattle factories produce furniture for regional consumption, rather than airplanes for a global market. Conversely, space within communities tends to become less bounded: workplaces are within walking or biking distance of homes, care for young children is provided within two blocks of homes, etc. Yet at the household level, such functions as cooking or personal offices are tending to move out of the household unit to separate buildings.

The achievement of this society lies not in any particular form of spatial structure, but in its ability to make spatial organization—like social boundaries—an object of social decision-making.

THE DIVISION OF LABOR

As these letters make clear, the division of labor intersects with virtually all the other key questions of what a socialist society would be like. The relations between old and young, men and women, different regions of the country and even the world—all are implicated. Indeed, one of the strengths of "Looking Forward" is that it shows that the division of labor must be addressed not just as an "economic" question, but as one involving politics, gender, age, race, and virtually every other aspect of human life. Because the division of labor is controlled by society, rather than by conflicting power centers and uncontrolled social forces, people have the opportunity to make choices that simply can't be made in today's society. Some of the lessons implicit in these letters can perhaps be drawn out by looking at division of labor in terms of these dimensions. I will start with the most intimate and move toward the most global.

Work and the Individual

A socialist society is not a fantasy world in which people's needs are met without work; labor remains a necessity. But how does the fact that labor is necessary get expressed at the level of the individual? It appears as a socially-imposed limitation on individual freedom. So there arises an inevitable tension between individual freedom and the necessity of work.

In the society described in these letters, labor is clearly considered compulsory. Guidelines have been established at a national level providing that each person of a given age shall work a certain number of hours. This is combined (at least in some regions) with a specified income to which all workers are entitled.

One question that would arise for a society implementing this approach would be the question of sanctions for violation of such norms. Would there be some kind of legal process for determining violations? Would those who were found in violation (say, by avoiding work) be subject to sanctions?

Related is the question of whether there is still a tie between income and work. What happens to an individual who, because of illness, age or other reasons is unable to work? Conversely, is the security of the individual's income established through her or his relation to a job?

The labor time guideline has the virtue of encouraging equality of contribution. But it eliminates all individual control over the question of how much time to work. One choice facing a socialist society would be whether to allow individuals and/or groups to increase or decrease their labor time and change their income proportionately.

This socialist society makes decisions on a regional basis that determine an overall social division of labor; a regional plan allocates resources to various forms of industry, community development, and the like. How do people's individual choices about what they want to do get coordinated with this overall social division of labor? In other words, what replaces the allocation function played in capitalism by the labor market?

Answers to this question could vary in terms of time. At one extreme, individuals could be rotated through every job in the community, changing frequently. At the other extreme, an individual could hold the same job as long as it existed. In the society described, individuals rotate through many jobs in their workplace, but not through different workplaces. But there is no reason in principle that job rotation or job bidding could not be extended beyond the individual workplace.

This is one of a class of trade-offs in which both individual freedom and the structuring of collective loyalties are involved. The fact that a worker is part of a particular workgroup is a limitation on individual freedom. It has the advantage that it tends to build strong workgroups whose members know each other, understand the unit as a whole, and share an interest in its future. On the other hand, this has the liability of its advantage: it tends to build loyalty to a particular workplace and workgroup at the expense of the community as a whole. The job rotation which is used within each workplace to reduce divisions within the workforce and let each individual appreciate the enterprise as a whole would serve the same function if individuals rotated through all the jobs in the community.

Another dimension concerns the role of individual choice in work assignments. In the furniture factory, for example, there is no equivalent to "job bidding." Individuals are assigned to work teams which are responsible for particular operations. This has the advantages of reducing "special interests" within the workforce and of reducing individual boredom, but it also reduces individual choice.

Another question is the kind of personal identification an individual makes with work activities. Present day society includes at one extreme the "professional" whose whole identity is wrapped up with a particular kind of work activity and its social role definitions, at the other extreme casual laborers who float among a large number of menial tasks without an identification with any of them. The society described in these letters seems to have chosen a third alternative: identification with a particular workplace and its collective. One appears to identify as a member of a furniture collective or a health team, not as a member of a particular profession or as an individual for whom work is incidental to personal identity.

It is important here to be conscious of the tradeoffs. The social-psychological structure of a "career" or a "profession" has certain virtues. It involves the idea of work as a "calling," not merely a burden, which partially nullifies the compulsory nature of labor. On the other hand, it creates a one-sided identity and a professional subculture that can be somewhat isolated from the rest of society.

To some extent, this one-sidedness is implicit in all work-based identities. The growth of a workforce composed of individuals with no identification with a particular workplace or work process has been an impoverishment, but it has also been a liberation from narrow, limited concepts of social role. There is something positive in considering oneself an individual or a member of society first, a worker of a particular kind only as an accidental matter. The questions of how work organization interacts with individual identities will play an important role in both individual life and political processes within a socialist society.

The society described has clearly decided to try to reduce the limitations that compulsory labor places on individual freedom, and to expand the realm of individual freedom to the extent that the wealth of the community allows. The industrial sabbatical, for example, is an institution which could be indefinitely expanded, and the labor time guidelines reduced, until work was a relatively minor part of an individual's total life.

Work and the Community

One obvious issue in a decentralized, community-based socialism is who is included in the community? Is it simply a matter of who lives in a given geographical area? If so, are there controls on the movement of people? What are the implications of this for equality, both within and between regions? Here again one can see a tension between individual freedom and community control. Massive influx of "outsiders" can easily disrupt a community, but a community's power to exclude me is a bar to my liberty. The New Jersey community deals with this by allowing immigrants but giving established community members preference in such matters as choice of housing. This of course creates a sort of class division between old residents and newcomers.

A related question is whether there is a sort of market, in which individuals "shop" for communities to belong to or regions in which to live. Do individuals move to places with types of schools or social organization they approve of, work they like, or a higher standard of living? If so, how does this affect the ability of communities to control their common life?

An important social decision lies in defining what constitutes "labor," as opposed to some other category of activity. Should, for example, tending the sick be "labor," or should it be part of non-institutional caring? Is it part of the "family," "household," or "industry"? What about other expressions of mutual or group obligations which lie outside the general division of labor? How will society decide that factory workers building furniture contribute to productive labor, whereas those preparing food, even in a communal kitchen which feeds several hundred people, do not?

Another group of questions cluster around the relationship between individual workplaces and the integrated regional economy. They are raised by Luke's statements about allocating capital and using productivity to "expand income" for a particular workplace.

Do particular workplaces have economic interests separate from the community or region as a whole? Do individuals receive benefits from the advances of their own workplace, or only from those of the wider economic unit as a whole?

Workers in the furniture factory, we are told, feel they are "working for themselves." But these words can have different meanings. An individual can feel she is working for herself because the product is something she herself will use, or because she will own the product and be able to use or sell it as she wishes. Similarly, a work group can feel they are working for themselves because collectively they will use the product or will be its possessors. People can feel that they are working for themselves because they are working for a society of which they are full members, so that they will receive a fair share of the benefit of society as a whole—something which might better be expressed as "working for each other." The sense in which one is "working for oneself" varies with the degree of decentralization. A socialist society requires a balance which leaves some degree of initiative in the hands of the communes, while providing social guidelines or limits within which that initiative can be exercised.

What sanctions, if any, are imposed on production communes which do not carry out the regional "production plan"? Are there forms of intervention from "above" when a workplace is not well managed? What happens when production teams do not fulfill their collective responsibility for work to be done?

These questions are brought forcibly to mind by the discussion of (p. 150) a conflict between workers and their management team. The managers propose overtime work, presumably in order to meet production quotas; the workers resist it. Evidently there is a conflict between the immediate interests of workgroups themselves and the responsibility for meeting the production plan. This suggests several questions: Where does the buck stop in responsibility for meeting the plan? Since there is a conflict between the immediate producers and the whole community, is there a place for unions? And should there be a right to strike?

One way to reduce this conflict is to have individuals rotate not only through one workplace but through various different ones in the community. This has the advantage of reducing "special interests" in the fate of particular enterprises, combined with the disadvantage of weakening individual involvement with a particular workplace and work group.

One also wonders whether there are not some skills that are really highly specialized, requiring special talents. Dentistry comes to mind as an example. Does it really make sense to rotate everyone in the health industry through a turn as dentist? Or does it make sense to train five or ten times as many people as dentists as are needed, so that they can work in other occupations as well? These are points at which the elimination of the specialized division of labor becomes extremely costly, and the trade-offs have to be weighed.

This problem is of course especially ticklish in the area of the economic and social expertise needed to deal with the planning process itself.

Work and the Region and Nation

Crucial decisions will concern the guidelines for overall social organization which in the society under consideration are set at a national level. We have little experience to guide us on which matters need to be settled at this level, which can be left to less centralized units. The guidelines described in these letters seem to pertain to the enforcement of certain basic norms of the society, such as the obligation to work and the elimination of racial and sexual inequality. Presumably others would deal with such questions as the reintroduction of wage labor. Still others would have to deal with questions of relations among different regions.

The society described is based on regional economic self-sufficiency. This involves trade-offs that will need to be weighed.

First, there are genuine costs to economic autarky. There are products for which large-scale production does indeed allow savings which would be lost in producing for a purely regional market. These costs would have to be weighed, not just ignored as a figment of capitalist economic ideology.

Second, there is the question of rich and poor regions. Regional differences exist both because of differentials inherited from capitalist uneven development and from differences in the resource base. A socialist society will have to weigh the value of decentralization against the regional inequality it implies (a conflict which has been very serious in the case of the Yugoslavian experiment with decentralized socialism). Evidently the society described has a strong drive to equalize incomes within each region, but is willing to tolerate substantial differences between regions. Such a policy needs to be considered both in terms of the egalitarian norms of the society and in terms of the impact of the movement of people from poor to rich regions.

Global Issues

Here the same issues arise as at the national level but in a more severe form. The inherited inequalities of developed and underdeveloped countries pose far more serious problems than those among regions within the territory of the United States. Natural resources are very unevenly distributed. The geographical division of labor is far more extreme, and the costs of eliminating it far greater. The movement of people resulting from disparities of wealth is likely to be a far more massive and disruptive phenomenon.

Further, mutual interdependence, as we have seen throughout this discussion, is one of the key factors that encourages people to pursue the general interest rather than special interests. Regional and national autarky reduces the interdependence and strengthens the tendencies toward a selfish consciousness on the part of regions and nations. This tendency needs to be balanced against the advantages of regional and national economic autonomy.

I don't think we can adequately address this question on the basis of the experience and ideas generated in the economically developed countries alone. For that reason I would like to urge that the dialogue which flows from this book include comrades from the Third World who will help us address this question.

THE HUMAN DIMENSION

Values

It is a common criticism of utopian projections that they are based on ideas and values that have arisen within the pre-revolutionary society, and therefore represent the past rather than the future. One of the best features of the society described in these letters is that it is based on freely developing needs and desires. There seems to be a general understanding that values about such matters as the desired level of consumption, the meaning of work, and the like will evolve over time through dialogue, debate, and experience, rather than being something that can be projected beforehand in "correct" form.

Further, there seems to be an understanding of the need to balance conflicting values. For example, the society described seems to have combined many of the advantages of communes and closed communities with the openness and variety characteristic of cities. The inhabitants seem to have escaped both the isolation and fragmentation of modern urban life and the claustrophobic ingrowness of traditional villages and isolated communes.

Nonetheless, it is important to recognize that this society is based on a high degree of cultural uniformity. There are no groups that represent, for example, strong religious or ideological beliefs that conflict with others: no fundamentalists insisting that Creation Science be taught in schools, no anti-abortionists picketing the clinics. This uniformity allows a high level of social consensus, but it restricts the variety of people one is involved with, and indicates significant limits on what is tolerated from individuals.

Life in general in this society seems very work-centered. Even in their free time individuals engage in activities we would normally think of as work. There is a prevailing mood of seriousness, even of "straightness." If anybody doesn't want to come into work because they really tied one on last night, we don't hear about it.

Such orderliness and diligence may be a cost of running anything as complex as a modern society democratically. But others have envisioned less Apollonian, more Dionysian futures—like Fourier's phalanxes, whose social relations are based on the variety of individual passions. Can a socialist society make room for a mad love affair that violates a contract, or a bereaved person whose only desire is to wander alone in the mountains for a couple of years? Could art be more important, production less? I think the answer to these questions is, again: these are the choices that people in a socialist society will finally have the freedom to make.

Human Relations

Runya emphasizes that "human nature" does change, and I think we can emphatically agree. But I'm not sure that we know enough to predict exactly how it changes, given particular changes in social structure. One of the few things described in these letters that did not strike me as immediately plausible was the absence of conflict in human relations.

I found this particularly dubious in the case of adolescents. It seems to me that there is a place for individual and collective rejection of the established social order on the part of adolescents, and that it can be a positive developmental force both for the individual and society. The rising generation needs to integrate with society not just on the basis of society as given, but also on its own terms, based on an autonomous decision.

Who would have predicted the massive generational conflict that arose in the U.S. in the 1960s? Certainly nobody did. I think we have to assume that this is one kind of phenomenon which will continue to be uncontrolled in a socialist society, at least for a long time, and one to which it will have to adapt—but which can also serve as a prod to its further development.

ON-GOING RANK AND FILE CONTROL: THE ONE EFFECTIVE WEAPON AGAINST BUREAUCRATS IN ANY SOCIETY

Stan Weir

I experienced a sense of excitement when I was told that this book was planned, containing writings about what socialism might be like in America. During the last forty years I have had opportunity to participate in informal and small scale discussion of this kind. But none of any greater scope were held either in the "Marxist" organizations with which I have been associated, or, to the best of my knowledge, in any others. With critical amendments, the early years of the Russian revolutionary experiment supplied the socialist model for all Trotskyist groupings. For followers of the Communist Party, the Russia of Stalin as adapted to the American scene provided the visionary goal for the future. Given the unique potential provided by the appearance of this book and the long wait, I have been forced to do some basic reassessment that might direct me while attempting a contribution to the discussion. I would like to begin by sharing some of the ideas which emerged in the process.

While still living in the old systems where the means of production are owned by private corporations or a government bureaucracy, and long before opportunity for changeovers have developed, it is presumptuous and elitist for socialists to lay down detailed blueprints of how new societies should be run. Blueprinting is not the point of this discussion.

No matter that conceptions of what a socialist society might look like will vary according to the experiences of the conceivers. If, when the time of power transfer from the old to the new arrives, the ranks of the population have not yet had extended debate on what they want their new society to be like, too many decisions will be made by the leaders without leadership from below. Thus, the leaders—even though democratically elected—must become bureaucrats.

Few things date faster than visions of the way people will actually live in the future. As a result, the most important aspect of visionary discussion emerges: the formulation of alternative democratic decision-making processes that might keep institutions abreast of the constant change in the way life is actually lived. More than anything else, methodology is what pioneer change seekers have to offer,

175

provided, it is also recognized that methodological needs are subject to change as well. The only real constants other than change are the need for freedom, and unity of ends and means.

By daring beforehand to dream about ways that a new society could bring greater fulfillment of the human potential, and then sharing those ideals, the resulting discussions allow participants to discover commonalities as well as differences of vision. Ideas held in common, in turn, become the basis for the formation of groupings by which to test the ideas in current struggles.

Anyone who today initiates a discussion of socialist futures can expect to generate responses from every point on the compass. We live in the longest period of successful frustration of attempts at democratic systemic change in modern history. Even though the initiators consciously put forth no more than a tentative basis for discussion, they naturally open themselves to broad disagreement. There is no precedent or common vocabulary for visionary discussion in this or the preceeding two generations of radicals. American socialists, among others, have not conducted extended public debate on this subject since the period prior to World War I and the Russian Revolution of 1917.

In the absence of this process, it is difficult to find an organized socialist tendency whose day-to-day activity directly concerns itself with the idealism which originally caused its members to join the socialist movement. The resulting condition guarantees continued isolation, increased pressures toward orthodoxy, and pessimism. Today, one finds more optimism about the capabilities of humanity in the ranks of the working class than among many socialists.

I have been asked to read and comment on only the contribution to *Socialist Visions* by Cummings and Greenbaum. They have touched on a number of aspects of what a socialist society might be like in relation to the problem of division of labor and how decisions affecting it might be made. I know both of them personally and obviously share widely in their ideas. I have therefore chosen to focus on possible differences, but for the most part I use their ideas as points of takeoff in order to project supplemental ideas. In what follows I will comment mainly on the question of length of work week, the separation of labor on "regular" jobs and community service work, and controls over the decision-making process.

The socialist experiment of which Luke, Jane, and Runya are part is twenty years or a generation old. The overall division of labor in their society is such that a 36-hour week has been set by "national guidelines." To me, the amount seems high.

The number one requirement for success in any socialist experiment is a steady growth in the quality and amount of goods and services available to all, together with an ever growing increase of *individual* as well as collective freedom. This definition merges two growth factors because the failure of all previous socialist experiments proves that both are totally interdependent. The pace of the growths can be irregular, but movement not for too long interrupted. And, the freedom factor cannot be solely measured by improvement of legal rights. Among other things, increased leisure time expands opportunity to become better informed.

The socialist experiment which in any real way meets the above requirement will release the labor force to make voluntary and vast increases in efficiency. No longer would there be the need for people to do as they did on oppressive jobs under either of the old (capitalist or Communist) systems, that is, to withhold their inventiveness in order to protect their earning power. Furthermore, production expertly planned by full participation of those involved would save billions of labor hours each year. Add to that the input gained by the elimination of the economic and social roots of racism, sexism, and ageism (inequality of young and old in the work force). Then consider what would be conserved if production of nuclear arms and the need to supply armies that police half the world, was stopped. Accomplish any of these savings and the growth of leisure time need not be modest. (It should be noted that early in this century, socialist thinkers were envisioning a real 20-hour week for a socialist United States, based on careful calculation and with only a fraction of the new technology available to us now. It was from this base that Jack London wrote his exciting and no pie-in-the-sky visionary novel, *The Iron Heel*.)

As I look upon it at this point, there are only three major problems which could cause a socialist experiment in an advanced industrial nation to retain a work week of a length near that demanded of us now. 1) The need to aid other countries which have experienced national disasters such as famine; 2) The need to give aid to embattled democratic-revolutionary movements in other lands, if they ask for it; and 3) The need to aid other socialist or democratic-collectivist experiments that have less industrial development.

It is assumed here that the highest of priorities in the aid-giving nation will have already been given to the problem of turning around the destruction of wildlife, wilderness, beaches, and clean air and water, as accomplished by the old systems. It is also assumed that efforts at resurrecting the environment and what can literally be the saving of millions of lives by international aid will, in turn, release still new meaning and enthusiasm for work. Not only will the efforts bring new self image, but they will decrease the possibility of failure in the industrially advanced nation. The principal lesson of our epoch is that socialism cannot be successful if it is forced to go it alone, isolated in one country.

The nationally set work week in Luke, Jane, and Runya's new America is 30-hours. But because all must contribute 6 hours to community work the actual work week is lengthened to 36. It is all work regardless of this major division. The new system has obviously not yet been able to end the artificial separation between "regular" work and the labor needed for services in the community. Both types of work have been enriched, but the gap dividing them remains. Not surprising. This same divorce is killing us in all present societies. Because of it we commonly meet persons who are radical in their rejection of capitalism in the context of their own workplace, but hold conservative ideas in relation to the problems of their community, nation, and world. People with-parallel attitudes are undoubtedly to be found in Communist countries. It is probable that an important part of this seeming contradiction exists because workplaces are shut from community view by physical location, architectural design, high fences, and inaccessibility to and denial of media coverage. It is not without reason that one of the primary demands of the Polish workers' Solidarity union is access to the press, radio, and television.

It is probable that many citizens of any new socialist industrial society will want new towns and cities, designed whenever possible around their places of work. In addition to the need for convenience is the desire in us all for a sense of neighborhood. As it is now, we are each driven to find an area to which we can escape in order to eliminate reminder of our labors. But as work becomes meaningful there is no reason why the neighborhoods of work and abode cannot be merged to a unified whole. This could be accomplished, in part, by relocating workplaces so as to integrate them with homes, schools, nurseries, stores, bars, restaurants, theatres, concert and meeting halls.

Geographic or physical integration of home and work "turfs" by itself is not enough. In order to eliminate the negative effects of the automobile revolution we have to be able to do much more of our task-travels by foot. On our way to and from sporting or cultural events by natural locomotion we should be able to catch glimpses of life in our communities' workplaces without special effort. Large ground level windows supply a partial answer. Let immediate outsiders look in and if their interest is caught, there should be easy access to interior observation areas. Factory hands, computer programmers, architects or bakers, at stage center turn to look at visitors and themselves become viewers. An end, for example, to the placing of industrial plants and movie houses in parts of town that are deserted at night. We need a new sense of what constitutes "the street." It might even be that some will want to take the integration a step further and locate some community facilities right inside selected workplaces. But by whatever method desired, it is as we build towns with automatic population "mixers" that we will have a society wherein relative strangers can socialize.

Yet another method of building cross-occupational contact is worthy of suggestion here. It can be stated briefly because of its simplicity: the creation of a special communication net between media workers' councils and all other workers' councils. In this way all forms of work can have advantage of that very special form of exposure which can be supplied by television, cinema, radio, and the press.

In Luke, Jane, and Runya's society, all get every fifth year off from their "regular" jobs, but not from community service assignments. I'm sure this would apply only to those who chose to stay at home during their earned year off. Otherwise, the right to travel is denied, community service comes to be seen as a drag and suffers further segregation. Broad new opportunity for travel is essential to the growth of internationalism. But more, people need to just get away if no more than to plotz by a mountain, desert, or shore, and there is little probability that socialism will eliminate the need. On the other hand it is impossible to estimate the increase in volunteerism that will occur in a democratic system. Under socialism, furniture workers, for example, while travelling here or abroad in cooperating nations might want to visit with other people in the most insightful way, on the job. If they wanted to pitch in and work a little in addition to swapping stories, it would be to everyone's benefit. With that kind of introduction it is probable that they would be invited to living areas and might even participate in some community activities or work. How interesting it would be as they returned home to us with their new stories. Dreams like this are what underlie the longtime demands of socialists for elimination of passports, all need for them gone as competition for jobs and markets is done away with.

At sixteen years of age the youth in Luke, Jane, and Runya's nation must spend a year in community service. This would not be like the present draft for the armed services. Rather, it would provide a period wherein young people could train themselves for participation in the life of community and nation. But isn't there serious risk that this would put an onus on community service work? It would still be a draft. One can see the logic as to why the idea might be raised in present societies. In socialist experiments all will have to work to reap the benefits collectively produced, but create a specially compulsory form of labor and great problems ensue.

Both literally and figuratively, the main troops of any massive movement for progressive change are the youth of the majority classes. Many who are much under sixteen enlist themselves. Delinquency begins to disappear. It is the young who are most able to fight, jump, run, hide, and fight again, attend long meetings and do without food or sleep for long periods. All who come to enjoy a socialist system will be in deep debt to them. They will not be denied the right to full active participation in society after the power transfer. To win that right is the main reason for the risks and sacrifices of life, limb, and youth they will have made. Anyone suggesting a special conscription for them could meet with the argument: "We are already among the most active in the development of the community and might point to others older than us who need . . ." It takes little imagination to see where those discussions would lead. In Russia of the very early 1920s, no coercion was needed to recruit the army of youth which drove eleven imperialist foreign armies from Russian soil. In fact, so heroic was the volunteerism they displayed that fifty-five percent of the leading youth cadres were killed off, a development which facilitated generational split and bureaucratization.

Is it possible to break through and foresee community service work divided into a series of "regular" occupations like all the others? Why not an attempt at the development of forces highly skilled in food service and chemistry, the maintenance of individual homes, public buildings, roads, child care, etc.? All work is community service. Socialism has the potential to end all denials of this truth. With short work weeks and communities where working and living are integrated, if the people of one workplace wish to spend part time in others there is no reason they couldn't move about. Temporary or even permanent job exchanges between individuals could be easily arranged. And, what is to stop the people of a workplace from granting special release time hours to those among them who have young children and wish to work in the indicated infant or child care centers part-time?

The ability to collectively handle special as well as routine problems related to the division of labor is all important and the people in Luke's collective have created a valuable model for the launching of discussion. Luke's people have set it up so that "regular" work is divided into three categories; mass production, craft, and administrative. In all three, the workers are divided into *Work Teams*. (Although not stated, it is probable that community service work would also be conducted by teams.) Thus, each individual has membership in at least three teams; these would constitute, in effect, three on-the-job families, each with its own informal team or group culture. As the people move from involvement with one family to another a rich communication network has to be the result. By the same process the group cultures merge to create a total workplace culture which is the sum of what individuals bring to the job from home and neighborhood; merged with what they create through interaction on the job.

Centralization of the power of all three categories of teams takes place as each team elects representatives to the workplace *Policy Council*. The general *Workers' Assembly* makes all final decisions.

Decisions of both the Policy Council and the Workers' Assembly are carried out by *Coordinating Committees*. Special *Sub-Committees of the Workers' Assembly* are formed to propose ideas for improvement of work methodology and benefits. Membership on all committees and the Council is subject to constant rotation. The committees do enough of the administration so that those assigned to full-time administrative work amount to no more than 5 percent of the total labor force of the workplace. Workers spend only three months on the committees every two years. The absence of detail on how all this might work out in practice supplies many important questions for discussion. I will comment on a few.

When there are full time administrators and others (the worker spends only part time in administration) the problem of bureaucratization arises. Can all the administrative work in Luke's workplace be done by workers on a part-time basis, six weeks a year? Possibly, in relatively small workplaces. But can the model be used in larger ones? Some continuity of administration is needed for ongoing efficiency, and for democracy. The Yugoslav works council experiment handles the problem of continuity for the sake of efficiency by keeping technicians and party representatives on the councils on a permanent basis. Workers' representatives to the councils, however, are allowed to hold office only one year. By the time they become fully acquainted with the work and operation of the councils, they have to go back to the job. It is an old ploy dressed up in synthetic democratic garb. It has many variants. One of them has been operating in the International Longshoremen's and Warehousemen's Union on the Pacific coast since the 1930s. Local union officials are allowed to serve two consecutive one year terms in office and then must return to the waterfront for a year before being allowed to run for office again. Great. But there is no parallel rule applying to the holders of office at the international union level. Thus, no local level leader ever gets to establish a broad enough reputation to allow him to run successfully against the long-incumbent top officials.

How can an official power structure be designed so that authority is always maintained from below? Does the Workers' Assembly in Luke's plant meet often enough to discipline the council and the committees? And, even though held often and regularly, are Assembly meetings adequate for control? General assemblies are a must. Without them the ranks are without this constant reminder of their collective power, without the ability to put the collective brain to work, and without an important vehicle for cross team communication. At the same time, mass meetings are such that there are limitations on the number who get to speak and the number of problems which can be discussed in detail. In addition, there is a limit on the degree to which team problems can be aired. After mass meetings end and the participants return to their groups, there are those who still have questions or want a chance to express their opinions. Thus, large portions of the democratic process get handled in the group on an informal basis, as well as in the formal-official general meetings.

It is imperative that control over the decisive segments of the power structure in the workplace be retained by the ranks, by formal design. The two places where the ranks can best work out their problems and articulate their point of view are: 1) in mass workplace meetings; and 2) in their informal work groups. There is so little precedent for discussion of the role of informal or primary work groups among socialists that I must define the term as used here.

> The informal work group is that formation which works together daily, its members in direct communication with one another—placed there by technology and assignment, and pushed into socialization by the needs of production. In terms of work, it is an on-the-job family, torn by hate and love, conflict and common interest. It is the basic "us" organization. All outside its numbers are "them." It naturally disciplines its members, most commonly by use of nurture or social isolation, ridicule or recognition. It has a naturally selected leadership, makes decisions in the immediate work area, and can affect the flow of production. (S. Weir, *Rank and File*, Alice and Staughton Lynd, Beacon Press, 1973, and Princeton University Press, 1981, p. 177.)

In an open society it is relatively easy to schedule regular mass Assembly meetings with large allotments of open agenda time, early on the agenda. But how build in a role for informal work groups in a formal power structure? By nature and definition the two types of organization cannot be mixed. It is not uncommon for a union official to select a particularly powerful informal work group and demand that it play an official role, for example, by designating its natural leader as shop steward. In doing so the official, most often unconsciously, temporarily monkey-wrenches the group's informal social, cultural, and political processes.

Informal work groups handle the personal lives of their members on too intimate a level to allow officialization. These groups belong solely to their members. They are the only organizations that cannot be bureaucratized. In any workplace crisis there are a number of analyses or "truths": the one that is the perception of the top local leaders, another that is the view of the departmental leaders or stewards, and the most telling perception, the one that develops within the informal work groups. But the latter seldom if ever gets direct consideration in the formal crisis solving process, often providing after-shock for offical leaders.

The innovation that would make socialism truly represent a new day, an actual democratic millenium, would be the creation of a power structure that allows direct expression to informal work groups. This might be done in two ways. First, by the holding of departmental meetings and team meetings in the immediate work area—right on the home turf of the groups. Second, and far more important, would be the innovation that makes all officials working officials. Do nothing to tamper with the autonomy of the informal work groups, but put the "leaders" regularly in face-to-face contact with the groups and thus subject to their feelings and informal discipline. Messages delivered in the context of production are most direct. If several times each week the officials must return to their "regular" jobs and spend time in their home teams, those not then serving in official positions will get a chance to either praise their formal—even if rotating—representatives, "give them an earful," or make their feelings known through other ways, while getting out the work.

The Polish Solidarity union now undoubtedly faces a crisis in this regard. Just weeks before this is written (January 1981), Lech Walesa announced that the union was about to move its central place of operation from the Gdansk shipyards to independent headquarters. No longer will the leaders operate within easy reach of the ranks, or deliberate in "goldfish bowl" meetings within vision of a large workplace collectivity. Mass meetings will continue, but as the top leaders and full time council representatives increasingly lose contact with the ranks, what can be done to make them responsive servants of those below? Will the rank and file be forced to take job action to get their ear? That should be their right, but by itself will it be enough?

The dozens of strikes and other actions by UAW members since the mid-1950s, for example, have gotten only the temporary attention of Walter Reuther, Leonard Woodcock, and Douglas Fraser. Shop-floor committeepersons are elected on a ratio of one to every 250 workers or major portion thereof, and they are full-time non-working reps. The International representatives who take over the handling of grievances at the decisive steps are full-time appointees of the International President and they rarely visit any particular and "regular" work area for more than minutes. Most UAW contracts do not allow for group stewards. The autoworkers have no body of working reps on which to apply daily pressure.

In the early 1930s, from 1932 to 1936, as opposed to the following years when the CIO became structured and signed contracts, the ranks of production workers in large part "spontaneously" organized indus-trial unions. Actually, there was nothing spontaneous about the process, it was just that they did it on the basis of their own independent preparations. In plant after plant, two of their main weapons were the formation of bodies of working stewards, one steward per foreman, and mass meetings on the job. The bureaucratization of industrial unions in America has paralleled the dismantling of these weapons.

Today, the national average attendance at local union meetings is just over two percent. Those who attend are forced to sit almost throughout as observers. Their main function is to okay reports of what the officials have done since the last meeting. By contrast, in the first organizing period of the '30s, the general meetings obtained maximum attendance because they were held right in work areas, plant cafeterias, or on company parking lots. Almost literally, full participation was automatic. Rather than an audience of individuals, the gatherings were actually clusters of groups. Genius for policy and strategy came out of the "crowds" at those meetings. Attendance demanded no special sacrifice of time or travel. Boredom was held to a minimum. It was possible for each person to feel that his or her presence made a difference. Each felt a power. The meetings, after all, were being held on the natural turf of the ranks, in places of *their* authority and expertise.

Later, as contracts were signed and meetings held blocks or more away from the plants it was not uncommon to lose the participation of over eighty percent of the membership. More and more, those who did attend were often either out of their element or seeking entry to spheres of official authority. Out of a much different history, the English workers have saved themselves from degeneration of rank and file unionism in significant part by forming the Shop Stewards Movement. It dares to hold on-the-job mass meetings (during work hours) from time to time when faced with deep crises. From those meetings and its councils the decisions are made on what actions to take, including strike. In short, the bulk of the organized workers in England have an independent organization, separate from official union apparatus and contracts, which enables them to handle many of the failings of their official unions.

Any socialist experiment in England or elsewhere will hopefully begin at least at the rank and file level, retain and expand upon the practice of having working representatives and workplace mass meetings. No matter the health of an experiment or the idealism of its leaders at the outset, the ranks have to remain forearmed. Otherwise the risks are too great. The experience of seeing movements become bureaucratic is so general that millions beyond the readers of Robert Michels carry somewhere within them the idea that bureaucratization may be inevitable. Challenge of the idea continues to go unmet precisely because socialist visionaries have failed to develop and spotlight possible counter-measures.

Alternative ideas for building in checks against bureaucratic control of new societies are particularly necessary for yet an additional and pressing reason. Unlike Greenbaum and Cummings, socialists of many tendencies still hold that a party should run a socialist government. Each feels it should be their party. They have turned the governmental form the Bolsheviks were forced to use out of failure into a model to be copied. This, despite the tragedies it has brought to all by its total failure in Russia, Poland, the rest of Eastern Europe, China, and more. If the idea persists in any future experiments, the ranks will have more than the usual need for every weapon which enables kicking of bureaucratic ass—at least till such time that they can eliminate party rule.

Experience in the last seventy years indicates that parties under socialism should be formations of people interested in propagating new ideas they have developed—but without the ability to turn membership in their party to governmental power or privilege. Otherwise, elite special interest groups will continue to make decisions on what the division of labor should be on all important matters.

It may well be that the concept which says that a society can be run by a network of on-the-job workers' councils composed of all who produce—whether the products be coal, autos, childcare, or poetry, and regardless of party membership or non-membership—is an idea whose time has come.

REJOINDER
Joan Greenbaum and Laird Cummings

We chose the letters format to help us capture the pervasiveness of the division of labor in our lives, and to personalize our vision of what living under socialism must be. Stan's and Jeremy's replies are most useful because they generalize and extend the discussion beyond individual experiences and perspectives.

For many years, we have met regularly with a collective studying the division of labor, the Work Relations Group. Our own visions of socialism have been strongly influenced by our discussions and by our collective practice. We are grateful to Stan and Jeremy, and all the others in Work Relations—Susan Reverby, David Noble, Peter Rachleff, Jill Cutler, Keith Dix, Rick Engler, Jim Weeks, Zeda Rosenberg, Robb Burlage, Len Rodberg, Rick Simon, Kathy Stone, and many visitors to our meetings—for their insights.

V. FAMILY & SEX ROLES

Lead Essay	Lois Rita Helmbold
	& Amber Hollibaugh
Responses	Ellen Herman
	Gloria I. Joseph
Rejoinders	Lois Rita Helmbold
	Amber Hollibaugh

THE FAMILY:
WHAT HOLDS US
WHAT HURTS US
The Family in Socialist America

Lois Rita Helmbold and Amber Hollibaugh

INTRODUCTION

The family is a profoundly complex institution. It forms the heart of our emotional landscape: sets our expectations and holds out promise of granting deep and critical needs. At the same time, it is a baldly economic institution: a foundation of patriarchy and capitalism, producing and disciplining the work force and consuming the system's products and services. The family is an institution that we need, and yet we are badly damaged by it.

In the first two sections of this essay, we try to analyze both the hold the family has over us and the harm it inflicts upon us. Only by considering both of these aspects will we be in a position to propose—as we do in the final section—alternative ways by which our needs might be served, enabling us to create a new vision of the family in a socialist America.

Families teach us to become a part of the culture. They also teach us strategies to survive its oppressions, particularly racism and classism. We feel both pain and respect for our own parents' attempts to educate us to survive in a system bent on our destruction.

We also see our own parents as earlier victims, molded by the families they came from, shaped by the lack of expectations that their sex and class demanded of them. We can't afford to be uncritical, but that doesn't mean we don't understand the pain they went through and are still going through, struggling with us to find a way to be human.

Lois: My mother, the oldest of six children, was forced by her father to quit high school at age 15 in 1934, in the depth of the depression, to go to work to support the family because he was not able to find work. She spent six years doing housework for the family of a middle class dentist before she married my father. It is no accident that I, her first child, am getting a Ph.D. because she wanted me to be able to care for myself financially, as well as have opportunities to use my creativity that were never open to her.

We are both white women in our middle 30s, from working class backgrounds, lesbians, feminists, independent Marxists, activists, intellectuals; neither of us are parents. This article will reflect those strengths and limitations. While working on this article, we each stopped living alone in order to move into collective households. We wanted to write the article that we could never find, that expressed our own ambivalences and hopes for those human relationships now called "the family."

Some people may find it disturbing that two lesbians have written about the future of the family. As lesbians, we don't partner with a person of the opposite sex, a major criterion of the heterosexual family. But it is precisely our exclusion from the traditional family that offers us insight as well as criticism. We are forced to consider the family time and again in its larger social context because we don't fit in, though we share similar needs. We also confront the shattered expectations that frequently accompany our "coming out" to our biological families.

Both the New Right and the women's movement have accurately understood that the family is in drastic need of change. They offer opposing solutions. Neither, however, has adequately described the contradictory nature of the demands placed upon, and the fulfillment one seeks (and occasionally finds) in that institution.

Amber: When I go home, I see the community that I came from, the things I still share, and the ways that I've grown apart and alien from the expectations we were all raised with. I am different there because I am known differently, I am Marge's daughter, a woman who herself has roots and memories which go back further than my own. That reflection changes the way I expect to be related to and the way I perceive myself. Going home is loaded with much more than the distance you travel or the people you see. When we are struggling to find ways of being new people in old institutions, that trip back is loaded with every fantasy we don't know how to let go of. At the heart of why it's so difficult to give up old notions is the sense of having a place we've come from, a place that can't be denied us.

Today, the myth of the family seduces with one hand, and rejects with the other. To develop new relationships in the future, we will have to find ways to solve problems that exist now. The rapidly rising number of households headed by women, for example, will continue. It is easier to describe what the clashes will be than to dream up the solutions. We cannot come up with all the alternative visions. What we can do is work to create a movement which frees people to create their own visions.

We have both tangible and intangible expectations for families. The possibility to have and raise kids, the right to have sex with another person, a viable economic support system, physical and mental care-taking are all relatively tangible. No less important though are the needs for affection, stability, continuity in relationships, inter/genera-tional and inter/sexual commitments, partnership, companionship and love. In order to see each issue and unravel their different intersections we have arranged the article around each "need" the family is respon-sible for so that we can begin separating and re-combining each desire to fit our own uniquely changing lives. By doing it this way we hope to expose both what holds us and what hurts us.

Child of Myself

from cavities of bones
spun
     from caverns of air
i, woman—bred of man
taken from the womb of sleep;
i, woman that comes
before the first.

to think second
to believe first
    a mistake conundrum
    erased by the motion of years.
i, woman, i
    can no longer claim
            a mother of flesh
            a father of marrow
I, Woman must be
    the child of myself.

Pat Parker, *Movement in Black*

PART I: WHAT HOLDS US:
THE EXPECTATIONS AND THEIR UNDERSIDE

Affection, Stability, Continuity

It's no wonder that we long for the family and mourn its absence. The family has become the repository of all the human needs we have. Many needs, formerly provided by families and kinship groups, have been taken over by a capitalist economy and sold back to us as goods and services. These range from child-care to therapy, birth, marriage and death processes. Anything that we want outside of the cash nexus, or cannot afford, we look to our families to provide. Everyone seeks affection and everyone needs to be cared for. Before and beyond sex, we all need loving care. Affection is one of the few things people can give each other outside of cash relationships.

Third world and working class families in particular are sustained by affection networks when the material aspects of life, such as jobs, remain outside our control. Having a place to turn to, people who care about what happens to you, makes life bearable. But these ways of caring are perverted by the power that men have over women, adults over children, younger adults over our elders, whites over people of color, and heterosexuals over gay members of families. Capitalism turns everything into commodities, and the power inequalities change wives and children into property, thus perverting loving relationships.

The romantic and sexual aspects of adult relationships are stressed in media and myth. But in reality, it is often neither romance nor sex but the development of long-term caring and affection which holds relationships together, in addition to the economic dependencies. To state this contradiction another way, if economics and children force families to stay together, it is made bearable by developing long term caring relationships, which may or may not be romantically or sexually satisfying. We create a human and humane dynamic in the midst of an alienating institution. Women may be angry and oppressed by the drudgery of housework, and by the energy drain of child raising, and by the emotional, physical, and sexual demands of relating to men; and men may feel trapped in jobs to put groceries on the table; but they cope with their despair by the love, affection, care, and regard that grow over the course of years. In families where this happens, the partnership softens the oppressiveness that the partners play out. This is possible; it happens all the time. It is one of the ironies of the family. *Oppression and affection coexist*, people help one another survive even while battling and bruising one another. One of the greatest obstacles to leaving the family is the trap that this contradiction sets. Where a partnership genuinely emerges, it is here that we can guess what might be possible under human, anti-capitalist conditions. Being in the family is often hard, oppressive, deadening, yet it is also there that we have learned to hope for the better lives our loving can create.

Even at its worst, what is known often holds less terror than what is unexplored and undreamed of. Young women frequently begin families in order to escape from the ones they were raised in. They hope that as recognized adults (since marriage and/or parenthood are the only clear marks of adulthood for women) they will have more power and control, that they will recreate only the "good" things they see in their own families, and not the bad.

> Lois: My mother once told me, "If I hadn't married your father, I'd still be keeping someone else's house." People make do the best they can.

We also want relationships we can trust to last. We want people we can rely on. Part of the appeal of long-term relationships is that they provide the opportunity to see yourself and your changes reflected back to you. This is most obvious between parents and children, but is also important in peer relationships, between partners and between siblings. Change, and not continuity, rule much of our lives, in jobs, geographical movement, friendships. The family is the only place we have left to look for stability. As political people, we cannot expect to be taken seriously when we question institutions if there are no other options for most people. The alternative to seeking affection in the family is often, tragically, to do without.

> Amber: My parents first met when they were 12 and 13. They have known each other over 45 years. I hope to have people whom I love and share with and whom I have known that long, 30 years from now. I secretly want a relationship that could move through such a stretch of my living and where I could see another person so intimately. As much as my politics makes me distrust the very idea of one person who could be so constant, another part of me holds on to this fantasy. In the face of divorce, job changes, health scares, and a general fear of the chaos I see around me, I cling to the wish to find a person or people I could love through years of my life. As I get older, this desire becomes more important. My own analysis notwithstanding, I am frequently gripped with the fear that I will never find this in my life and will be lonely and unsustained.

Out of the fury of feminist and gay experiences in the family and the twisting traps of love/hate we found there, we have not given credit to an important dimension of family dynamics, forcing us to appear unsympathetic with the real reasons people are drawn towards such institutions. Not all that people seek in the family is false consciousness.

Love

> Love becomes complicated, corrupted or obstructed by an unequal balance of power. Love demands a mutual vulnerability or it turns destructive: the destructive effects of love occur only in the context of inequality.
>
> Shulamith Firestone, *Dialectics of Sex*, p. 130

Myths had to be created to make the notion of ownership as the ultimate act of love more palatable. And in this mythical tale of capitalist romance, love requires: (1) women and men only; (2) debilitating need and dependency; (3) ownership; (4) sanctioned sexual violation; (5) fear, to be portrayed as pleasure; and (6) children as investments.

But before we can have healthy love, people must be self-sustaining and autonomous. The idea that you are only half of something without a partner, that you need someone else to complete you, demands involuntary dependence and servitude. To love someone, to feel deeply committed and responsive, to sustain caring and passion, to be a friend without restraint, these are some of the unfettered feelings of love separated from ownership of another person. Love is greatly shaped by money and power in this society. As feminists, we have no intention of giving up love, but we cannot afford to give *ourselves* up in order to discover it. As long as women are taught to believe in love, and men are taught to believe in sex, heterosexual relationships will be based on oppressive dominance and manipulation.

Partnership

Having someone to share with, to consult and make decisions with, helps life immeasurably. Much long-term partnering is this agreement to take things on together instead of trying (or being forced) to go it alone. There are few collective solutions to help us build our lives, so it becomes critical to find someone to share the tasks. Much of the joy in a relationship is built on thousands of tiny experiences. Even when partnerships dissolve, the family is one of the few institutions that make the attempt to develop intimacy valid.

The only emotional long-term partnership that is sanctioned is between wife and husband. Other partnerships have narrow boundaries, such as business partnerships, close friendships (which one is expected to put aside upon marriage, or to relegate to specific functions such as hunting trips with the guys, card games with the "girls"). The assumption behind marriage vows is an unending partnership. And though the divorce rate belies this assumption, many people enter serial monogamy to escape the fear of being alone and without someone to count on. Some partnerships are forced to remain hidden. One way to silence gays (and others) is to pretend that they have not created their own structures of survival.

> Amber. In the brashness of my youth, I asked my mother, "How could you stay married to the same person for 40 years?" The longer I have lived my life primarily responsible for myself, the more I understand the choices my Mom and Dad made to keep their marriage together. They were in it together for the long haul. They compromised, but so do I in being single. My own pain comes from always being forced to choose between those two poles. I don't know how to live well with a lover without giving up a lot of myself, but living alone to sustain other parts of myself is not so great either.

This tension is all around us. The woman who lives downstairs with her small son left her husband because "she was dying and nobody saw it." Friends are scared of collective living, but still think about it. Lesbians and gay men fight for state recognition of homosexual marriages. Many mid-30s feminists have gone back to "permanent" relationships with men, and are trying to be strong there. We are all looking for people with whom we can share our love and need.

We are especially vulnerable as women to the emotional burdens of family relationships. Women in heterosexual marriages confront and resolve endless problems in raising children and running homes. They may also be raising their husbands. The reality is different from the promise of partnership. The illusion that marriage or a permanent partner genuinely makes you less lonely is often unrealistic, given how many people feel terribly alone inside their relationships. They also feel crazy for feeling that, because they do have someone of their own, and the world out there alone seems even more threatening and lonely. Part of the threat of being a single person or parent is that aloneness. There is no one to share disciplining the children, fixing the leaks, dealing with doctors, the social workers, or the child's teacher.

For women, the most graphic image of this fearful loneliness is the shopping bag lady. She is unprotected by a family, unconnected, poverty-stricken, desperate, outside human caring, with nowhere to sleep. She is HOMELESS. The image terrifies us because it suggests how vulnerable we all are when we confront this culture by ourselves.

> At the center of my bleakest fantasy is the shopping bag lady. Invariably she clutches her paper shopping bags close to her. From a distance, her face looks black, her skin gray. I know I am not unique in having this fantasy. I have heard many other women express it, perhaps not always in terms of shopping bag ladies, but in terms of old age insecurity. It is not surprising because we are living in a period of depression when everyone is worried about money and jobs, about the possibility of surviving in some decent way.
>
> Irena Klepfisz, "Women without Children, Women without Families, Women Alone," *Conditions: 2*

In a world controlled by men, to be cut off from men is to be without power and consequently without pride, rights, home, or roots. For women in generations before us the best a single woman could hope for was to be a maiden aunt dependent on male family members to sustain her or piecework, fieldwork, or labor in another woman's house. Unless she came from money, there were no alternatives. If she had neither father provider nor husband she was stranded in a male world with no rights. Some women passed as men or were forced into religious institutions. This situation obviously made real partnership nearly impossible. That some genuine love and bonding has nevertheless occurred is a tribute to human perseverance and creativity under the most negative of circumstances.

Lesbian/Gay

Lesbians and gay men are the outlaws of a heterosexual system. Raised inside traditional families, we seek out others who share our desire only when we can redefine the assumptions we have been taught by our parents or guardians. We must then "raise ourselves" again, through lovers and gay communities. Many gay people never survive this journey. Until recently most gay children and adolescents were without any support in their search for a healthy sexual self. The very silence imposed on the knowledge of homosexuality in children and teenagers is proof itself of the terror this culture entertains at the thought of same sex partnering.

No one yet knows why anyone is heterosexual or homosexual. What we do know is that our culture encourages a rigidly self-destructive gender system; one each of us, regardless of sexual choice, suffers inside of. Those strictures which outline "genuine masculinity" and "real woman-ness" bypass or deform critical portions of actual human potential. The fear and oppression suffered by sexual minorities forces many gay people to renounce their own sexual and emotional desires to try to hide them inside frantic marriages or celibacy. The other options are equally unwelcome—institutionalization by the state through juvie hall, mental wards, or jails, as well as probable rejection from heterosexual families and communities.

The relations between homosexual men and lesbians with their families is an issue exacerbated by realities of race and class. Third world and working class people need the communities from which they come in order to survive. The threat of expulsion carries greater weight as does the sense of responsibility to help one's communities thrive. While the possibility of upward mobility can make the allegiances of white working class people to their origins murky or shifting, racism makes identification and connections with communities and familiies crucial for people of color. Minority communities sustain values and existence through caring for elders, nurturing or having children, fighting for language and culture, and passing on the skills to outwit or withstand racism. Often gay people walk a continual tightrope between two necessary support systems, not able to be whole in both. The dangers of expulsion from the family are multiplied and the threat of exposure ever-present.

There are other differences to grapple with when challenging gender silence. The gulf between boy's/men's right to be sexually experimental in order to learn about sex and the corresponding disapproval of such behavior in girls/women creates a more difficult search for conciousness of a sexual self for lesbians than gay men. It is precisely because women are not the owners of their own sexual desire that the discovery of lesbianism may take longer, be more shocking or never be allowed to surface. The threat of being a single woman in a heterosexual culture, without a man, and aging, is used to quiet female and lesbian sexual rebellion and reinforce male privilege.

Yet we have begun to build a new version of the sexually possible through a radical lesbian and gay movement. This movement has dramatically altered cultural sex/gender notions and is helping to create a bridge for lesbians and gay men back to their own roots. It is a Beginning.

A History of Lesbianism

How they lived in the world
The women-loving-women

learned as much as they were allowed
and walked and wore their clothes
the way they liked
whenever they could. They did whatever
they knew to be happy or free
and worked and worked and worked
The women-loving-women
in American were called Dykes
and some liked it
and some did not.

Judy Grahn, *The Work of a Common Woman*

Sex

Men see themselves as sexual, most women do not. Women see
themselves as the *object* of sexuality, but not the active one
sexually . . . . Women are not encouraged to see themselves as
erotic, to see their erotic capacity, so they don't think of a
partner in sexual terms, but more in emotional, social, or
economic terms. . . . For most women, sexual potential is not
even an option or a question. It is not something women walk
around thinking about in a way they can resolve. Not that
women don't think about it, it's just that it's a luxury and you
cannot use it to make choices you need to make for survival.

Amber Hollibaugh, "Sexuality and the State: the Defeat
of the Briggs Initiative and Beyond," *Socialist Review*, #45

Not only is the family the only sanctioned place for sexual
relationships, carefully and specifically defined, but the family is also
the sexual socializer, teaching us with whom and under what circumstances sexual relationships are possible. This power is overwhelming.
We learn that mommy and daddy can do it, and the only way we can do
it is to grow up and become half of a girl/boy couple. Heterosexuality
denies people sexual knowledge whether they are gay or straight,
particularly to women. Nevertheless, the heterosexual family is the
only legitimate and moral arrangement allowing sexual expression,
forcing marriage to be the primary place where sexual experimentation
is allowed for most people.

Sex or the promise of sex may get people into marriage, but it isn't
what keeps them there. Women often compromise around sex in
marriage, maintain the relationship for other reasons, and see sex as a
duty to their husbands. Men may compromise, but they have other
outlets available. For women, the compromise can mean the end of

their sexuality. Women, children, and gay people have all been profoundly affected by not having autonomous sexual identities. Discovering what you are capable of sexually gives a sense of pride and
competency which most women have never had. The irony is that
women frequently marry to have the right to be sexual in the first place.
While standards of how far you can go, or with how many partners,
have loosened up in terms of premarital sex, the ongoing demand is that
a woman return to sexual fidelity within marriage. As long as women
are taught that their own legitimate sexual responses are primarily as
the receiver of other people's passion, a radically freeing female and
male sexual experience remains to be created. The "Need" to be sexual
cannot be denied; the "Right" to be sexual, for women, children, and
gay people, remains to be won.

Children

Having children is a primary reason people give for marrying or
living together permanently. When one or more adults live with
children in any fashion, it is called a family. This major commitment to
living with children radically alters your life; it is an all or nothing
proposition. When a woman decides to have a child, or finds herself
pregnant and decides to continue with the pregnancy, there are few
other people who accept the responsibility and weight of that decision.
Often a husband or other partner is the main or only other adult to
share the change. For women (especially third world women) whose
extended families help with responsibilities, a mother, older sister, or
aunt may also take part in the work. This is an example in which the
standard model of a white middle class TV family differs markedly
from the realities of some people's lives. On the other hand, geographical mobility today makes receiving support and work from an extended family much less likely than it was a generation or two ago.

Having a child is a long-term project, a connection that outlasts
many marriages and other life changes. While other people may
become support systems, usually the primary responsiblity for the
child's welfare is on the parents, and in the final conclusion, on the
mother. Likewise, the responsibility for failure in this task rests on the
mother. On the other hand, adults who are not biological or adoptive
parents have few opportunities to relate to children. There is little
flexibility in our links with children in a society that privatizes and
possesses them.

Similarly, the decision to have children is made in a haphazard
manner. Most women who are mothers have their children before they
ever have a notion that they have a choice. Most women we grew up

with were engaged, or trying to be, while they were still in high school, and got married soon after. By their early 20s they usually had two kids and were considering a third. Though some had abortions, if they were still in high school, many had kids. Now in their middle 30s, they have 16 and 17-year olds.

The idea of "choice" in having children (as in many other decisions) is class and race determined. Most working class and third world women and men work out independent relationships with children after they have had them, not before. It is not a choice of child or career, but rather an issue of how long a woman will remain outside the labor force, if in fact she has ever left it. This reality forces the woman to make accommodations between motherhood and a paid job, or else forego a higher income in order to stay at home with the children. For all but the most privileged women, decisions about having children shape the rest of their adult lives.

To compound the harshness of the "choice," a woman's worth as a woman is judged both by her physical ability to bear a child, as well as by her willingness to do so. To not want to have children is sacriligious even today.

If a woman then is an empty vessel to be filled, the lack of filling by a man or children, preferably both, is tantamount to not being a complete woman. This is a major source of the fears about lesbianism as an incomplete female experience. A woman is not defined in terms of herself, but rather by the people to whom she gives her time and energy: her husband and children.

For men, the exclusion from primary relationships with children is also severe and damaging. Contrary to the new myths being promulgated, *Kramer v. Kramer* is not the norm; rather, it is the single-parent household headed by a woman. The case of single men adopting children is so unusual that it still gets media attention. Meanwhile, there are 8.5 million households headed by women. The growth rate of female-headed households increased 51 percent in the 1970s.

Culturally, it is never demanded of men that they assume the same responsibility for children. Economic realities as well as sexism and racism make it likely that relations with children will be superficial or sporadic. Men are in pain from this lack. Not only do they miss the joys and growth of relating to children, but their own emotional development is stunted by being removed from others' emotional development. No part of the society encourages fathering similar to mothering. Men give less than they can to children because they have the privilege to decide not to. They are also controlled by the work they must do to keep a family together, a family to which they are frequently emotional strangers. The costs are high.

Physical and Mental Care

The family is expected to provide special care for its members in two circumstances: in life stages requiring special care, namely childhood and old age; and when physical or mental disability prevents a person from being an independent part of the public, working world. Not only is the family expected to provide all the necessary care, it is also a storage place for immature, damaged, or outmoded workers, until they are capable of entering or re-entering the labor force, or until they die. The family is capitalism's major holding pattern.

> Lois: My sister, who was brain damaged at birth, is currently in a mental institution. My parents soon will have neither the physical nor the emotional stamina, to say nothing of the financial means, to care for her. My choices are between meeting some of my own needs versus a kind of financial stability that will allow me to meet more of her needs. The choice feels like no choice. No one else will care for my sister. The state provides minimal care at best, which will surely decrease in an age of economic contraction. The family is the only source to turn to. My mother says not to make my sister my main responsibility. I point out that she did that for the 27 years that Rachel lived with her. "Yes," she says, "but she was my child."

Changes in the family and its breaking down expose the lack of options for persons mentally and/or physically needy and disabled. Previously, the family, including its extended forms, was expected to absorb the suffering and care for its individual members. The family did not absorb these needs without great costs, usually to the lives of women. And while this activity remained within the family, it was one more part of women's work that was ignored, denied, and undervalued. The inability of families to provide this kind of care, because of the decline of the extended family, women's high labor force participation rate, and divorce, has now made the provision and financing of health care and social services a public issue.

In heterosexual marriage, once you have children, you owe them care, both emotionally and legally. In exchange parents own children, all their labor power and decision-making rights. Legally and morally most children are powerless and trivialized.

At the other end of the age spectrum, deteriorating health and forced retirement unrelated to desire or economic needs also make old people dependent on families. Mandatory retirement and the inadequacy of Social Security payments compel economic dependency. Many elderly people are not sick, nor are they physically strong enough to do all the tasks that living alone and isolated require, from carrying home a bag of groceries, climbing up to change a lightbulb, dealing with bureaucracies of pensions, social security, etc. This society gives no one a community to age in. Old age means enforced obsolescence. But most people can do many, if not all, of the things necessary for their survival. What they can't do becomes family work, work that is not profitable to include in the market economy. If no family members are available and/or willing, this work doesn't get done. Before the proliferation of old age homes, if a person couldn't make it on her/his own or with the help of their families, they were forced into a county poor farm, a state mental institution, or simply were forced to die, sometimes of cold and hunger.

Generally, life for a physically or mentally disabled person is better at home than in an institution, unless the family is wealthy. Most institutions are inhumane warehouses. Alternatives that meet needs are almost non-existent, and financially prohibitive when they do exist. Besides the lack of real choice, there is the burden of guilt that a family feels if it gives up on the attempt to care for a disabled member. The idea of giving up on one of your own is anathema to most people. If a main function of the family is to produce perfect workers (wage workers and houseworkers), then having produced an "imperfect" member is a deep source of shame. Whether the disability is caused by birth, illness, or accident, it profoundly affects the life of the family, making the disabled person a central focus of concern, adding un-dreamed of burdens to women's work and men's financial responsibil-ities. The movement for independence among physically disabled and retarded people still has little public financial and material support. When independence is not feasible, for a wide variety of reasons, families and institutions are the only places to meet needs.

The claim that we have on our families' lives makes the assump-tion that disability is a family responsibility, regardless of impossible circumstances. This is true for short-term health crises such as a broken leg or a nervous breakdown, as well as life-long disabilities.

Intergenerational Relationships

Most daily activities segregate us by age: in workplaces, schools, child care centers, old age homes. Only in the relationship between parent and child, and with members of one's extended family—grand-parents, aunts, uncles—do we have the opportunity to participate in intimate relationships with people of other generations.

Our personal connection with history is our connection with our families, where they came from, what they have seen and survived.

These are parts of how we've been taught to respect ourselves. Stories about the family's collective past can lead to a sense of ourselves. Jewish children learn about the pogroms that led their grandparents to flee Russia. Racism, fighting in wars, options for birth control are all the types of information we learn from family stories. Dating of important events happens by family crises. People's history is eradicated unless we know stories of the ways our families participated. An underground people's history is kept alive by the story telling. Everything from wars to the depression or the horror of unwanted pregnancies is passed through family circuits and gives us possible sources of pride and models of resistance. Outside Black Studies classes, few people know about the Black nationalist movement of the 1920s unless a family member was in the Garvey movement. Our family histories tie us to the larger world. The intimacy in family intergenerational relationships distinguishes them from intergenerational relationships in other places. But we need more connection to older people than families alone can give us. Unfortunately we are often refused even the knowledge of how important this can be to our own lives.

PART II: WHAT HURTS US

In this culture, most people, having relatively little power, can survive only by remaining in the family. This is especially true for women and for people whose age or physical or emotional dependence makes them most vulnerable. Family care and responsibility serve all the crises that people stumble over in their lives: unemployment, alcoholism, illness, "acts of God." This is precisely the way the family works to trap us, and that makes it such an untenable place to be. Alternatives are not a luxury, but a necessity to express the different needs people have in their lives. One institution is supposed to encompass all the emotional needs of a lifetime, but our needs and desires are not the same at 5 as at 20, 50, or 75.

The farthest that capitalism has allowed us to stray from this institution is a brief period of early adulthood. It is now socially acceptable and economically feasible for many young people to live outside their families of origin before starting families of procreation. Formerly, young people went directly from their parents' home to the home they would make with their spouse, and many still do, especially women. But capitalism has tolerated a period of rootlessness and unconnectedness to the discipline of either family because it can make a profit from the new market of the individual single young consumer, and from the vulnerability of that isolation.

If not actually hating their family, most people have experienced the desire to leave it at some point. The possibility of acting on this desire is a function of class, race, and sex, and the privilege or lack of privilege which that gives you, both economically and emotionally.

Countless hidden crimes occur within the family, such as woman battering, rape, incest, forced child bearing, craziness, economic servitude, and child abuse. Because the family is a private institution, these crimes have not come to public light until the women's movement exposed them. Because we have all internalized the ideology of the family, we have barely been able to admit to ourselves or our closest friends or family members that these terrors existed, and we have had to continue to live with them. The official mythology is that the viciousness of family life happens only in rare and isolated circumstances, not that it is woven into the texture of families. Because this ideology is so pervasive, people see few ways of resisting the oppression of life inside a locked system. Women, children, and gay people have no way to resist the terror they experience as powerless members of that institution because they believe it is an individual problem.

Because of the overwhelming need to sustain the family as an institution, social agencies and religious organizations fight to keep the family intact as an establishment, rather than find other ways to sustain people who are being harmed. "Can This Marriage Be Saved?" the *Ladies Home Journal* asked throughout all the years of the 1950s. Predictably, the answer was always yes, and still is. Since the family is such a pervasive institution, the sense of personal failure and worthlessness if you can't hack it is overwhelming. It is the standard model against which you evaluate yourself, against which you figure out your own self-worth and self-value. Since it is the lifeline to so many facets of your needs and your ability to give and receive love, the idea of doing without it or criticizing it seems outside the realm of the possible.

Even when you know that your family does not meet many of your needs and never will, it frequently is the only place you have to turn to.

> Lois: When my 20-year-old cousin, unmarried, separated from the father of her two small children, without a high school diploma and little work experience or skills, found herself increasingly up against the wall, she moved 2500 miles back across the country to her home town. There she had to face the censure and disapproval of her family but she could also receive some support, emotional and financial, some sense of belonging.

> Amber: Similarly, my aunt, after the failure of her third marriage, and when arthritis had made it impossible for her to

work, moved back in with her 85–year–old mother, the best alternative.

Economic Survival

Whatever the myths of love that surround the family, it is economics that defines much of the interactions. Money determines how you feel about relationships and whether you stay in them. Dependency for services is forced on children to survive. Most women are dependent on husband, partner, or the state (welfare) for support, or for a standard of living marginally above poverty. Men, while above women in the financial hierarchy, depend on women for the unwaged labor that in fact keeps everyone going. Women earn 57 percent of what men earn, children are marginalized from the money economy; their services are free, or at best earn them a pittance. We stay in jobs we hate because there is no other choice, and we stay in relationships for the same reason.

Yet the model of working husband, housewife, and 2.4 children is increasingly a myth. Between 1973 and 1978 alone, 6 million additional women joined the labor force. Half of all women are working for wages. This means that women have two jobs, rather than one, and that the cost of survival is so high that the ideological value placed on the non-working housewife (the one who has only one job) must take a seat behind necessity.

Although more women are in the work force than ever before, only 40 percent of working women are employed full-time; the other 60 percent work part-time or part-year, moving in and out of the work force as the economy and the family allow and demand. Thus, the challenge to women's economic dependency provided by the increase of women earning money is very incomplete, for relatively few of us can survive on women's incomes alone, let alone support children.

Women are the possession of men, both economically and physically. Under capitalism, most men own little, but they possess their wives, and together the adults possess the children. In most states, the rape of a woman by her husband does not legally exist. This is only one example of the physical dimensions of the ownership. No matter how strong and independent a woman may be, as long as she is economically dependent, she must compromise her choices. For children, there are no choices.

Hetero/Sexuality

The attempt to keep people ignorant of their sexual needs until marriage finds two people facing each other technically ignorant and emotionally terrified to explore the range of feelings that emerge between people when they make love. Although men and boys are expected to experiment before they finally "settle down," the knowledge of how to sustain an ongoing responsive sexual relationship is not part of that experience. For women, *True Confessions* or Harlequin romances, movies, and soap operas are the models for sexual fantasy and the how-to manual for what to expect of and what to feel for a lover.

We learned, as children, that the only conceivable reason for sexual intercourse was for having children, but were not taught about sexual pleasure. Even the ideological change in the fashionably sensual '80s never deals with the completeness of the human being confronting the needs of another person as a peer and partner.

Silence by women and power in the hands of men have been the terms for most heterosexual relationships. While changes are occurring, there is no equality between men and women. Sexual equality cannot be imposed. For women with no other sexual outlets, marriage is the only place to go. Men can find sexual options in hookers, pornography, occasional partners from bars or work, other men, and/or baths and brothels. For women, the choices are not the same, nor are the values. Sex is a *commodity* for men to purchase, outside the family, and for women to create. Being a sexual *commodity* means that women must create the personality and physical presence that will appeal to and lure a partner. Appeasing the need is a similar process, whether the price is direct cash, a few drinks, dinner and the movies, or a wedding license. Either active or passive, a woman's ultimate power to determine her sexual partner generally resides only in marriage.

Since the desire for marriage often has little to do with sex, and much more to do with other needs, most women's true sexual capabilities are least recognized in this institution. To say it another way, sex is often the expendable element of a marriage. Because heterosexuality is a monolith, it forces everyone to cooperate within unchosen boundaries irrespective of the needs and desires they may feel (or want to feel) in their own bodies. It is a vicious trap and often denies the true sexual pleasure man or woman can create sexually together, nor does it encourage growth and good sexual information.

Family Violence

When middle class parents are alcoholics, they have a well-stocked bar in their dens and no one knows about it except their children and their spouses, who aren't talking. When a working class parent is alcoholic, he/she stumbles to the corner liquor store in his/her pajamas late at night, and is found in the street by the neighbors while everyone on the block talks. The difference class can make is the difference of control over your so-called private life. The more privilege, the more likely it is that your problems are exposed only to the intimate family circle, and perhaps the paid help. The less privilege, the more your failings are exposed to the world. It is assumed that there is more violence in working class, poor, and third world families. Classist and racist assumptions in the women's movement and the left ignore the fact that poorer people have less ability to hide their lives from others.

We are both white women from working class families and know how painful this stereotype is. We do not want physical violence to go unchallenged but feel that it's no accident people of color and white working class people always take the rap, while those with more class protection remain hidden from social criticism. As well, it sometimes seems easier to avoid looking at certain power issues in the family because they are so painful for us. A grim example is battery and/or rape of women and children by men. Inside the cycle of physical violence are children who are powerless to stop their father's attacks on their mother and themselves; women who are powerless to stop attacks on themselves, and because of economics as well as emotional training, feel powerless to stop or even acknowledge the rape of their daughters. All conspire to pretend that none of this exists. The multitude of stories women have told to explain black eyes, fractured ribs, and bleeding vaginas, or the excuses used in admitting a child to a hospital with unexplained bruises, testify to our inability or powerlessness to acknowledge the reality or know how to escape it. In poor neighborhoods, we experience the weekend police siren, when someone calls the cops as a man is beating up his wife. Working class women describe a good relationship with a man by his lack of violence against her or the children. "He's a steady worker; he doesn't drink; he doesn't hit me." (Lillian Rubin, *Worlds of Pain*)

There are other acts of violence as well. If the countless times a woman said no and a man didn't listen were considered rape, virtually all women who have slept with men would be included as rape statistics. One of the most painful areas of power struggle between men and women is exactly this area of coercive sexual exploitation. Until recently, the notion that a husband could rape his wife was so shocking even to the woman who had just been raped that it was rarely acknowledged. There have been a few newsmaking acquittals of women tried for killing husbands who had consistently beaten them. The acquittals were newsworthy because this verdict is so new, and is a product of the women's movement.

But even if we are not directly bruised by physical violence, we all carry the results of the emotional violence of those things that were never named or discussed. In less dramatic form, we all have ambivalent feelings about our families. There are the rules laid down without explanation (Do it. Because I tell you to do it. When I tell you to do it.), the sexual invalidation, the family's inability to allow people to have personality differences. For a family to function smoothly, it must ride roughshod over many traits important to individuals. The family demands the same taste in food, clothes, and entertainment because it can't afford economically or emotionally to support differences among family members. Our identities are built in the family against our will. The same dynamic holds true for the family as for any power dynamic—we are pushed and shoved to become certain things we have no way to resist. The family as the main acculturation agent gives you your values. The narrowness of what the family thinks is possible works to destroy the individual's potential.

Summing Up

Our struggles as adults spring directly from the deformed and constrained possibilities that the family was forced to offer for the future. It is frightening to need the love and nourishment that only the family seems to provide, and yet be an exile from it in order not to reproduce the viciousness that the family has taught us.

As women, we learn our second class status in our families. Mothers are expected to teach the same values to their children that damaged them and so destroyed their own sense of worth. We are forced to internalize the values that make us less than human, and then to pass them along to the new generation. We find it unthinkably painful to see women raising their sons to have contempt for women, and their daughters to have contempt for themselves.

In the same ironic way that women are forced to teach their offspring to hate femaleness, so are people of color and of the working class forced to teach their children an ambivalent relationship to their race or class. To escape color and class boundaries, people are forced to leave behind, geographically and emotionally, their families, as they climb the ladder of upward mobility. Upward mobility offers success to the individual only, separated from the group. The best is to share that success, to bring over other family members from the old country, to buy a house for your parents. But it is success to the "worthy" individual only. We learn from our families to go upward, but to leave them behind.

I was educated, and wore it with a keen sense of pride and satisfaction, my head propped up with the knowledge, from my Chicana mother that my life would be easier than hers. I was educated; but more than this, I was "la güera": fair-skinned. Born with the features of my Chicana mother, but the skin of my Anglo father. I had it made.

No one ever quite told me this (that light was right), but I knew that being *light* was something valued in my family (who were all Chicano, with the exception of my father). In fact, everything about my upbringing (at least what occurred on a conscious level) attempted to bleach me of what color I did have. Although my mother was fluent in it, I was never to learn Spanish at home. I picked up what I did learn from school and from overheard snatches of conversation among my relatives and mother. She often called the lower-income Mexicans braceros or "wet backs," referring to herself and her family as "a different class of people." And yet, the real story was that my family, too, had been poor (some still are) and farmworkers. My mother can remember this in her blood as if it were yesterday. But this is something she would like to forget (and rightfully), for to her, on a basic economic level, being Chicana meant being "less." It was through my mother's desire to protect her children from poverty and illiteracy that we became "Anglo-ized," the more effectively we could pass in the white world, the better guaranteed our future.

Cher'rie Moraga, "La Güera," in *The Coming Out Stories*, Julia Penelope Stanley and Susan L. Wolfe, eds.

Finally, the most common, understood, and feared measure of the family's strangulation of its members, especially women, is the soaring divorce rate. Today one marriage in three ends in divorce. Between 1970 and 1978 the proportion of women living in traditional nuclear families with husbands present dropped from 73 to 64 percent. That the traditional institution of the family is no longer sufficient to meet human needs is obvious. What is available to take its place, however, is not so obvious, as the attempts of the '60s and '70s to create alternative living situations can show.

PART III: THE NEW FAMILIES IN A SOCIALIST AND RADICAL FEMINIST AMERICA

The institution of the family and the people who enforce its rules and uphold its values define the lives of both married and single people, just as capitalism defines the lives of workers and dropouts alike. The family system divides us up into insiders and outsiders, as insiders, married people are more likely to identify with the established order, and when they do, they are not simply expressing a personal preference but taking a political stand. THE ISSUE, FINALLY, IS WHETHER WE HAVE THE RIGHT TO HOPE FOR A FREER, MORE HUMANE WAY OF CONNECTING WITH EACH OTHER. Defenders of the family seem to think that we have already gone too far, that the problem of this painful and confusing time is too much freedom. I think there is no such thing as too much freedom, only too little nerve.

Ellen Willis, "The Family: Love It or Leave It," reprinted in her new book, *Beginning to See the Light*, p. 168.

The Women's Movement has been daring. Feminism looked socialism right in the eye and demanded answers to questions of daily life. This radical confrontation has set the stage for what will be one of the most creative tensions that a new radical america will draw on, ten years after the revolution. While socialist movements in this country have talked vaguely about society after that revolution, feminism went beyond talk to demand the beginning of that future starting now, a demand to begin changing how we live today. It asked that people examine the role of the family, the sexual division of labor, women's bodies, unwaged labor in the home, misogyny, parenting, violence against women's bodies and minds, sexuality/gender and homosexuality. Feminism has been an explosion which opened up areas socialism addressed only tangentially. Feminism also created new arenas for analysis and activism. Because of this it has altered the whole debate about the world we want to create.

As well, feminism has stated that the *way* revolutions get made, the process of radical transformation, is equally critical to the final outcome. In order to create a vibrant alternative in this new society, we must create the conditions in ourselves and our communities to develop new values and priorities. One of the most insidious ways capitalism remains in control is by constricting our imaginations. We literally "can't imagine" things any other way. The feminism and socialism of a new future must break the silence that this culture has imposed on our imagery and invention, and challenge us to take chances on each other; to develop respect, automony, and independence as equal needs to our desires for love, companionship, and communities.

There has never been a feminist movement equally committed to socialist revolution. And the extent to which socialism has met the needs of women either in socialist countries or socialist movements and theory leads us constantly to reaffirm that socialism is a necessary but *insufficient* condition to the liberation of women and gender. Our feminist demands must be inseparable from our socialist assumptions that each *person* has the absolute right to a decent life, a home, health care, equal and accessible economic support, meaningful work, joyful play, and a caring community. It is the success of merging these goals that will dictate our ability to give birth to this new society in the first place.

Socialism speaks directly to questions of economic re-organization. Toppling capitalism's money–before–people priorities opens up our human labor to create for fundamentally equalitarian purposes. Feminism then asks where and how women's labor will be employed and to what degree a revolution in the USA would allow women to decide for themselves what they are capable of. Marxism has always recognized the need for women to fully join the workforce after the revolution, but rarely has that knowledge been extended to include a structure where women have equal power in shaping and governing that workplace as well as all other institutions. As well, we'll need agreement in this new society to pour our energies and excitement into devising countless ways to struggle against racism and sexual oppression by fully including women/people of color who are often unrecognized as members in good standing of "the working class."

In this re–organization, we should see no person penalized for living alone or in collective situations, as well as more traditional family settings. Similarly, no woman must ever need ask husband or father for money, no child should judge her or his own worth by what material possessions they are surrounded by, and no person should ever be chosen for a particular job because racism or sexism has deemed this work uniquely "theirs." Human relationships can only be reshaped if economic, racial, and sexual differences go unrewarded in this new socialist society.

Yet 10 years is short time indeed to imagine that we can undo hundreds of years of destructive work that capitalism has grafted onto our values and perceptions. The process of ordering our priorities shares the difficult challenge all revolutions face between economic necessities and utopian desires. We can see the experiences of other socialist attempts in the world as well as our own history of socialist struggles, especially through the last 15 years, during the decline of American imperialism. When we no longer consume 50 percent of the world's resources with only 7 percent of the world's population, when the greed of a consumer culture is replaced by humane values, we suspect that work, living space, environmental and ecological sensibilities as well as personal life, sexuality, and relationships will be freed up and our notions of what constitutes a good life within our communities liberated.

Our vision of socialism is a socialism which reorganizes the economics of our culture to provide for real, not created, needs and desires and which makes people independent and resourceful rather than dependent on the state. Our communities will then be able to relocate their values and aspirations in the strength and vitality of their differences as well as the common expectations which our various socialisms share.

Feminism has addressed many of these questions. It has challenged the labor patterns of capitalism and the consumer patterns of imperialism. Thus the insurance industry, for example, which manipulates real needs and fears about our future survival, could be done away with. The army of women who now do the clerical work of the insurance industry would be able to do other work, more necessary to survival.

It is hard to envision just how much intense and emotional areas like personal relationships will change after 10 years of socialism. We can only guess at the new expectations and possibilities if the struggle to survive became instead a struggle to create. But as women whose lives have been radically and permanently altered by the feminist and lesbian movements of the past decade, we think that examining feminist and gay issues has given us a barometer to appreciate where change and struggle will be happening 10 years after "the revolution."

Already, feminism has redefined the terms on which women and men meet each other in this culture. Precisely because its issues hit us all in our daily lives, feminism now demands (and will in the future), that we take seriously the thousand and one chores that go into supporting and caring for other people and ourselves in a new society. How would daily tasks be broken up in our new living situations? How would we encourage long term and ongoing commitments between people (lovers, children, parents, friends) and still provide flexible options so that no one was forced to stay in one place or relationship when they were burned out or unchallenged? Who would cook breakfast? Would only one person work primarily in the home, assuming the thousands of responsiblities from cooking for a sick neighbor or packing lunches to waiting at home for a repair person or telephone installer? Would some categories of work be more legitimately considered labor than others and command a higher wage or more status? Would constantly repeated (and therefore often "unseen") chores like cooking, laundry, or house cleaning continue to center in individual homes, or could each block or neighborhood collectivize its washing machines? Would we want blocks to collectivize child care? Would the people who cared for children be paid equally to a chemist? Would you know who was lovers with whom, and who wasn't? What would be considered erotic? If you lived with children, would they see your sex life visibly? How would children express their sexuality? If all these things changed, would we still carry with us drastic power imbalances from our old oppressions? These are all difficult, challenging questions, ones that we will still be approaching 10 years after socialism is a reality.

Collective Living

Experiences in collective living during the past fifteen years have given varied evidence of success. It has proven much harder to live our lives in new ways than to dream of them. Yet for all the disappointments between parents and non-parents, the houses broken up, the children hurt from not understanding, still collective living has never been worse than the nuclear family. The criticism that children suffer most from failed communal living situations ignores the reality that women and children are being brutalized daily in the nuclear family. This criticism of collective, communal child-rearing undermines feminist analyses of the nuclear family.

Clearly, the bitterness of failed communal solutions is out of proportion to the few years and little help we had in attempting to live differently. If we submit to that despair, we condemn women forever to the nuclear family as the only model and continue to make child-rearing a women's-only task. Feminism is then great as a theory, but cannot give us the tools to change the way we really live. All of us in the women's movement and the left should examine closely the reasons we are so willing to condemn our "youthful" experiments, while spending a fortune in therapy to deal with our own childhoods! We have been too willing to fall back into an institution that has not met our needs for 35 years, but give up on alternatives after 2, 3, or 4 years as failures, not worth understanding or trying again.

But this experimentation has exploded on many fronts. In projects and tracts across the country are battles to live truer to our real needs and hopes. Not everyone is equally alienated from their families of origin, or the ones they are creating. Some people have always had more extended families. Those people already have a head start in building alternative forms for the future, because their past history is less confined. Extended families and friends and neighbors who shared in the welfare of the children, rural communities that didn't so clearly and cruelly segregate adults and children, give models outside the narrow structures of poppa, momma, and baby bears. For most working class and people of color, the media reality was never their own experience. Their families could not and did not exist in that structure. The nuclear family was an image we were supposed to want, not a lived reality. We have had to adapt to survive.

> Lois: My experience in living in heterosexual collective "fam-
> ilies" is that even when the women and men attempted to share
> equally the cooking and childcare, work on the garden and
> repair of cars, still what remained, and was even more artfully
> disguised, was the emotional responsibility laid on the
> women, the fact that emotional work was still women's work.
> Men could pride themselves on mending the slipcover on the
> couch, but couldn't recognize or struggle over the reality that
> women still initiated and fought through the emotional strug-
> gles. Many human issues, such as loneliness and tiredness, are
> not sex-specific except to the extent that they become part of
> women's emotional burdens. We need space and commitment
> to work out these problems.
> Amber: My own terror of the family has always, at least
> subconsciously, been the feeling that I would inevitably be
> encircled and enclosed by its values, forced back into relation-
> ships with my parents that I always wanted to change, back
> into dependency and vulnerability I had no way to alter. That
> nightmare has nothing to do with loving or not loving the
> individual members of my family, but with knowing what
> happens to relationships that are based on overwhelming need
> and dependency, where no one is given a choice in the ways in
> which they care for each other. Yet at the same time it is a
> foregone conclusion that if something happened to my father I
> would immediately return home and live with my mother
> indefinitely. It's exactly that contradiction between needs and
> responsibilities for support and caring versus my own inde-
> pendent life that makes the family so painful for me as a
> woman and a lesbian. It is frequently the subtle forms of
> demand that the family makes on its members which we hate
> and cannot escape.

It is against this backdrop that we will be struggling to overcome and
redefine our lives.

Revolutionary Tumult
Feminism and Socialism Engaged

The family, because of what needs it promises to fulfill, is always a
volatile institution to try to change. Ten years after a revolution what
will likely exist is a combination of tentative beginnings, new and
alternative ways of living and loving with people's energies freed up to
start looking at the world differently while living and acting in new
ways. Concurrently, a conservative reaction is likely to appear with

some people arguing that we should hold on to the family as it was in the old culture, even if oppressive, because it's known and familiar. People may more readily change the structure of decision-making at their jobs than in their homes. There was an old feminist slogan which said "A revolution in every bedroom" and we think that feminism will be challenging some of our most cherished (and oppressive) notions while it looks for alternatives that are as meaningful for women as all others who group together to create a family. Community fears and pressures in conservative directions must be dealt with by all of us building socialism. Social change and personal transformation are slow and difficult and cannot simply be legislated.

Most revolutionary movements to date have been more than willing to compromise on what they have considered "personal" issues rather than issues of work or politics. It is just that juncture to which feminism speaks and why feminism must not compromise or subsume its relationship to socialist struggle but be a continuing pivot for our very notion of what constitutes making revolutionary change. Most socialist countries to date have been economically and culturally colonized. The material conditions they faced in deciding revolutionary priorities were radically different from the society we will be fighting against and rebuilding in a highly developed capitalist setting. While we do think that the necessity for economic survival was partly the cause for the Soviet Union and China to create the revolutionary societies the way they did, we are suspicious of their unwillingness to move beyond that and challenge notions of the family or personal life with vigor and commitment. American economic development gives us fewer economic obstacles to changing family and personal life.

Relationships will change slowly though in any case. And they will change in proportion to the support and security afforded the changers, as well as our ongoing consciousness of feminist/socialist goals. If for example women are educated to understand and therefore control our own bodies, we would know about our own physiology and birth control; our menstruation process would not be a taboo hidden away from men and fearfully accepted by women; there would be reproductive rights, good, non-judgmental sex education, and knowledge of lesbianism would be the expectation not the exception. Moreover, women from early age will have been encouraged to learn ways to defend themselves so that the control of their own bodies included the knowledge and techniques to physically control our environment and resist attacks and assaults should they occur.

Both of us are active and usually over-extended. We suspect that living in a revolutionary culture would continue to demand enormous energy. What then will we do without wives? The idea of wives as it's now constituted is appalling, but activism and commitments demand a support system in our personal lives and chores. We will all still need people to come home to that we love and respect and the nurturance that close friendship, lovers, and biological families can offer. Here it seems feminism has much to offer in its notions of the quality of life. It has asked what a genuinely supportive community would look like. One answer is that it will make space for people to have a cyclical relationship to the work force so that not everyone has to work constantly (or 9 to 5 each day) from economic necessity or fear of not being able to get back into the workforce. People then could choose periods in their lives when their work was where they lived and assume more, though not all, responsibility for friends, lovers, kids, comrades, and neighbors who themselves revolved through their work and back into the homes of this new society.

It is important to appreciate the pain that change brings as well as the benefits. We know how difficult the last 10 years have been in attempting to redefine our notions of female and male. Too often the left and the women's movement have not developed support systems to care for people in the midst of personal upheaval. One solution as a support institution will continue to be autonomous organizations. Women, lesbians, people of color, physically challenged people, etc., will need to speak directly to a still unresolved future and a longed-for connection between people who share a past and are committed to continually dreaming and struggling with folks of their own sex, color, etc., as part of their socialist vision.

The family, too, will have different and autonomous structures. One model for all of us will not suffice. The family is different in every cultural, racial, or class group in this country. People must be free to dream up varied tactics and structures for support and change in personal issues and home lives.

Feminism is not a temporary goal, any more than the eradication of racism. We think there are many ways to struggle against sexual or racial oppression, but *no* way to defer it. Various communities must challenge sexism with feminist answers developed by women and gay people in each of those communities. We are not advocating that "real" feminist change means everyone suddenly lives collectively or in women-only or men-only households, but rather it means an ongoing acknowledgment and struggle for feminist values, whatever the structures of personal life look like.

Lesbians and gay men will have much to offer this new culture as it tries to answer questions of how to live outside the now established boundaries. We have developed friendship networks which rival or over-shadow individual love relationships because we have had to. "Lovers may last or not, but it is your friends that get you through." (An old gay saying.) Because of that, intimacy is a more shared emotion than just with a lover, and "family" has become those people with whom you have gone through years of loving, taking care of (or being taken care of), eating with and living. Ongoing need for continuity then occurs between people who are peers and who choose each other freely rather than get born together. And these families will probably resemble large extended families of today, with some parts of those groupings stable while others come inside and leave again more regularly.

But all families will have a broader definition than the assumption of one woman and one man. Though we think that some people will choose to live in male/female single dwelling families, even this will be different because the block they live on could include for example three communes, two buildings of single people living in separate units but eating together in a communal kitchen, three gay men raising kids in the corner house, two older couples (one straight, one gay) living in the duplex next door, one independent household where teenagers on the block have set up a youth house for no one older than 17, and all buildings being redesigned by physically challenged people so that each block and living option is truly an option for everyone. And this would just be one block.

We expect that autonomous groups based on sexuality, race, and/or gender will also develop independent living situations, perhaps on their own land or in city areas which they claim. Since this new society will have a stake in assisting communities to develop their own unique characteristics and identities, surely the family and living plans will be a part of that surge for identity and independent culture. Our guess is that people will move back and forth between different communities, autonomous ones based on color, sex, or class, and more divergent communities freely chosen. Since gay and lesbian people will be in each of these communities, we will be struggling in each of these cultures as well as our own independent lesbian and gay neighborhoods. We expect that non-antagonistic separations will continue far into the future because each of us will need communities of peers to work with as we attempt to alter ourselves and experiment with form and content of the new families we create. Our autonomy is vital to our future.

In a society where divergence from the norm is tolerated, accepted, even encouraged, it will be an asset to people to know gay people. Not only will such circumstances enrich straight people's lives, but children will be exposed to a full range of possible role models. If sexual questions and issues of sexual identity are openly acknowledged, discussed, laughed about, and incorporated into the culture in open rather than derisive ways, the possibilities for newer generations to know and explore themselves and their sexuality are beyond our imagining. We do know that as long as people are bound to oppressive notions of femininity and masculinity, a genuine searching through of sexual/emotional desire for someone of the same sex is impossible.

A socialist and feminist society will offer increased possibilities for all kinds of relationships between people of the same sex. Today such relationships are mostly confined to family members and peer groups, especially before child-bearing, or to the unacceptable category of homosexuals. Forming close and ongoing friendships with persons of the same sex can include love, caring, intimacy, and sex, or not. Women's friendships today do not take priority. If a husband or male lover changes jobs, the assumption is always that that relationship takes precedence, and friends will be left behind.

We need to value friendships in a way in which they too will be reason for changing our habits. Children, for example, might choose to live with their mother's best friend, if they both felt comfortable with her and did not want to live where their parent(s) wanted to go.

The family is a stressful institution because it is the source for all our needs being met. Feminism has exposed the bankruptcy of the notion that one person, one lover, is capable of meeting all our needs. In addition, enforced heterosexuality damages. Homosexuality challenges the assumptions and forces people to rearrange what they considered important, desirable, natural. Because heterosexuality has been so incredibly pervasive a social system, invading every part of people's lives, a struggle against that system is intimately connected to our vision of socialism and women's liberation. Family is a euphemism for institutionalized heterosexuality today. If heterosexuality is made explicit as an institution, not the "natural" form of human relationships, and thus totally implicit, homosexuality will be real. Sexuality will be real. Sexuality will become realizable.

Part of women-hating is women hating each other and themselves, as well as men hating women. When there is no economic reason to internalize the hatred of oneself and other women, women will have the option to like, rather than compete with, other women. As well, when women are each others' partners, it will not be strange to see two (or more) women raising children together, building houses which they live in, and generally assuming that women's relationships to each other, whether sexual or not, can and will be primary. If it doesn't take the slinkiest body, sexiest smile, most stylish clothing, to attract partners to care about, women won't have to compete with one another for lovers. What will it be like when women are models for other women? Women can teach other women to cross the barriers femaleness is assumed to imply. Beauty standards will likewise disappear as we know them. Rather than having *standards* of beauty, there will be individual assessments of how and why each of us is beautiful to another. Obviously, physical beauty won't disappear as an aspect of our desire and appreciation of each other, but the false definitions (like thinness, shape of breasts, even teeth, hair type) will become integrated into a personal desire for a certain person or a sexual connection. We don't think that the revolution has to do away with beauty or sexual attraction in order to challenge sexism.

But the centrality of the family today is illustrated by the consequences of not having one. Orphanages, foster care programs, the juvenile justice system, and other institutions are all sad testimony to the inability of this culture to support young people outside the family. Adults outside families at least have the power to create alternative institutions. Our elders are put into warehouses to await death. Everyone whose needs cannot be met by a family loses out, unless they have families with wealth. These categories include physical and emotional disabilities and problems, people labeled crazy, retarded people, prisoners, gay people, alcoholics. Every age of life brings its own terror about not fitting into the family. If a middle aged wife is thrown out, what are her choices?

In previous centuries, many more marginal people were maintained by their families. The contemporary family usually has neither the continuity nor the physical space nor the personnel in the home (with more women in the labor market) to meet these needs. If the family cannot meet these needs, we are forced to rely on the inadequate offerings of the state. "Marginal" people offer a potent threat to everyone else. We want a society in which the well-being of people labeled marginal is not dependent on the financial or emotional resources of their families. Independence and autonomy over their own lives, combined with options of aid from family, friends, and community, will allow everyone to have better lives. Only a system which is committed to both socialist and feminist values could provide ways to deal with differences without trying to erase them.

Today, the best that we can hope for from a socialist country is that its culture does not rely on denigrating women. But this is a far distance from being informed by a feminist vision. In *Portrait of Teresa*, the highly acclaimed Cuban film, the conclusion leaves an unanswered question about whether Teresa has an extra-marital affair while her husband is doing that very thing, and whether she will accompany her husband when he moves away to a new job. Her questions extend to issues of personal autonomy, having a life outside the control of her husband. But that life is a substitute for her life with her husband, another man in a series. Possibilities such as her living alone, or not having responsibility for the children, or living with other women, are not raised. Her problem is familiar—being superwoman, juggling the demands of husband, children, paid job, and political work. But the only option presented is to trade in one man for a better model. While it is exciting that a film twenty years after the revolution considers these questions important, the narrowness of the perspective is shocking for what it leaves out.

Both *Theresa* and our society tell us our only choices for survival and happiness lie within heterosexual institutions, perhaps somewhat rearranged. But we can have so much more. The challenge of changing the family is difficult and demanding. We don't think it will happen over night and we know that it will take shapes we've never even guessed were possible. Our commitment to feminism and socialism is asserted through our equal desire for our liberation as women, as lesbians, and as workers, and we have a corresponding need to rebuild the institution of the family and the needs it answers in our lives into a place where *we* can live *our* lives to their own potential, not live through others' power. It is about destroying old and painful stereotypes and values, but even more, it is about creating our own visions of freedom as women in a new and possible future—a future that frees us all.

LUST AT LAST
Ellen Herman

At last. Sexual politics has entered the arena of legitimate political debate. For too long, the left has refused to engage in even the most elementary discussions of sexual politics. Leftists can justly claim a heritage ranging from ignoring feminists and gay liberationists to outright accusations of self-indulgence and "bourgeois decadence." To my way of thinking, there is nothing more radical or potentially relevant to a new society than feminism's central concerns with individual autonomy, personal happiness, and sexual gratification. If the left pursues a course of puritanical and reductionist thinking about everyday life, we will not succeed in even envisioning changes in the most superficial conditions of human life, let alone generate the enthusiasm and commitment necessary to fuel a revolutionary movement.

It is increasingly clear to people in many quarters that our society is experiencing crises in sexuality, morality, and authority. The New Right is busy reacting hysterically to feminism's dangerous perceptions about the nature of the nuclear family. The pro-family left has emerged as the guardian angel of "progressive" virtue and morality. Parts of the women's movement itself, notably the anti-porn activists, have begun to wage all-out campaigns against "male vice" and for "female values." These feminist crusaders are characterized by an unattractive tendency toward biologically determinist thinking about gender differences and sexuality. It would not at first seem that the discussions about sexual politics occurring in these diverse camps have much in common, but underlying them all is some degree of commitment to the appropriateness of the masculine/feminine polarity and a decided unwillingness to dig it up by its roots. Unfortunately, this is not the lesson to learn when finally getting around to making gender and social relations the material of practical and theoretical political controversy.

When we project a vision of a better way to live, sexual politics must mean much more than adding a few discrete items like child care, equal pay, and civil rights for gays to our list of required changes. A revolutionary vision must give full consideration to the dimensions of human experience addressed by feminism and gay liberation in particular: the fabric of daily life and personal interchange from its most individual detail to its most sweeping social consequence. This will mean attention to modes of thought, feeling, and practice, as well as to certain topics of inquiry: for example, crediting imagination, irrationality, and spirituality, as well as stressing the importance of a liberating "process."

The article by Lois Helmbold and Amber Hollibaugh undeniably pushes questions about the family and personal life into the realm of political debate. One of their main points is that "the family is a stressful institution because it is the source for all our needs being met." They focus on what these needs are specifically, why the nuclear family cannot possibly meet them, and how they might be met in a different, better society. Helmbold and Hollibaugh are particularly insightful in pointing out that working class and third world families and kin networks differ significantly from the middle class norm and have indeed been the source of sustenance to individuals and sometimes also the source of resistance to capitalist work and patriarchal social values. This is fine as far as it goes. My own feeling is that the family and the ideology of the family are far more than simply insufficient for satisfying people's real needs and desires. The patriarchal family, in all its variations, actively destroys women, children, gay people, and all possibility of anyone's ultimate sexual freedom.

Helmbold and Hollibaugh do take seriously the power of "non-material" forces like sexuality and emotion in motivating human choice and behavior, but they end up slipping in the direction of economism nevertheless. When they get down to it, "it is economics that defines much of the [family's] interactions. Money determines how you feel about relationships and whether you stay in them." This trend (usually in more extreme forms that leave out or subsume feminist politics completely) has enough of a history on the left to make it thoroughly familiar and entirely boring. Also wrong. The challenge of vision-making is to move us beyond the convenience and/or dogma of our pre-fab categories (whether marxist, feminist, nationalist, or whatever) toward an integration that is closer to the reality of our political, economic, cultural, and sexual selves.

A summary of the broad feminist critique of the family would have to include several important points: that in a patriarchal, capitalist society men have control over and access to women's reproductive and sexual bodies; men have the right to women's domestic labor (not recognized as work) and emotional sustenance; men (and parents in general) have absolute control over their children's lives and over those of the elderly, who are infantalized; the private world of family and emotion and the public world of work and rationality are maintained as separate spheres; procreative heterosexuality and the nuclear family are institutionalized to the point that they are considered the sole possibilities in life.

I would like to proceed, using this summary as a starting point, to follow through on some of the questions posed by Helmbold and Hollibaugh about (1) the relationship between reproduction and sexuality, (2) lifestyle, and (3) the authority of adults over young people and the aged. The context for these and other areas of life must be a society that guarantees each individual the material, cultural, emotional, and sexual means of survival, positive (non-sexist, non-racist, and non-class biased) socialization practices, and real choices of sexual self-expression. Some of the needs discussed by Helmbold and Hollibaugh are for affection and stability, love and intimacy, partnership, sex, children, physical and mental caretaking, and inter-generational contact. What will happen to these? My sense is that some will disappear altogether and some will remain. In all cases, individuals will have many more options about where and how to meet them, and this factor will change the meaning of "family" and "personal" needs entirely.

REPRODUCTION AND SEXUALITY

The assumed, intrinsic relationship between reproductive activity and sexual activity (whether rigidly enforced or subtly understood) is a major contributor to sexism and gay oppression. The New Right and the pro-family left alike are convinced that the only form of family making a genuine contribution to society is the child-bearing one. This implies that society has a different, *and lesser*, responsibility to women who aren't mothers, to gay people (at least gay people without children), and to non-procreative family units of all sorts. The hierarchy embodied in this assumed relationship would have no place in a liberatory society. Such a society would neither organize itself nor distribute its resources on the basis of reproductive activity or desire. The decision to bear and/or rear children would simply be one choice among many—not a prerequisite for attaining personal fulfillment or making a social contribution.

By the same token, the profoundly repressive and anti-sexual undercurrents of our society would be transformed into a celebration of sexual diversity. Sexual activity would be its own justification, and thus would have a completely original role in human experience—that of pleasure. There would be no requirement that sexual encounters take place only within loving relationships or have as their goal reproduction. In fact, in a society comprised of truly independent individuals, there might well be a tendency toward casual sexual interactions of many varieties and with many different partners. Lust would lose its moralistic undertones and the expression of honest physical desire would be normal.[1]

Heterosexuality would not exist as an institutional category. Sexual liberation demands not only the right for certain people to be gay, but the acknowledgment of everyone's freedom and potential to be "queer." (Hence, the New Right is right and the pro-family left is wrong in labeling homosexuality as anti-family.) It is possible to speculate that oppressed sexual minorities like gays have for various reasons and to varying degrees escaped the repressive sexual socialization of the larger society, and therefore may be *more* indicative of what sexual practice will look like in a new society than ordinary heterosexuals. Nevertheless, the real oppression currently associated with violation of compulsory heterosexuality is the price tag of a gay or "sexual freak" lifestyle: the increasing incidence of queerbashings, the self-denial of being "in the closet," the incredible risk of coming out on the job or in one's family, the lack of even basic civil protections, etc. (Some would say that the boredom and dissatisfaction of many heterosexuals is a price exacted by compulsion too.) This concept of deviance, which ruins individual lives and painfully marginalizes masses of people, has no place in a vision dedicated to both sexual choice and variety for individuals and maximizing the potential of a whole society.

Tastes now considered "exotic" (at best), such as S/M[2] and fetishism, would not necessarily fade away, but might become one of many ways to express oneself sexually. Of course, the debate about S/M in particular—whether it is sick, symptomatic of sexism, or revolutionary—rages on. I am not sure that the power plays so characteristic of S/M are unrelated to the oppressive power arrangements of our society. I am sure, though, that purging S/M people involves pointless individual anguish, strategic stupidity at a time when we confront a socially reactionary movement of some proportions, and a political narrowing of a feminist vision of sexual possibilities. Like tastes, the character of a given sexual encounter— passionate, tender, cathartic, frivolous, indifferent—would not be preordained by the sexes of the participants or the depth of feeling of the relationship (or lack of relationship) in which it occurred. The people involved would just be expressing their desires and feelings of the moment.

I feel strongly that developing a feminist politics of sexuality means holding out for all the choices, including but not limited to the "unladylike" ones which have been repressed or experienced in shame: pain, power, and willful loss of self-conscious control. It is not clear that this adds up to an endorsement of every imaginable variety of sex, but neither does it mean coming to consensus about which varieties are in the revolutionary vanguard of sexual practice, while ruling out all the rest as "politically incorrect." I should think that in a better future, we would all experience sexuality of many more kinds than we do now, though preferences might remain in some form. What will not remain are the dynamics of oppression and repression that contaminate the majority's perception of sexual minorities in a society such as ours. In sum, the elimination of institutionalized heterosexuality and homophobia will mean more and better sex for all of us.

LIFESTYLE: DEFINITIONS OF FAMILY AND COMMUNITY

The concrete ways in which people choose to live—where and with whom—were among the first issues examined by contemporary feminists. Lifestyle, however, has become less and less a subject of political scrutiny. I can only understand this silence as a retreat from a radical feminist critique of the family. Helmbold and Hollibaugh are so right when they point out that recent experiments in alternative living have never hurt women, children, or gay people as much as the nuclear family has. The personal justifications for retreat—weariness and frustration, the expressed longings for security, legitimacy, and children (these often go together)—speak poignantly to our need for creative, energizing vision. The fact that 70 percent of U.S. households live in non-nuclear family arrangements (according to the 1980 census) points simultaneously to the actuality of lived alternatives and to the baffling power of family mythology to keep us feeling like we are missing some crucial piece of happiness.

In a socialist-feminist society, the material needs met by families (child care, care for the elderly and disabled, food, clothing, shelter, etc.) would be collectivized, organized perhaps by block or neighborhood. Living arrangements would vary in type and size: individuals would live alone or in groups comprised of all combinations of ages, sexes, and races. They would be long term and short term. Perhaps there would be an occasional heterosexual couple with kids.

Helmbold and Hollibaugh discuss many other needs that are currently met, however imperfectly, by the family: needs for "community," a sense of continuity and history, intimacy and friendship. In a society devoid of economic, emotional, and sexual dependence there would be no reason for the locus of these needs to be the family. The privatization of emotional and sexual life would be radically challenged. People might be as likely to ask for and receive support or sex from neighbors as from co-workers as from lovers, thus changing the very nature of all these relationships. There would not exist the pressure to meet needs for sex and love in the same place or at the same time. The ideology of romantic love which now burdens sexual relationships with economic and emotional baggage and vice versa (especially for women) would disappear. This does not mean that love and intimacy would disappear, just that the role of sexuality would be less distorted and scaled to a more realistic size, making chances for sexual and emotional satisfaction much greater. Monogamy would suffer as a result, since long term partnerships would no longer offer a unique emotional safety and refuge from a dog-eat-dog world, nor would they be the locus of most living arrangements.

AUTHORITY OF ADULTS OVER YOUNG PEOPLE AND THE AGED

In order to forge a vision that will challenge age oppression, we must take up the questions of socialization and sexuality as they apply to young and old people in particular. In a sexist and homophobic society, the issues of young and old people's sexuality, and above all inter-generational sex, are hopelessly muddled in repression and denial. For one, young and old people are not generally accorded the dignity of any independent sexuality at all. When they are perceived as sexual beings, it is almost always in coercive, inter-generational circumstances. Of course, there are real reasons why incest and rape are sometimes considered the only ways that young people relate to sex. During a time of challenge to family and sexual norms, it is not surprising that enormous confusion and loneliness emerge. These feelings can partly account for the prevalence of suicide, "mental illness," drug and alcohol abuse, and definitely incest and battering, all of which come down very hard on young people. There is the additional factor that genuine youthful or aged sexuality is considered illegitimate and embarrassing. For these reasons, "consent" has no meaning because it is thought to be inconceivable for a young or old person to freely desire a sexual encounter with someone much younger or older than themselves. Homophobia has made sure that the popular image of inter-generational sex is of a drooling old man or a sleazy middle-aged man and an innocent young boy; the fact that abusive inter-generational sex is an overwhelmingly heterosexual and incestuous phenomenon cannot touch this myth.

All of this would change. As independent actors, both young and old would be free to choose how and with whom to live and how and with whom to have sex. Obviously, the very young and elderly in need of physical and emotional care-taking would be dependent on others. The experience of this dependence will necessarily be transformed when such care-taking is not a personal or family burden, but a social responsibility of some value. Like others, young and old will exist in an environment sensitive to the sexual nature of all living—from birth to death. Included in this spectrum will be an affirmation of the sexuality of disabled people, something I imagine will greatly influence our standards of beauty and eroticism in the direction of individual tastes and away from prescriptions dictated by oppressive standards unrelated to real life and sexual practice.

The daily, material aspects of child-rearing will be taken care of through collective living and child care arrangements, making biological parents no more than biological parents. People who want to have contact with young children will do so, whether or not they give birth to babies themselves. The important work of socializing human beings will be designed with attention to extending individual potential: intellectual, creative, etc. All people will have the skills to operate on a behavioral and emotional spectrum encompassing the entire male/female polarity as we now know it. Masculinity and femininity will have no real life basis as distinct concepts. Decisions about how to live, with whom to make love or have sex, what work to do—will all be individual ones. Decisions to do mechanical work or clerical work or intellectual work,[3] for example, will occur because one choice really appeals more than others at a given point in time, not because one kind of work is more appropriate for someone of a certain age, gender, class, or race.

Information about sexuality and the opportunity for sexual experimentation will not only be available to young and old people, but controlled by them. There might be community centers, functioning partly to provide people with extra places to sleep, eat, have sex, hang out, or work, when they wanted to.

*   *   *

For those of you skeptically shaking your heads, I am not engaging in some wild fantasy (or nightmare, depending on your perspective) of 24-hour-a-day drug-like euphoria. Nor do I mean to imply that good sex, caring relationships, and positive family situations are not possible for us now, with a great deal of work. Fear, anger, frustration, sadness, to name just a few, will remain part of human experience. Maybe even a bigger part because they will all be wholly permissible for all of us. But in a society where people can really feel and express themselves, great sex, intimacy, and frivolity will be both possible and probable. I can't think of anything I'd rather dream about or fight for.

NOTES

1. Words like "loving," "casual," and "lust" have obvious, value-laden connotations in a sexist society. If possible, I mean them to describe equally satisfying, if different, emotions and interactions.
2. S/M is a form of eroticism based on a consensual exchange of power.
3. Like "loving," "casual," and "lust," "mechanical," "clerical," and "intellectual" are words that imply a hierarchy of what is good or important work. This meaning would no longer hold.

BLACK FAMILY STRUCTURES: FOUNDATIONS FOR THE FUTURE

Gloria I. Joseph*

Writing a comprehensive article on the family as an American institution from a progressive-minded perspective in 1982 is a most formidable task. In my opinion the two authors, Helmbold and Hollibaugh, tried to do the near impossible in "What Holds Us and Hurts Us," and like most attempts at near impossible tasks, their success was mixed. The authors show that they are knowledgeable about the family as an institution from the disciplines and viewpoints of Sociology, Child Development, Psychology, Feminism, and Socialism, but what I found disturbing was the lack of serious and sensitive treatment of racism and classism in the development of their ideas, themes, and creative ventures. To simply mention race and class as crucial issues of a topic is not enough when doing a critical analysis. Racism and classism intrinsically have tentacles that reach out and permeate, influence and are influenced by, all and everything that they touch.

A second problem with the article was that I was never quite sure what was meant by "family," or what was a family and what wasn't. Unless the authors initially set forth their operational definition of the family and then proceed, much of what follows about the nature, the goods and bads of the family, could sound irrelevant to the "realistic" family that many people experience. Nor could I understand the authors being apologetic for being working class, single, lesbian, feminists. They apologize for writing about the family. How odd!

Where you live, whom you live with, and who raises you— THAT is your family—and everyone, even feral children are considered to have a family. Surely these two authors grew up in some social setting. Their families should be considered as legitimate and valid as any other family structure, whether the members were working class, leftist, feminist or not. I refer to family as a social group, related and bound by either common ancestry, marriage, or familiar-

---

*The author wishes to acknowledge and give thanks to Dr. Roseann Bell for her "special effects" in the writing of this article.

ity, and with moral and economic rights, duties, and responsibilities to one another. These members provide sources of intimacy and live under a common roof (or sky) for extended periods of time.

In writing about the family at this time in our history, the problem is not so much one of looking for NEW family structures, as it is one of recognizing, and accurately describing those family structures that already exist and realizing that structure does not impute function. For too long, we the conditioned citizenry have been media victims, seduced by models of so-called "typical" families—"typical" in their composition, structure, roles, and functions. The authors, although knowledgeable about how society seduces us, fell right into the hands of the corrupters. They too selected family characteristics and labeled some good and some bad based on old-fashioned criteria, without giving sufficient attention to the functions of certain family forms.

In the remainder of my response to the article, I shall focus on one of the major omissions in the article—black families and their inclusion and integration in the "Families in a Socialist and Radical Feminist America." Although blacks are the focus of my response, other non-white families (Chicano, Native American) could be similarly addressed. It must also be stated that it is *working class* blacks (employed and unemployed) who are the major contributors to the dominant family structures discussed. The experiences of these blacks have fundamentally been the experiences of poor whites as well.

The discussion of any and all subjects in the U.S. must specifically address blacks and therefore racism. This is necessary because our American society is in actuality two societies—one black and the other white. (For further discussion of this, see my essay in *Women in Revolution*, edited by Lydia Sargent, South End Press, Boston, 1981, pp. 91-106.)

During our lifetime we usually experience two different families—the one of orientation (the one we are born into), and the one we establish either after marriage, through our own procreation, or simply by leaving the nest and "going it on our own." There are certain characteristics of the family that are universal to all societies, such as common ancestry through blood or marriage, economic support, source of intimacy. Naturally, there is variation among the characteristics across cultures. Black families in America certainly exemplify variations from the so-called typical American family. (Other ethnic groups also are at variance with the "typical" American family, but my focus is *blacks*.) Despite facts to the contrary, "typical" refers to that oft-described but only occasionally actualized nuclear family with two parents, one male and the other female, with a certain number of children (2.5), with the male adult the *bread winner* and definitely the head of the household. The children are pretty much assured that their lives will be better than their parents' or at least as good.

I do not think that the family as an institution—regardless of how it is described—is dying. Nor are there drastic changes in the kinds of family structures that exist. What we have happening today is a SHIFT, a numerical shift within the already existing family structures, which are being called "New Types of Families" or Non-traditional Family and Marriage Forms. Families—a conglomeration of associations and relationships that exist among a group of people for the purpose of fulfilling certain needs (economic, emotional, physical, and sexual) and as a source of psychological and material survival—have always taken many forms in America. Those families whose configurations deviated from the "typical" nuclear family form simply were not popularized as legitimate, American-style desirable households. They were given feckless names with derogatory connotations, like broken homes, welfare homes, fatherless homes, matriarchal households, culture of poverty homes, and deprived homes.

The history of black families in America will show that there have always been: extended families; single parent families; (biologically) parentless families, female heads of households; households with women (some of whom were lesbians and others not) raising the children; and families with both parents working and at times living apart due to a scarcity of jobs. And there is no scientific proof that one family form produces "better" children than any other. We do know that our society with its capitalistic self and gross income inequalities contributes more to the delinquency of children than any traditional or non-traditional family structure does.

Blacks (families) like any other groups in America that have never been fully integrated economically, socially, and politically into the basic threads of the American way of life experience the effects of monumental changes in the society in ways that differ from the effects that the changes have on mainstream white families. For example, during the Industrial Revolution, (white) extended families lost their meaning in the sense that nuclear families flourish in societies where individualism and personal achievements are valued. The extended family continued to flourish for blacks long after the Industrial Revolution. This is not to say that the economic phenomenon had no effect on black families; it is to say that other forces in the lives of blacks so outweighed the forces/influences of the Industrial Revolution that the extended family flourished and is still operating, although at a lesser level. For numerous reasons, but largely due to racism which influenced the economic conditions, black families have wittingly and skillfully constructed their unique family configurations based on common sense and the need for survival in an alien and hostile society.

Since the initial kidnapping of Africans to American s(p)oils, a variety of family forms have existed: The extended family is as old as Africa; common law marriages were never a lost art among blacks; black women have been heads of households for centuries; black women, widowed by "death or left" or "never been married" have raised children on their own (with a little help from their families and/or friends); two career marriages are definitely nothing new— black adults have been working not only two but frequently three jobs in a two-parent household; living together sans vows, or plain old "shacking up" has been a popular practice for decades upon decades; gay males, either very flamboyant or hiding behind marriages, are old hat; swingers—ask any jive-ass Negro about that! Today we are seeing these family forms flourishing among white families but with updated, "respectable" titles. These modern day non-traditional family and marriage forms have very few "new" options to offer black families. Observe the following chart:

Non-Traditional Family and Marriage Forms or Alternative Life Styles—The Changing American Family	*Traditional/ Historical Black Family Forms*
1. Communal Living	1. The extended family which often included members not related by ancestry or marriage.
2. Two-Career Marriages	2. Traditionally both black parents worked for economic survival.
3. Single Parenting	3. Black women frequently raised children on their own. A very frequent practice since the 1800's.
4. Co-habitation	4. Common law marriage or "shacking up" or "living with."
5. Open Marriage	5. A variation on "running around" or "slipping around" or two-timing with or without the knowledge of the other partner.
6. Double Domicile or Double Residency; parents working and living in different locales. (E.g., college professors teaching at different institutions.)	6. Black men have historically had to migrate in order to secure jobs. Black women doing domestic work ("sleep in" jobs) were separated from their families.

7. Swinging—The exchange of sexual partners among two or more married couples.	7. This practice although not new to black life was not categorized or characterized as a legitimate family arrangement.
8. Lesbian/Gay Households	8. An increase in the numbers who are openly admitting their non-heterosexual dimensions.

And two recent "new" trends in living arrangements in the black scheme of things are: the single status "whole" woman and the poly-nuclear family.

The U.S. family rather than being in a true state of transition, more accurately speaking is in a state of shifting categories that have long existed in black communities. In the past it was predominantly black families that felt the severest burdens of economic oppression— low incomes, underemployment, unemployment, no income. These conditions forced blacks to initiate and practice, out of necessity, living and family arrangements that met their monetary, social, emotional, and sexual needs. Under the current government administration, increasing numbers of non-black families are experiencing economic conditions similar to those previously experienced by blacks. Consequently they are adopting so-called non-traditional marriage and family forms and "new types of families" which basically are traditional black creations. In addition the women's movement has undeniably played an influential role in shaping the changing attitudes towards family forms, living arrangements, and personal life styles.

In this final section I will concentrate on some of the ways blacks have responded to their social environment.

One unquestionable finding of recent research is that black family structure is experiencing an increase in the proportion of black female-headed households. They are almost as prevalent as those families headed by black males. The proportion of black families headed by women with no husband has doubled since 1940. These families constituted about 35 percent of all black families in 1975 compared to 18 percent in 1940.

This finding is doubly important because many of these families live in poverty. In 1959 about 30 percent of all poor black families were maintained by women. This proportion grew to 54 percent in 1969 and reached 67 percent in 1974. (See Jeanette Jennings, *An Analysis of Black Working Poor Female-Headed Families* [paper presented at the 8th Annual Conference of Black Families in America, Louisville, Kentucky, March 12-14, 1981], pp. 2-3.)

The increase in female headed households among blacks may be attributed to four *main* factors: (1) Black women not getting married. Never married women comprised about 9 percent of all black women heading families in 1950, but increased to 22 percent in 1975. (2) Married men leaving home. The degree of misunderstanding, frustration, and anger that is expressed between males and females in their intimate relations frequently results in male aggression and violence which often leads to separation. (3) Black women widowed. Death from the military, the street (drugs and bullets), jails, and early natural causes. And (4) Divorce.

The category "single women households" includes the working poor (i.e. low income women with children) and upper income women with or without children. Both groups include women who are developing and creating meaningful lives in their single status, but by far the majority of single women households are the working poor. These women face severe economic problems. In particular, the black female-headed household, while becoming increasingly prevalent, has many serious problems. It must not be assumed that these working class poor females are associated with the "joys of freedom of choice" or the "liberation from the kitchen" or any other such proclamations. These women have a lower median earning than their white counterparts, and are more heavily concentrated in low skill, low paying jobs. In 1900 women represented only 18 percent of the total labor force. In the same year, black women had a labor force participation rate of 41.2 percent. In 1975 women were 40 percent of the labor force and 49 percent of black women were in the labor force. In 1974, black families headed by a male with a wife in the paid labor force had a median income of $12,982; with a wife not in the paid labor force the figure was $7,773, whereas a female headed household with no husband present earned $4,465.

Children present a double problem for the low wage black female worker. Poverty rates for children in families headed by females were 52 percent as compared with only 9 percent for males in a similar situation. In 1974, the poverty rate for black children under 18 years of age was almost four times that of white children (41 percent and 11 percent respectively). The vast majority—70 percent—of these poor black children were in families maintained by a woman. So we can see the grim life that is in store for the black woman who is head of her household. It is a situation brought about by the classist, racist, and sexist order of American capitalism. Black women do not willingly opt for a situation of poverty, excessive hard work with few rewards (exploitation), and all its concommitant miseries.

The reasons for the increase of female headed households is part and parcel of the reality of the male shortage. In 1971, black sociologist Jacquelyn Jackson conducted a study of census records over the past 50 years and concluded that

> there are not enough Black males for Black females and since non-Black males rarely marry Black females, a sufficient supply of males for Black females is not available at this point in time. Hence, in line with one prominent social policy, even if all available Black males were to amass highly significant gains in their educational, occupational employment, and income levels tomorrow, some Black females would yet be without mates. Thus, there is a critical need to concentrate not only on improving socio-economic levels of Black males so that they may be in better positions to support their families . . .; but there also must be simultaneous concentration on improving the socio-economic positions of Black females who are likely to be bereft of mates, so that they too may improve significantly the opportunities to be derived for themselves and their families. (Jennings, p. 3.)

As mentioned earlier, all the single black females are not in the working poor category. A growing number of black women are developing and creating meaningful, "whole" lives in their single status. The majority of black single sisters still hold on to the elusive American dream of finding at any and all cost Mr. Right, (or Mr. Wrong if the "right" one doesn't come along) and settling down with a home, car, children, and work. But the trend set by the "new" single woman with the "new" outlook is becoming increasingly more popular and attractive as black women face the reality of their situation. These "women identified women" are using their energies developing new attitudes and are taking new strides that do not include the incessant search for a husband. They are realizing the importance of female networking and the value of female friendship which can be as endearing and sustaining as any other relationship. They are learning to strike a balance between their sexual and emotional needs. Men are still very much a part of the lives of many of these women but there is the realization that they can become whole and satisfied individuals with or without a man as the center of their lives and well being. They are experiencing satisfaction in their friendships with both males and females on the platonic level; they are raising children if they so desire; they are living in lesbian relationships; they are purchasing homes and seeking satisfying careers. They do not see themselves doomed to the role of an "old maid" if their lives are not dependent on, dedicated to, or dominated by males.

It was interesting to note that very little research on black women includes lesbianism as a viable way of life. Usually if lesbianism is mentioned, it is rapidly dismissed. Lesbianism is definitely a way of life for a growing number of black women, and that fact should neither be denied nor ignored. On college campuses, where the influence of the women's movement and the politics of lesbianism flourished much more than in black communities, the increase of young women who refer to themselves as lesbians is particularly noticeable. You will find black females, many of whom are the most politically and intellectually astute among the female population, openly declaring a way of life that does not place men in the center or near center of their scopes. They depend on women to fulfill their basic emotional, sexual, spiritual, psychological, and intellectual needs.

Counter to the position of single women or lesbianism as whole life arrangements is the position of certain black scholars who feel that the root and quality of black life is in the relationship established between men and women. One such male writer is Haki Madhubuti. In his book, *People of the Sun: Men-Women Relationships* (Third World Press, 1981), he analyzes and assesses the black male/female relationship in America. After examining monogamy and polygamy, Madhubuti concludes that the most suitable family form for blacks is the poly-nuclear family. The poly-nuclear family is described as consisting of one male and two or more wives and its advocates claim that if functioning "properly" it will solve many problems that both black men and women now face on a daily basis. Quoting from Madhubuti's book, the poly-nuclear family would "provide economic and physical security; household help; help raising the children; release severe depression and loneliness; eliminate adultery; eliminate prostitution; aid in intellectual development for the children; provide stable fathers for children; develop a collective attitude in adults and children." The ideal housing would be a large house of two or three apartments with many rooms so that each person could have their own space to develop an expression of their own individuality. The possibility of each wife maintaining her own apartment would not be ruled out.

The poly-nuclear family theoretically offers solutions to the male shortage, and the economic, social, and political problems facing blacks. However, it is formulated on a questionable initial premise: namely, "That the root and quality of black life is in the relationship established between black men and women" (p. 48). The theory is also seriously lacking in a class analysis. It seems that with black women currently seeking a new equality in their relationships with black men and economics being a fundamental problem facing blacks, then what black women need are better paying jobs—not sharing a man! Madhubuti makes the statement that "Within the poly-nuclear family the male would still be the head of the household but decisions are to be made in *consultation* with the wives." The question must be raised as to why the male should uncontestedly be designated as head of the household? The poly-nuclear family as a new solution to current social and economic problems facing blacks fails to take into consideration: black feminist ideology, a class analysis, and a realistic understanding of the cultural and social values of Afro-Americans.

The concluding section of Helmbold and Hollibaugh's article is a discussion of "Revolutionary Tumult: Feminism and Socialism Engaged." How black families fit into the Socialist Radical Feminist America will depend on the extent to which the "new" American deals with racism. Black family forms are diversified and have proven their resiliency and flexibility and adaptability. They have also accepted most other forms of family arrangements. Black families would not have much difficulty fitting into a new Socialist society that contained a variety of living arrangements. It would be a welcome comfort to be "legitimized" for a change.

As traditionally defined and practiced in U.S. society a family is neither a necessary nor rewarding social force. It is only the roles assumed by the individual members and the misuse of the power assigned to those roles that makes a family a negative or undesirable force.

REJOINDER
Lois Rita Helmbold

Today, three years after we began work on our essay, both the right and the left attack women's rights and alternatives to traditional families. Right-wing proponents of repressive and authoritarian families use anti-abortion, anti-ERA, and the Family Protection Act to wage campaigns to force conformity to their standards, at the same time cutting social welfare benefits and programs. On the left, white heterosexual men attempt to wrest away from the women's movement the issues of family and the quality of daily life. Feminists, hippies, and some leftists have self-consciously tried to create new ways to live; among the entire population there has been increased divorce and single parenthood. Now the boys, such as Michael Lerner of Friends of Families and John Judis of *In These Times*, are attempting to exert their hegemony over this arena, defining politically correct ways in which people should form traditional relationships and families and then stay in them, a position which many sectarian Marxist-Leninist groups have long advocated.

The economic crisis, our own aging, and our personal/political experiences have changed feminists and leftists. I have spent my adult life living in self-consciously collective households, sometimes calling ourselves a family, and alternately living alone. Recently, a year of unemployment following two years of marginal employment pushed me to move 2600 miles across the country for a job. Not having a wife of either sex who would follow me (and not wanting such a relationship either), I live alone, desperately missing my extended "family," which consists mostly of white lesbians, but includes black and white, gay and straight, men and women, adults and children, some of whom have shared life with me for twelve years. I miss supper table conversations; figuring out with roommates how to replace a flooding hot water heater; help with problems, mundane and serious; and people who listen to my day's worth of stories while I listen to theirs. I am afraid that economic and political pressures will make it increasingly more difficult for me to construct such a life again, as nuclear monogamy, both gay and straight, becomes the norm, and collectivity a relic of our hippie pasts.

Ellen Herman's response continues some of the arguments for future creativity and growth which Amber and I originally made. I agree with Herman that emotion and sexuality are key motivations in life. With the exception of religion, the family is the only realm considered appropriate for the expression of emotion in this society. Herman's view of the future is similar to ours: an openness to invent what we do not have, the risk-taking to experiment and to hope. Yet Herman's ideas are pie in the sky. I want to share that pie, but we need more thought and practice on how we are going to get there. Herman simply states the way that life will be after the revolution; she does not offer insights into the process, the forces that will support change, nor the forces that will impede the realization of hopes. Herman, Joseph, and Amber and I all share this shortcoming. Neither Herman nor Joseph addresses the dynamics of families which are so hurtful. We will not rid ourselves of these oppressions so easily.

Gloria Joseph rightly criticizes our failure to offer a clear definition of the family. Her definition—whom you live with and who raises you—is a useful description. Her argument that the multiple forms which we envision in the future already exist in the present in black communities is a point well taken, a valuable addition to the topic. Yet she fails to address the fact that the family is a normative institution which prescribes and proscribes certain behavior. It is this institutional demand for conformity to narrowly specified behavior which must also change: the social context as well as the composition of particular households.

It is in this context that Amber and I have addressed the family. Not only do we think that our perspective as lesbian, non-parent, white working class intellectuals living outside traditional families is unique and valuable, but also that it is rare. When the left has finally come to grips with issues that involve both economics and emotion, it is as a backlash to the women's movement (parts of which have also retreated from earlier more radical stands). It is white, heterosexual men who are defining the territory, the same people who always defined the territory. Rather than being apologetic, our intent was to make clear why our perspective is different, and why we believe that, as persons excluded from families, it is so valuable.

"WHAT HOLDS US AND HURTS US" A LAST WORD

Amber Hollibaugh

Lois and I sat down to write the article three years ago. Seeing each response makes clear how the analysis of the family has changed and deepened during that time. Our article and the two responses are a start towards a new way of exploring the diversity of experience as it's lived and understood through class, race, gender, and sexual preference. Each responder used the original article as a jumping off place for her own work and each developed ideas about the family that Lois and I had not grappled with. Together they make up an exciting discussion of the family.

The original impulse behind writing the article was our discomfort with left and feminist explanations of the *experience* of the family. We were ambivalent about the role and meaning of "the family" in the past and for the future. We did not want to rush in and snatch the family from the jaws of the New Right like Michael Lerner. Our criticisms are much too serious for that approach. But we had also been nourished as children raised in working class homes and didn't want that reality shelved either or just called false consciousness. It was exactly because we were uncomfortable everywhere we looked that we thought to try and unravel the puzzle of the family another way: we would try to name each need that the family was responsible for and separate that genuine reaction from the structures that imposed all needs on the family unit. We were foggy in our definitions of the family but right on track in our focusing in on the powerful needs the family responds to.

Certain questions seemed to rise right off the pages as I reread the article and responses. . .

> How can we really recognize critical differences in form and meaning of "family" for people of different class, race, and gender experiences?
>
> Would the struggles in the family be similar in the long run or would the different structures that the family has assumed for different groups historically change the direction of the future?

Would the New Right's vicious responses to sex and gender (like its newest campaign against Herpes taken up now by the Eagle Forum) finally force the left and the women's movement to develop a radical notion of pleasure and desire?

How is pleasure radical? With whom? Why?

My list could cover pages. Looking back at our work in the paper there are holes and missing understandings I would take on were we writing it today. At that time the "pro-family" drift of segments of the left had only just begun. Issues of class and race have come more in focus for me in the widening discussions of "Difference and Diversity" that is now called the Politics of Difference by feminists of color. And finally, I would try to take apart the reactionary sentiment that is surfacing in parts of the women's movement on issues of sexual variation and sexual desire.

But this was a beginning for both Lois and me . . . a place to set down developing questions that we thought were critical to any ongoing discussion of the family. The responses pushed the boundaries of our work far beyond its original abilities. Now it is for other writers to take this and develop it anew . . . to continue taking up these issues that go to the heart of shaping the visions that encompass such radical issues as love, community, passion, difference—that can begin to describe what the world could be for all of us in the future. It is a challenge that engages: the thought of a culture where these sorts of issues are the priority, not missiles; where change is a welcome notion which is part of our need to grow and become. It is this combination of change and continuity that will be the basis for our new ideas of family, our new ideas of community, our new ideas of trust.

VI. THE ECONOMY

PARTICIPATORY PLANNING

Michael Albert and Robin Hahnel

INTRODUCTION

For many people socialism is an economic concept synonymous with public ownership of the means of production and centralized planning of economic activity. But admittedly this working definition implies different things for different people. For *anti*-socialists public ownership and central planning eliminate the critical safe-guards of individual liberty—private property and freedom of contract. Therefore, for them "socialism" is totalitarianism. For most *pro*-socialists public ownership and central planning eliminate economic exploitation, class divisions, and economic decision-making according to the profit principle. Moreover, for these socialists, since the economic "base" is presumed dominant in the long run, "socialism" also implies eventual economic and political democracy and an end to alienation. But the total failure of public ownership and centralized planning in the Soviet Union—there is neither economic self-management, political democracy, cultural diversity, or social solidarity—has led a growing minority of socialists to reject economistic definitions of socialism. Many are critically examining the institutional implications of public ownership and central planning, and searching for alternative economic forms more consistent with a broader socialist vision.

As members of this growing minority we refuse to minimize the failures of "existing socialism." Considering the alienation and power-lessness of Soviet workers, the ignominious history of the Soviet Gulag, the complete secrecy shrouding Chinese Communist decision-making, the material privileges of the economic and political elite in Eastern Europe, the failure to overcome patriarchal injustice throughout the "socialist" bloc, and the innumerable instances of national chauvinism being accorded priority over international solidarity in the foreign policies of all "existing socialist" states: it is painfully obvious to us that a socialism characterized by self-management, solidarity, and diversity has yet to materialize. Nevertheless, we do *not* count ourselves among those in this minority, such as the dominant tendency in international social democracy, who are so bedazzled by the failing of "existing socialism" that they become re-blinded to the horrors of capitalism to the point of settling for private ownership "moderated" by a Swedish-style "safety-net" of welfare programs. *Nor* do we count ourselves among those like the Yugoslavs who reject planning and embrace free markets as the only mechanism capable of breathing self-management into a publicly owned economy. *Instead* we count ourselves among those committed to a broad vision of socialism including not only an economic transformation but also a transformation of political, kinship, and cultural/community relations.[1] And regarding the economy, the primary subject of this essay, we consider ourselves among those in the tradition of the council communists, syndicalists, and guild socialists, convinced that *both* public ownership *and* planning are necessary though not alone sufficent ingredients for a socialist economy.

In other words, while "existing socialism" is certainly not "socialist," its problems are *not* due to public ownership or planning per se. Nor is a solution to be found in tolerating private ownership or free markets. The problem is with hierarchical central planning accompanied by political authoritarianism, ongoing patriarchy, and "cultural homogenization." For in combination these yield new forms of class division and new ruling elites. The solution *for the economic sphere* is to be found in a different kind of democratic planning, capable of expressing collective economic self-management, and therefore compatible with the development of participatory and democratic political, cultural, and kinship relations.

CAPITALIST ECONOMIC RELATIONS

In all economies there is production, consumption, and some means for getting what is produced by some people into the hands of others who use it. In capitalism production occurs primarily in privately owned corporations, consumption occurs primarily in households, and allocation between different corporations and households occurs via more or less competitive markets. As a result, under capitalism the distribution of wealth and income is highly unequal and cycles of unemployment and inflation cause great dislocation and hardship. But, in addition, below these readily apparent problems there lie other layers of failure knitted into the very fabric of capitalism.

In capitalism people do not conceive, manage, and coordinate their own economic efforts. Instead the great majority sell their ability to work to others who must constantly strive to squeeze as much work as possible out of people who have little or no say over what they will produce or how they will produce it, and who do not directly benefit from whatever success their efforts might yield. This hardly reads like a formula for *either* high economic productivity *or* meaningful economic activity (for workers endowed with the capacity to conceptualize, analyze, and evaluate the effects of their own actions) but for an economic system full of contradictions and alienated workers. This is a system in which the interests of workers and capitalists are fundamentally opposed both regarding the selling price of the commodity they exchange—the worker's labor power—and regarding the use that will be made of this commodity once it is sold. It is in the capitalist's interest not only to negotiate the lowest possible real wage today, but to organize the work process so as to minimize the workers' bargaining strength in the future. It is in the capitalist's interest to maximize the quantity of work effort extracted from his employees' laboring capacities irrespective of how debilitating the effects might be on the worker him/her self. And it is in the capitalist's interest to organize work today so as to preserve his ability to direct it and benefit from it in the future. On the other hand, it is in the worker's interest not only to negotiate the highest possible real wage for selling his/her labor power today, but to have this power used in ways that minimize drudgery and maximize personal satisfaction, and that enhance her/his bargaining strength over wages and work conditions in the future. Besides their ownership of the means of production and ideological propaganda, the principal weapons capitalists use to keep wages down, extract as much work as possible out of "their" commodity, labor power, and preserve and expand their power to do both, are their ability to control the choice of technology and the internal system of supervision and reward. It is only logical that capitalists would utilize these prerogatives to deskill workers, make them more docile, limit communication among them, and pit them against one another. And of course, any divisions among workers that *originate outside* the workplace will necessarily be exploited within it. Women will be paid less than men and used for "women's work," which will be less rewarding and less empowering. Black, Chicano, and other third world workers will be paid less than whites and saddled with the most dangerous, demeaning, and debilitating jobs. In a society in which kinship and community relations are oppressive, expectations and attitudes on the shop floor will embody both racist and sexist stereotypes.

The general point is that economic institutions are not neutral devices with no effects of their own. Rather they structure the *kinds* of outcomes we can generate through our economic efforts. Private ownership of the means of production inevitably implies not only material inequality and production for profit instead of human need, but also the progressive dehumanization of work. But markets, the other hallmark of capitalism, also impose restrictive role requirements. The market forces each of us to consider only our own personal well-being, and not that of people who produce what we consume or consume what we produce. Knowing only prices and nothing about the situations of others, each individual has *no choice* but to make decisions that are completely self-centered. Not only will we suffer if we fail to act competitively, but we do not even have the information necessary to act differently. For the market gives us no information concerning the situation of others. When we eat a salad the market systematically deletes information about the migrant workers who picked it. We thus come to see "things" as but means to self-centered material ends. We go all out for "number one" in work and consumption because *within the system* this is the sensible thing to do, however anti-social and ultimately destructive the collective results may be—Adam Smith notwithstanding.

So like private ownership of the means of production, the market too is not a neutral institution. It affects our very personalities and desires. Markets provide few social goods such as parks, public transportation, clean air, and public health care, relative to private goods such as lawn fertilizer, automobiles, and "beauty" aides. Each individual must accommodate to this situation. To some extent the system does deliver what we ask for. But it is also true that we largely confine our requests to things which we have good reason to believe will be available. When living in a market society it makes sense to develop market-oriented tastes. Trying to buy dignity or a sense of collective solidarity at the new shopping mall is futile, so it is advisable to let these desires weaken and go unexpressed. Over the counter it is much easier to get a new lawn trimmer or a bottle of beer. Better to cultivate and express these tastes which can be met.

Love Canal is a poisonous sewage pit; we have spent one and a half trillion dollars to create a military capable of killing everyone on the planet twelve times over; there were 20,000 murders in 1978, 2,000 committed by people under the age of 18; 30% of the elderly poor have no indoor flush toilets; auto styling changes from 1956 to 1960 cost $24 billion; and approximately 250,000 households buy pet food for people not pets. This is testimony to the crimes built into the fabric of capitalist economic relations. And, at the extreme, far from being a deplorable error, the bombed out defoliated moonscape that covers substantial portions of Southeast Asia is a natural "product" of capitalism, a system which is equally capable of leaving to ruin its own cities and citizens when profit so dictates. That something must be done is becoming ever more widely recognized, yet for a variety of reasons socialists are in disarray. Not the least of our problems is that whatever their accomplishments, and these are many, the countries that call themselves "socialist" do not exert a great attraction for our fellow citizens. Is this due to our neighbors' ignorance or their perspicacity?

"EXISTING SOCIALIST ECONOMICS"

One alternative to capitalist economic relations is to nationalize ownership of society's means of production and establish central planning according to socially agreed criteria. Some of the benefits of this are evident. Unemployment, business cycles, and inflation virtually disappear. With the major cause of unequal wealth socialized, material inequality should be considerably diminished. Production need no longer be for profit but could serve social goals.

It's no wonder that this model has exerted considerable *intellectual* attraction as an alternative to capitalism. At the same time, at least in the U.S., it has exerted little *popular* appeal. Despite the theoretical advantages of socialized ownership and central planning, the Soviet Union and other "existing socialist" countries are anathema to most in the United States. Is this entirely due to anti-communist propaganda?

What is the situation of a Soviet worker? Income is steady, but worklife is remarkably like that in the U.S. As here, there is a dictatorship in the workplace—a manager exercises unchallenged authority. Soviet workers no more determine the organization of the workplace, the pace of work, or how funds will be invested than do U.S. workers. And like U.S. workers, for the most part their motivation to work is individual material gain with very little concern for the effects of their economic activities on others. As here, the situation of Soviet workers leaves them no other options. And even if Soviet political life were to become democratic—which would be an immense advance—Soviet economic relations would still be dehumanizing, and the limitations on worker power and personal development severe.

In the Soviet Union, planners decide on economic projects according to two major criteria: the perceived well-being of various sectors of the population, and the furtherance of the planners' own interest including maintenance of their monopoly of economic decision-making power. Planners, managers, and intellectuals enjoy many advantages compared with manual workers. And the economic programs they choose enhance these advantages by expanding the bureaucracy and increasing its monopoly of knowledge relative to everyone else's. For the planners, huge military expenditures or nuclear power development, both of which require elite management, are more desirable than such things as locally manageable solar energy programs.

The possibility of democracy in the Soviet workplace is precluded by the existence of command relations between local economic units and the planning center. The planners make all the most important decisions; the units must carry them out. The units may often negotiate with the planners, in particular providing information (and disinformation) about what they can and cannot do. But the units do not exert national decision-making power, and are even denied information needed for making local decisions socially in light of the needs of others. Clearly, it would be disadvantageous to the central planners for workers to meet in democratic councils to make local economic decisions. From the planners' point of view, it is necessary to have an agent of the planning board—a manager—within the factory to tell the workers what they *have to do* and to insure that they carry out their appointed tasks effectively. This manager can be held accountable by the central planners, whereas a democratic council would be a permanent threat. No wonder the Soviet workplace looks so much like its U.S. counterpart. In both there is institutional pressure to keep power from the work-force. In the U.S. it is private ownership and the market that accomplish this; in the Soviet Union it is the central planning procedure and "one man management."

Does the Soviet Union also have a class structure? By a class we mean a group of people that has an economic position that gives it shared interests, consciousness, and even personality types different from and opposed to those of people occupying other economic positions. By a ruling class we mean a class that attains dominance over the determination of economic outcomes in a society, and that uses its dominance to accrue social, psychological, political, and material advantages.

Under capitalism the capitalists are the ruling class which has power over the working class. There is, however, another class of considerable importance in advanced capitalism which is frequently unnoticed. Managers, engineers, technicians, highly placed academics, bureaucrats, doctors, and lawyers occupy economic positions that are different from those occupied by workers *or* capitalists. These people have considerable power over their own work life and often over the work life of many clients or subordinates as well. They do conceptual labor, defining the set of policy options available to tackle problems. They often define or administer the economic activity of others. They don't generally own significant capital, and, like workers, are frequently employed by capitalists. But their income vastly exceeds that of other workers, and they have not been de-skilled but are the recipients of those skills previously residing in the population at large. These conceptual workers with high incomes and security, relative autonomy in decision-making, and a near monopoly on advanced education constitute what we call the "coordinator class." Against capital they seek higher wages and greater autonomy, up to and including control over economic planning. Against the working class they struggle to maintain their relative monopoly of administrative skills and scientific knowledge. Moreover, under capitalism, in between this intellectual elite and the workers themselves there is a large "middle element" which is more or less caught on the fence. Teachers, social workers, nurses, and technicians: these people share much in common with both coordinators and workers.[2]

So in the U.S. we have three classes—the capitalists, the workers, and the coordinators—and also a rather large group situated between the latter two. But when speaking of modern economic systems only two kinds are mentioned: capitalism and socialism. The first is obviously the system in which the capitalists are the ruling class. The second is the system in which the workers rule. But what of "existing socialist" economies? Who rules them? And since it isn't the workers, why call these systems socialist?

We have already described how planners determine economic goals in the Soviet economy and how managers within each factory oversee the implementation of these goals. There is a division between the conceptual work performed by planners and managers (and other intellectuals such as scientists, engineers, ideologues, etc.) and the executionary work of the working class itself which carries out the plans and orders of others. The Soviet economy does not put the workers in control, but rather the coordinators. Thus it is not a socialist but a coordinator economy. The central plan has replaced the market as the chief allocative mechanism. But one thing clearly has not happened: all have not become workers and workers do not manage the economy in their own material and spiritual interest. The division of labor between conception and execution has replaced private ownership as the key to class struggle.

In the early years after an anti-capitalist revolution, revolutionary élan will be relatively successful in eliciting workers' cooperation. But if workers do not control their economy, and if instead the coordinator class consolidates its power and expands its privileges, after a time élan fades and a different motivation for work must be found. If the coordinator class has consolidated power, socialist solidarity will not be the motivating force because this would require eliminating the workplace hierarchy, thereby undermining the "reason for being" of the coordinators. If the coordinators permitted the social relations of factory life to alter enough to generate socialist motivations, work activity would create people no longer willing to accept the centralization, elitism, and authoritarianism intrinsic to the system of coordinator dominance. Self-destruction has never been and likely never will be a ruling class program.

As under capitalism, there is an intimate interaction between factory structure and allocation relations in coordinator economies such that each limits the possible forms of the other. With the possibility of a cooperative self-motivated worklife ruled out, the coordinators must turn to material rewards to get the working class to carry out their allotted tasks. But for personal income to be valuable enough to motivate hard work, two conditions must be met. First, the society must produce an ample supply of consumer goods for purchase by *individuals*. And, second, there must be no readily available *social* means for attaining comparable or more fulfilling lives than private consumption allows. The trend should be clear: in addition to authoritarianism, extreme individualism and consumerism also appear in this "planned" economy, though in a new non-capitalist guise, serving the interests of a new, non-capitalist ruling class.

So, as Marxists should anticipate, the U.S. working class's hostility to what goes under the name "socialism" proves to be more than a mindless response to propaganda. The system workers dislike is not "their system." U.S. workers' distaste for the Soviet economy parallels the hostility they rightfully feel toward the coordinators within capitalism itself.[3] If socialism is to appeal to workers, it will have to be something other than an extension of domination by a coordinator elite.

Nor will it suffice to simply do away with the central planners by substituting a market in their place while keeping property socialized—as in Yugoslavia. As we have argued above markets are not neutral. They have negative implications built into their very role requirements. Those who wish socialism with markets preserved want, as Marx put it, "competition without the pernicious effects of competition." They "want the impossible, namely the conditions of bourgeois existence without the necessary consequences of these conditions."

With central planning the individual is subordinated to the whole; with markets the individual is isolated from the whole. In neither case do individual wills come into contact with one another to alter in the light of new insights and to then resolve themselves in the development of a "collective will" that is the sum of many reformulated contributions. To replace planning with markets merely replaces the central coordinators with local managerial coordinators and does little to allow workers to socially define their own economic existence. They still take orders from superiors and suffer economic consequences beyond their reach.

LESSONS FOR SOCIALISM

A socialist economy—one that manifests the power of workers and consumers over all economic outcomes—cannot allow the maintenance of capitalist private ownership. But neither can it allow the knowledge advantage of coordinators to replace the property advantage of capitalists as the new locus of economic power. There must be a way to ensure that knowledge and the capacity to plan and conceive social options are also "socialized"—that is, made accessible to all and not the "property" of a privileged few.

Furthermore, replacing the market with a central planning bureau, while allowing for a more conscious approach to economic decision-making, does not permit different groups of producers and consumers to initiate and coordinate their own economic activities in a social way. The market assumes that many pairs of parties, through exchanges, will reach an optimal outcome, but it ignores the impact the exchanges might have on people other than the two parties involved. It treats all economic decisions as if only two parties were affected by the outcome. (For example, the market does not take account of the social costs of an agreement in which a firm sells a polluting car to a customer.) The best central planning can do is sum up people's individual preferences for final goods and calculate the optimal work plan to achieve those goals. This does not permit workers in a machine shop in Massachusetts any more say over their own work than they have over what and how things will be done in an assembly plant in California. Nor does it allow a social dialogue between economic actors so that their respective desires may take account of one another's needs and potentials. In effect, even a genuinely democratic central plan treats all economic decisions as if everyone were equally affected by the outcome of each decision, and as if desires were most respresentative of deepest personal needs and capabilities when expressed in ignorance of their impact on other people. But since most economic decisions affect more than two parties, but not all parties equally, neither markets nor central planning can provide each party with decision-making input in proportion to the degree to which it is affected. And since ideally desires should be informed so that they can reflect social interrelationships as well as private dispositions, again neither allocation mechanism is optimal.*

Consider the following simple example. Three people wish to go to the movies together. Which movie should they go to? Under a market mechanism, the one with the money decides. Under central planning, if the planner determines that two out of three prefer *Modern Times*, then that is the one they go to. But if instead the three people spoke to one another—as friends would do—they might find that two have only a slight preference for *Modern Times*, while the third saw this very movie just the night before, or they might find that as a result of their dialogue their desires change, partially in mutual compromise and solidarity, partially owing to new information. Only with this knowledge of the social dimension can decisions be reached that are truly optimal.

Therefore, for us, a socialist economy requires: (1) the abolition of private ownership of the means of production; (2) the elimination of a fixed division of labor between conception and execution; and (3) an allocation mechanism that promotes decision-making that is both participatory *and* collective. Where central planning makes workers passive and markets make them individualistic; and where an economy dominated by *either* central planners *or* local managers will eventually resort to material incentives—socialist allocation must promote worker initiative, consumer sociality, and increasingly rely on solidarity and self-management as the dominant incentives to work. We think the system we shall now describe meets these three requirements. We present in turn how production, consumption, and allocation might function in a socialist economy.

---

*Technically, one could argue that a benign central planner armed with each individual's preferences in light of every possible social context could in fact find the optimal plan. This argument is irrelevant, however, because the communication of so much information—literally an infinity of preferences for every individual and unit—is impossible, and also because it precludes social interaction, thus ensuring that over time individuals' personalities will become so asocial that the drift of society and the economy will once again be individualistic in the worst sense. Our solution makes all this information manageable without excluding its essential social aspects, aspects that are necessarily excluded under a market or standard central planning mechanism.

SOCIALIST PRODUCTION

The most general decision-making criterion of a socialist work-force should be to maximize the fulfillment and development of every worker consistent with equal consideration for all. Each workplace would seek to increase fulfilling work activities, minimize drudgery, and distribute the differential human effects of work equitably. Assuming there are no constraints imposed by the allocative mechanism (to be discussed below), how would we structure a factory, office, or service center to promote fulfilling work?

First consider the problem of democratic decision-making. We can group decisions into two general types. Some affect the whole workforce more or less equally: for example, decisions concerning the length of the work day, the introduction of a comprehensive new technology, or the timing of breaks. Others might affect primarily only a small group, for example, the division of tasks within a subdivision of a workplace, or a change in machinery in a single operation in a plant. To have participatory democracy within a workplace means that the whole workforce together makes decisions. For the first type of decision we require one person one vote. But for the second type the most directly affected groups must be allowed greater influence.

In a capitalist firm with accounting, finance, production, research, and personnel departments, decisions might be made by a board composed of department heads. Each officer would have relative autonomy in his/her division, bringing decisions that were already tentatively made to the board for ratification. Of course the board might decide that a departmental decision impinging on the whole operation had to be reversed, but presumably this would not happen often. With regard to general policy, the department heads would deliberate and finally vote—perhaps following the lead of a dictatorial chairman, but perhaps not. From a socialist perspective, the problems with this approach are its aims and its exclusion of the workforce. However, this is a function of ownership, class relations, and market pressures; the concepts of voting, departments, relative autonomy, and "oversight" are adaptable to a socialist economic system.

For example, in a socialist workplace there could be a general workers' council composed of all workers, division councils, and work groups composed only of those people who were immediately involved with one another during the work day (though, of course, the definition and purpose of divisions would be different than in capitalism). Each unit would make decisions relevant to its own operations within the context of decisions made at more inclusive levels. There could be committees to prepare written comparisons of proposals that were too complex for simple treatment. There might be a whole divison for addressing technological innovation, job redefinition, etc. But the principal point is that all decisions would be made democratically with all concerned parties free to express their opinions and vote, roughly in proportion to the extent to which they will be affected by the outcome.

But what if only a few individuals dominate at each level? What if initiatives come from only a few individuals, who dominate discussions, and votes follow their lead almost automatically? When meeting attendance inevitably dwindles, won't we have returned to a situation reminiscent of capitalism but without owners?

This potential "internal evolution" of the most democratic workplace structure leads many people to conclude that all efforts to create non-hierarchical, participatory institutions are doomed. But what would cause such a degeneration of participation into an unequal division of power? Why would such a class division—between coordinators and workers—evolve?

The simplistic answer is that some people are inherently more intelligent, aggressive, and capable than others, so sooner or later they would inevitably come to dominate. But this view is ignorant. First, the right to make decisions about one's own circumstances does not rest upon being the smartest or most knowledgeable on every question. Second, it is *never* the case, unless institutional relations make it so, that *the same* individuals will be best informed and most knowledgeable about *all* aspects of the workplace. Third, it can *never* be the case that a small set of individuals knows the feelings, desires, and capabilities of everyone else, better than people know these things themselves, yet it is just this information that is most critical to decision-making of the sort we are discussing. And fourth, and for our purposes most important, to the extent that differences between people—in their capacities to make decisions, plan, and conceptualize—are so great as to promote patterns of dominance and submissiveness, they are socially produced, *not* genetic.

There are at least three social factors accounting for these differences. One is obviously an unequal distribution of income which allows differential access to intellectual and cultural involvement and time for reflection. But under socialism this would disappear for reasons that will become clear when we discuss allocation. The second factor is schooling. To prevent the development of a division of labor between conceptual and executionary work it would be essential that *all* students in a socialist society became well-educated in general studies and well-versed in critical thinking. "Liberal arts" under socialism would be precisely that knowledge and experience that was a prerequisite for participation in democratic decision-making at all levels of society.[4] The third factor that promotes unequal development of decision-making capacities is the structure of the workplace itself.

For example, if workers in a production department do only rote manual work, while a few others are responsible for redesign and coordination, then obviously the second group would continually enhance its conceptual skills and the first would just get more and more bored.

At this point the cynic might say, "Even if you are right, what would you have us do? I suppose you'd like to see everyone do all jobs on a rotating basis every day. What naivete!" But even though there is a very significant place for job rotation in socialism, this is too extreme a proposal and an obvious "straw man." Jobs that are boring, debilitating, dangerous, or otherwise undesirable, as well as jobs which are unusually gratifying, skill inducing, or empowering, must be shared equitably among the whole workforce. These would be rotated, *within the constraints of the difficulty of learning them and the human and material costs incurred by discontinuity*. But there would be other reasons for job rotation on an optional basis. First, individuals would benefit from learning a variety of kinds of work over their lifetimes. Second, plant operation as a whole would benefit as each individual became personally familiar with more of its diverse aspects and their interrelations. And finally, democratic decision-making would be enhanced as people became accustomed to different aspects of the work process and could therefore better understand and empathize with the situation of others.

So for both "defensive" and "positive" reasons technology would be designed and job allocation determined to meet three goals: (1) Every individual would be regularly involved in *both* conception and execution. (2) No individual would long occupy positions that presented unusual opportunities to monopolize influence or knowledge. (Indeed, jobs which permitted such monopolization would themselves be progressively eliminated by the restructuring of technologies, work roles, and workplace social relations.) (3) And there would be an equitable distribution of the human benefits and costs of work. The point here is straightforward: To avoid class division, and eventually a new form of class rule, it is necessary to avoid institutional relations that bestow differential conceptual capabilities and managerial powers in a regular pattern. Just as private ownership of the means by which we must all produce and survive cannot be allowed if there is to be material equity, so fixed hierarchies of social planning and decision–making power cannot be permitted if there is to be real economic democracy.

But what are the implications of what we have said for issues of racial, sexual, and political hierarchy? Each of these hierarchies contains dynamics that are oppressive in different, but no less important, ways from class hierarchies. Their *roots* lie predominantly outside the economic sphere, but, nonetheless, when these kinds of oppressive hierarchies exist within a society, they inevitably appear and are reinforced within the economy as well. In capitalism, for example, patriarchy has its roots in kinship relations, but is exacerbated by the sexual division of labor in the workplace, unequal incomes for men and women, and other economic factors. In societies with coordinator economic relations, the authoritarianism of the political sphere is aggravated by the command character of economic relations, and sexism and racism are reinforced by an unequal division of work burdens and rewards along sexual and racial lines. To eliminate sexual, racial, and political hierarchies two things must be done. The principal task is for socialists to directly transform the social relations that produce these oppressive dynamics in their individual spheres of origin. That is, kinship, political, and community relations must be changed to no longer generate hierarchical divisions. But the economic system must be transformed as well so as not to continue promoting racism, sexism, and authoritarianism.

We believe this second task can be carried out by the kind of economy we are describing. In a society in which socialist values come to prevail in the kinship, political, and community spheres, features of our economic system—material equality (still to be discussed), elimination of fixed divisions of labor, and self-management—would all enhance the anti-racist, anti-sexist, and anti-authoritarian character of social life. But initially special safeguards would have to prevent sexist and racist outcomes. Briefly, minorities and women would constitute social groups with special interests with respect to which their influence would be accentuated, even within the operation of participatory democracy. In this essay, however, we are focusing on the operation of a well-established socialist society and its economy.

SOCIALIST CONSUMPTION

How should consumption be organized under socialism? In general we seek a context in which consumers can maximize their fulfillment and development with equal consideration for all. To accomplish this we suggest formation of consumers' councils at the level of the neighborhood, ward, region, and so on. To promote participatory decision-making that is socially responsible we want outcomes to be decided by people at the level most affected, but subject to review by councils at more inclusive levels.

What kinds of consumption decisions would arise? Individuals would have to choose between different kinds of relatively private goods and services. Neighborhoods would ask for things like parks, clinics, or new centers for study or play. And regions might request new transportation vehicles, major housing renovations, etc. With decisions at the higher, more inclusive levels made first, the structure of layered councils allows all concerned at each level to participate equally in the debates and voting on options.

Consumption is inherently a social process. The consumption of one item instead of another affects which irreplaceable resources will be used, what workers must do, and the human characteristics of the consumers themselves, and thereby the social relations they will be able to form with others. Some consumption induces social interaction and solidarity, while some is highly private. Compare communal music or sports facilities with the sight of a jogger running along with headphones.

The ideal situation would be for individuals and all larger units to assess their desires in light of the implications for others. Likewise, we would wish a household to question an individual's preferences, a neighborhood to question a household, and so on, whenever socialist norms seemed threatened. But we would propose that the larger units only be permitted to overrule the consumption requests of the smaller units when the request impinged unduly upon the rights of others. In other words, whenever someone felt that a consumption request was not in the best interests of the group making the request, in terms of socialist values, there would be room for the kind of discussion that takes place among friends today. But only when a proposal was judged unmindful of the right of others to have their needs addressed on an equal basis would social pressure be brought to play.

In any case, the freedom to consume what one desires, within the constraint of its being producible at a reasonable social cost, and the right to influence the consumption choices of larger groups of which one is a member would go far beyond what the average consumer enjoys under either capitalist or coordinator economies. This follows from the most striking and unusual feature of the consumption model we are presenting: one's consumption does not depend upon what work one does. Rather, to consume the means of life and development is treated as a human right, to be exercised in the context of everyone else's equal right, and not to be abrogated or threatened because of anything that happens in some other area of daily life. But to see how this could work, we need to describe our model of socialist allocation.

SOCIALIST ALLOCATION

Let us first simplify the problem by considering a world of a hundred people. Let us assume they value egalitarianism, democracy, and variety, and have designed political, cultural, and kinship institutions embodying these values. How might they organize their economy?

They could have a contest, a lottery, or perhaps a brawl to determine who would own all the resources. The "losers" would then hire themselves out for a wage to the "winners." But such a system would obviously guarantee inequality, hostility, competition, and the degradation of work. In short, it would be capitalism.

Or they could make the best educated or most ruthless responsible for planning the entire economy for the rest of them. These planners would carefully determine (mostly by asking everyone a lot of questions) what work people could do, what people liked and disliked, and what the stock of resources was. Then the planners would calculate a plan that everyone would follow. But if the planners, and a few others they might appoint to relay their instructions, monopolized leadership positions surely they would begin to see themselves as more knowledgeable than those who merely carried out decisions and surely they would come to substitute their own desires for those of the populace. Gradually differences in skill and knowledge would become enlarged to the advantage of the few and the detriment of everyone else, and the planners and their aides would ask fewer questions of the citizenry and give them more and more orders to obey. In other words we would have a coordinator economy with an elite class of planners wielding disproportionate power over all economic decisions.

In any case, neither the contest nor elite planning approach could possibly help everyone discover how their work and consumption fit together with the work and consumption of others. Nor would either of these approaches build empathy and solidarity. Even if we could prevent the development of antagonisms between people who won the contest and those who lost, or between people who plan and those who must carry out their plans, neither arrangement could meet the positive requirements of a socialist economy.

The solution, we believe, has the virture of simplicity. Instead of providing the central planners with the information they need to calculate a plan, people could talk *to each other*. Different people could do different things after talking to each other about what each needs from the others in order to carry out his or her work and the human costs and benefits of all the different possible activities. If everyone contributed to their capacity, all would have an equal claim on the product in order to meet their different needs.

Each group of workers (those doing farming, making clothing, or housing, etc.) would inquire about the needs and desires of all the others. Consumers' projected benefits would be taken into account by each work group alongside their own benefits and debits from doing the work. Moreover, considerations such as environmental impact and the effects on social values and relationships would be given their fair weight too because, as we shall see, there is no incentive *not* to consider these things in the system we are proposing. For example, a debate over alternative energy options would not only address the relative efficiency of the different options in providing electricity or other forms of energy, but also their effects on ecological relations, health and safety, and even problems of culture and political relations. By means of this dialogue, everyone would learn the social consequences of their activity and make proposals for what they would prefer to produce and consume.

Obviously the "initial" proposals of all the work and consumption groups would not "mesh" and form a "feasible plan." Instead some things would be in over-supply, but most things would be in excess demand. But based on reports about what everyone thought about the initial proposals, and based on calculations of what the average consumption request and average work commitment were, people would make new proposals. The key incentive in this process of proposal revision and resubmission is that ultimately each group's proposal must be accepted by all the other groups. If a consumption request unjustifiably places a significantly greater burden on society's productive abilities than the average request, there is no reason to believe that it would be accepted by the other consumption groups. Similarly, if a work commitment falls below the average effort others have agreed to, it would be rejected unless accompanied by a reasonable explanation. In other words, it is in the interest of every group to convince all the other groups that its proposal does not imply a higher regard for the well-being of its members than for the rest of the participants in the economy. Yet the "social iterative" procedure we have outlined for "converging" to an economic plan preserves the right of initiative for the individual groups who will be carrying out the activities agreed to.

A repeated sequence of iterations —proposals are made, assessed, altered in light of the assessments and new information, assessed again, etc. for a few rounds—would ultimately "converge" to a feasible plan, not by magic, but because the iterations would progressively whittle away excess demands by reducing unjustifiable consumption requests, increasing unfair work commitments, and shifting resources and labor from low priority tasks to higher ones. But the process would also involve all people in deciding on the plan, increase everyone's knowledge about the situation of others, sensitize everybody to each others' needs, and prevent emergence of an elite group of planners or managers.

But is such a system adaptable to a large, modern, complex economy? Or does its feasibility rest on the small scale we chose for the model—100 people—and the possibility of face-to-face negotiations? Can a society with millions of products, hundreds of millions of people, intricate technological choices, and immensely complicated interdependencies engage in an allocation procedure of this sort? Is there just too much information for each council to take into account? Does the number of people and distance between them preclude empathy and solidarity?

Clearly these are serious questions. But the solution cannot be to label the vision utopian and fall back on some variant of central planning or markets. For we have seen that these are intrinsically incompatible with socialist aims. The fact that we know how to establish these systems doesn't mean that we should rush to do so. We mustn't seek to solve the problem of overwhelming information by leaving out the most important information of all—the human consequences of economic activity—as both central planning and markets do in their different ways.

We believe that the model described here *can* provide the basis for a system of socialist allocation for large, modern economies. Of course the give and take of information exchange would have to be carefully streamlined. The process of sequentially assessing plan proposals and making new ones would have to be organized in a way suited to a relatively prompt convergence to a collectively agreed set of actions. But this is possible. Elsewhere we have discussed how, by using the information contained in the previous year's plan, the material consequences of different proposals involving tens of thousands of different items can be compared and evaluated by workers' and consumers' councils themselves. We describe how adjustments can be made in the evaluation components taken from last year's plan during the planning process to hasten the shifting of labor and resources to more productive activities. And we describe how computer terminals and storage systems already well within the scope of present computer technology can readily assist the councils and federations of councils not only in calculating quantitative implications of proposals with immensely long sequences of consequences for other councils, but also in storing and accessing the more complicated but more critical information concerning the human and social consequences of different economic choices. Actually, technology far more powerful than that required to carry out the kind of planning we suggest already exists. It is now possible, for example, to create a book sized computer device with a screen into which one can insert cassettes containing pre-recorded books, musical scores, or other forms of stored information and art. Indeed, with such a device and just a few cassettes an individual would literally be able to carry the entire offering of titles in a major library in his/her pocket, and have a retrieval capacity greater than any modern library affords. If it isn't misused such technology is grounds for optimism not only regarding the possibility of storing and accessing large quantities of information, but also for making available much more knowledge and culture than has ever been in reach of the public before. The main problem is not technically processing the quantity of information associated with making social economic decisions in even the largest, most complex economies, but summarizing it in ways that will allow each council to take it into account in decision-making. However, this too is possible, as we have elaborated in some detail elsewhere.[5]

In any case, every step made toward inclusion of more qualitative information is an improvement upon what is now done in modern planning and market economies. It is essential to remember this. The seeming advantage of the "quantitative approach"—the numbers are objective, verifiable, manipulable—is gained by ignoring the human aspect of economic activity. That is, by ignoring that which must be central to a socialist social order.

The socialist planning system we envision involves a social, iterative procedure. Each council uses past experience and an accumulated record of prior planning communications to estimate the kinds of efforts others would have to expend to provide a proposed list of inputs, and the uses to which others could put a proposed list of outputs, and then makes its own initial proposal. Upon seeing all other units' first proposals, the council would get new information to work with. It would immediately be told whether each good or sevice in the economy was in excess supply or demand. Descriptions of human inputs and outputs would provide improved information about the human effects for others of different options. Cross-council comparisons and averages would show what were typical production proposals and consumption requests, and how far each council diverged, either above or below the average. And this is precisely the kind of information that is required for the members of each council to collectively reassess their own proposals and amend them in light of concern for themselves and for other participants in the economy as well.

A person who worked in a plant producing bicycles, for example, might find out that many more bicycles were desired than bicycle councils as a whole had proposed to produce. It would thus be socially desirable to increase production if it could be done without incurring great difficulties in the workplace. But should one's particular plant increase output? You would want to check your proposed output and inputs against that of other bicycle plants to see how you compared to the average in the industry, for output could be increased either through greater effort by those already working there or by an increase in the amount of resources and labor used. You would also want to check the degree of excess demand for bicycles compared to other items to see if a transfer of resources to the bicycle industry was warranted or if the excess demand for bicycles was simply the result of aggregate excess demand to be expected in early iterations. On the other hand if you were in a neighborhood council requesting bicycles, you would want to consider cutting back, and one of the first things you would check is whether your request was under or over the general social average. In the next round bicycle producers would either increase their proposed output or conclude that the needs of consumers did not warrant either a shift of labor and resources or an increase in the intensity—and therefore danger and/or unpleasantness— of work in the bicycle industry. Consumers of bicycles would make similar assessments and either cut back or persist in their requests.

To design a system of this kind, prevent it from getting bogged down in endless haggling, and ensure that it will converge in a reasonable time to a desirable social plan is no mean task. But then no one ever claimed that socialist planning would be easy. Our own feeling is that the major amendments to the simple structure described here will involve devising mechanisms for shortcutting information processing and forming federations of councils at many levels in each industry to allow for larger scale planning and coordination between similar units. One way to see some of the possibilities is to consider how the planning system would handle three often irksome problems of economic coordination: (1) unforeseen changes in needs or production failures; (2) designing major new production techniques; and (3) making choices between major economic projects that substantially affect resource and labor allocation over long periods—for example, rebuilding cities versus retooling a major industry.

If a production council agreed to a year-long plan but unforeseen conditions led its members to feel they wanted to make revisions, they would communicate to the industry wide council their wish to cut back production, their reasons, and request that other firms in the industry take up the slack so no consumption plans would need to be altered. But if other units in the industry could not make up the shortfall, the industry federation would have to request that consumption federations cut back their use of the good in question. Similarly, if a consumer council agreed to a plan and then for some reason wanted to change its demand for food, for instance, its new request and the reasons for it would be communicated to the appropriate agricultural councils. Perhaps they would agree to meet the new request, or perhaps they would be unimpressed. In any case, the basic give-and-take procedure would be similar to the initial planning process itself. By building some slack into production quotas, and recognizing that often changes would largely counter-balance one another, we can see that the economy could be organized to handle this sort of uncertainty fairly smoothly. In any case, this is a practical problem which plagues the operation of any economic system, but can be handled at least as efficiently in material terms, and more efficiently in social terms, by participatory planning than by other models.

The problem of designing and implementing new technologies is more complex. Many times workers in plants would come up with new ideas themselves. Yet the fullest elaboration of such ideas, the careful calculation of all their implications, and the conceptualization of certain new innovations will require investigation using expert skills of particular sorts for extended periods. Workers bearing the responsibility for current production will not be in a position to perform all the tasks necessary for making rational decisions about new technological possibilities. So while it is not desirable to create a specialized economic strata of technologists who design society's future by designing its new technological infrastructure, some division of labor seems necessary. The solution to this conundrum is the creation of research and development departments in all production and consumption units and federations directly responsible to those units and staffed by people who serve on a rotating rather than permanent basis. The kind of research that would be carried out would of course vary from council to council and depend on the size of the federation the R&D department was attached to. But the principles of a rotating workforce and oversight by the council or federation would be the same in every case.

Finally, although we have not dwelt on the interface between the economic and political institutions of a socialist society, the economic system we have described would only be compatible with a state that was truly democratic and participatory in the broadest sense. We would expect that some of these political channels would be employed along with the federations of economic councils in setting broad economic priorities. Not all desirable economic transformations can be carried out at the same time. Cities will need to be restructured. Whole industries will need to be redesigned and retooled. Broad issues of greater fulfillment now versus development for later benefit must be addressed. Although the federations of production and consumption councils and particularly their research departments will bear the major responsibility for formulating the alternatives as well as tracing their expected long run implications, the major media institutions and political bodies will play a critical role in facilitating the fullest and most informed public debate on these issues as well as ensuring that the final decision regarding an ordering of these social priorities is reached democratically. When these decisions are finally reached they will entail production commitments extending through many planning periods. These commitments would simply be incorporated into future planning efforts as decisions that had already been agreed to.

TRANSITION

We have not dwelled on the kinds of problems we can expect to encounter in trying *to establish* socialist economic relationships because that was not the purpose of this essay. Yet before concluding some mention should be made of "transition problems," even if only very briefly.

The usual worry about transition is that the old capitalist class will somehow reassert its hegemony. We think this is an almost ludicrous fear, at least in the advanced industrial economies. When a truly socialist movement grows sufficiently to challenge and win power from the current rulers of society, there will be little danger that these same rulers will later reassert themselves. On the other hand, there will be another very real danger that will pose many complex problems. That danger is that a revolution that overthrows capitalism in the name of socialism might still fail to create socialism and give rise to a coordinator society instead. The skills and knowledge largely monopolized by coordinators and middle strata are often overrated, but not so overrated that we could reasonably make a case that these individuals' services can be dispensed with in a period of socialist upheaval. Rather, these individuals will be called upon to play an important role in providing expertise and training at many levels. How to welcome their involvement but prevent their dominance over social reconstruction is going to be a difficult problem.

Similarly, citizens used to economic life under capitalism are going to find many of the organizational impositions of socialism demanding and sometimes annoying. In the face of this inevitable disorientation there will be a deep tendency on the part of all sectors within the economy to gravitate toward old and familiar ways of doing things. Sometimes this will be to avoid disruption, sometimes it will stem from ingrained habits and/or fear of unfamiliar circumstances. But to create a climate suitable for the most vigorous experimentation and growth of consciousness and knowledge is going to be very difficult even though it is of the utmost importance. Opposition to the most egalitarian and democratic aspects of socialist economic relations is not going to come only from people whose mind-set is geared toward establishing a coordinator economy, but also from many of the most

conscientious working people themselves. Consumerism, individualism, and self-doubts run deep in all of us, not to mention racism and
sexism which will also remain significant problems for some time in the
new society. And in addition to negative carry-overs from capitalism,
some of our best instincts, such as the desire for efficiency, will often
work against pursuit of participatory economic relations. In sum,
without pretending to have addressed transition in any kind of depth,
the point we wish to make is that "transition" has meaning as a concept
only as a bridge, and as a bridge it must touch ground at both ends. The
problems of transition are a function of this necessity—that programs
respect people's immediate needs and inclinations and yet also aim
without compromise for socialism and not some pitiful, oppressive,
false facsimile.

Returning to socialist allocation as we propose it, the idea should
now be clear. Participatory planning allows units to coordinate their
activities democratically, consuming according to need and in light of
the social relations of production, and producing according to capabil-
ity and in light of the social worth of consumption. It is a means of
social planning without centralization or competition, but with a
dynamic that reinforces empathy between democratic councils. Decisions are made in light of all their human implications—both for
immediate fulfillments and for the development of people's capacities
and tastes over time. What to build, what technologies to create, how to
structure factories, neighborhoods, and even whole cities, how to
conduct day-to-day economic activities: all are determined in accord-
ance with people's desires and skills. The economic plan is socially
determined yet its various aspects are at every step proposed and
elaborated directly by people most intimately involved with carrying
them out. We believe the participatory, iterative model is the only
economic form that embodies *both* self-management and social solidarity as central aspects, and that can reinforce both of these attributes in
democratic councils and in all people who engage in economic activity.
We believe it is the only economic form which addresses the criticism
of capitalism expressed by Karl Marx in the *Grundrisse:*

> The social character of activity and the social form of the
> product, as well as the participation of the individual in
> production, appear here as alien material things in opposition
> to the individual; not in their behavior to each other, but in
> their subordination to relations which exist independently of
> them and arise out of the collisions of indifferent individuals.
> The universal exchange of activities and products has become
> a condition of life for each individual and the bond between
> individuals appears to them as something alien and indepen-
> dent, like a thing.

Through the iterative mechanisms we have described, councils will have to take account of the well-being of all in drawing up their economic plans. Each worker's activity will have to benefit society at the same time that it furthers the worker's fulfillment, and each consumer's request will have to reflect a sensitivity to workers' situations as well as to the consumer's own needs. In sum, individuals and groups will have to be motivated by very different values and understandings from those that now prevail. Is this possible?

HUMAN MOTIVATION UNDER SOCIALISM

While we have not, in this essay, addressed the possibility of attaining socialism against all the forces of the capitalist state, culture, etc., it is incumbent upon us to address another question about possibility: Can people behave in a socialist manner? Is it reasonable to expect people to act as we have described, taking one another's needs and potentials seriously, being active yet non-competitive and un-selfish?

We must admit that in our current experience whatever "good behavior" we might encounter, there is also a vast amount of lazy, envious, competitive, racist, and sexist behavior going on all around us, all the time. Greed is one of the themes of capitalist daily life, not a fiction of novelists searching for interesting plots. At the same time, the common assumption that all this anti-social behavior and consciousness is a function of innate programming embedded in our genetic structure, is unwarranted. It is logically just as possible, and theoretically far more compelling, that this anti-social behavior is embodied in the institutions around us and imposed upon us by the constraints of having to act within those institutions and the roles they offer us. Sociobiology notwithstanding, there is simply no scientific nor even remotely compelling argumentation to justify an assertion that personality types of any sort are wired into our genetic structure, let alone that anti-social dispositions have a priority place there. On the contrary, it can be argued quite forcefully that many of our most basic institutions have built-in tendencies impelling us toward adopting anti-social traits. Even in this short essay we have shown, however briefly, that allocation through competitive markets or central planning inevitably leads to anti-social behavior. So it is our contention that in a socialist society, where institutions are redesigned to promote solidarity, variety, and self-management, and where survival is assured, people could be sociable and empathetic, and both human nature and social forms would make oppressive behavior as irrational as most humane behavior is in our present context.

Under socialism workers will work because they understand the importance of their tasks and the ways they interrelate with other people's efforts, because they self-manage their own labors, and because of the direct rewards of socially valuable, self-managed, collectively shared creative activity. Painful jobs will be rotated, their assignment and definition continually reevaluated. Artisan values will be prevalent and workers will be able to take pride in their efforts. The free time generated by eliminating wasteful production will go in part to increasing leisure and in part to allowing more artistry in useful work which people would rather not automate. In short, workplaces and work processes will be conceived with human need and scale in mind.

As a worker under socialism would you hold back your energies, or try to honestly commit your capabilities to meeting society's needs? Everyone has an interest, and understands their interest, in the overall well-being of the community. Consumers recognize when work is painful and try to moderate their requests accordingly while the character of worklife has changed dramatically. In these circumstances we believe workers will seek to ensure that *everyone* benefits from their efforts to the greatest possible extent. We think collective behavior will come naturally under socialism as we have envisioned it because it would be in each worker's interest to behave this way just as competition, authoritarianism, laziness, sexism, and racism are standard defensive responses of people seeking to survive and rationalize worklife under present day capitalism.

Likewise, as a consumer under socialism would you ask for all that you could dream of? Or, given your knowledge of the social relations behind the products you seek, the investment patterns society has chosen and their rationale, and the importance to the whole community of cooperative behavior, wouldn't the pressures of the council system as well as your own desires for community mitigate against excessive requests and cause you to assess possibilities in a socialist manner?

Contrary to the situation prevailing now under capitalism, in a socialist society a person's well-being would not be a function of the number of goods he or she possessed. One needn't accumulate goods as a buffer against unemployment and hardship. Nor would accumulated goods impart status or power, or be necessary as a substitute for the otherwise unavailable goals of community, sociality, or love. On the contrary, by pursuing consumption that was unnecessary but caused producers considerable difficulties, a person would be risking loss of friendship and empathy to no purpose. Under capitalism you try to squeeze as much as you can out of a system hostile to your needs; under socialism you try to further a favorable system of which you are and feel an integral part. This, we believe, explains the possibility of the economic relations we have described.

The obvious benefits that will derive from the transition to socialist economic relations include material well-being for all, self-management, improved conditions of work, skill enhancement, sociability and solidarity, and human scales of technology. Some benefits, however, are more derivative and subtle.

For example, the relationship of work to community and kinship will alter. All economies produce not just things but also social relationships and human characteristics. In capitalist society, class dynamics both embody and enhance patriarchal and racial divisions, and are in turn embodied and enhanced by these. For example, capitalist jobs are culturally and sexually stratified in ways that are dysfunctional for workers and adopted only to enhance capitalist stability and reproduce white and male supremacy. But under socialism there is no owner to profit (nor coordinator to manage) and so the economic bases of racism and sexism are overcome. And if community and kinship relations are also directly revolutionized—for they are not simply functions of the economy—then racism and sexism can be fully uprooted.

Furthermore, there will not only be changes in interpersonal relations of all kinds, but in the relations between people and nature as well. In capitalism nature is regarded only as an object to be used. The capitalist drive to accumulate makes ecological failures inevitable in two senses: first, we exploit nature so rapaciously that we endanger our very existence by ignoring environmental limits and dangers; and second, we break all bonds with nature, destroy ecological balance and variety, and thus diminish the *quality* of our surroundings. In a coordinator mode little of this changes. The manipulative approach to life remains, and so does a drive to accumulate and the ecological consequences have been equally disastrous. But under participatory socialism we will have an economic arrangement which neither compels growth nor propels instrumentalism. This is not to say that socialist economies will not *choose* growth that is both desirable and ecologically balanced, but only to point out that socialist economic relations will sensitize people to the processes behind consumption and production. Our pleasures will relate to the final good *and* to the chain of its development. This will enhance our empathy with other people's capacities, needs, and desires, and it will also promote consciousness of natural balance and of the merits of the evolution of our planetary ecology as against the short-term experimental guesses of "scientific experts." The resulting ecological awareness, both a sensitivity to natural limits and to a balance with nature and the earth, will support projects aimed at human scales of production and technology, and the replacement of sprawling metropolitan centers by networks of townships which physically and psychologically embody the advantages of both city and country life.

In short, the advantages from a change to a socialist mode of production and consumption seem varied and to penetrate every aspect of life. Beyond material well-being and equity—each critically important in its own right—there will also be many qualitative advances; and the need to elaborate the socialist vision so that these might become more readily apparent is a practical political priority.

We are certainly not contending that the model presented here is complete. Nor, obviously, have we even broached the difficult problems of revolution itself, or more than touched upon the complex initial stages of construction of new economic relations when old habits still prevail. But the fact that the model seems to require immense changes in our understanding of economic activity, huge advances in communication and information processing, and other similar leaps into an only loosely charted future cannot be reason for shunning further investigation. Moreover, even if our model does prove flawed in some essential way, a critical point of this essay will be unaffected. For an economic system to embody self-management and solidarity rather than class rule by a few, it will have to preclude all fixed divisions between conceptual and executionary labor. But this requires the abandonment of markets and central planning as methods of allocation. Likewise, the pursuit of the positive goals of self-management and solidarity exclude markets and central planning. So even should the model we have put forward prove less viable than we currently believe it to be, the implication is *not* that as socialists we should re-embrace either "old model" seeking to reform it in a "progressive" way. Neither enlightened market allocation nor enlightened central planning can provide a fertile breeding ground for socialist economics in a new society. A new model, whether ours or another, is a prerequisite to further progress.

Are we being utopian? It *is* utopian to expect more from a system than it can possibly deliver. To expect equality and justice—or even rationality—from capitalism is utopian. To expect social solidarity from markets, or self-management from central planning, is equally utopian. To argue that competition can yield empathy or that authoritarianism can promote initiative or that keeping most people from decision-making can employ human potential most fully: these are utopian fantasies without question. But to recognize human potentials and to seek to embody their development into a set of economic institutions and then to expect those institutions to encourage desirable outcomes is no more than reasonable theorizing. What is utopian is not planting new seeds but expecting flowers from dying weeds.

NOTES

1. We call this broader perspective a "holistic approach" and it is elaborated in detail in our *Unorthodox Marxism* (1978), *Marxism and Socialist Theory* (1981), and *Socialism Today and Tomorrow* (1981), all published by South End Press, Boston. Many of the arguments and ideas expressed in this essay are developed in one or another of these three volumes, often at greater length and with more practical and historical examples. There, too, the reader will find extensive bibliographic materials.

2. A full, multi-sided discussion of these issues appears in *Between Labor and Capital*, Pat Walker ed. (Boston: South End Press, 1980). Our own contribution is titled "A Ticket to Ride: More Locations on the Class Map."

3. See *Between Labor and Capital*, especially Sandy Carter, "Class Conflict: The Human Dimension."

4. Although we have many disagreements with Rudolf Bahro's views as set forth in his *The Alternative in Eastern Europe* (London: New Left Books, 1977), he does address this question in detail and with much sensitivity. Also relevant is the work of George Konrad and Ivan Szelenyi, *The Intellectuals on the Road to Class Power* (New York: Harcourt, Brace, Jovanovich, 1979).

5. Albert and Hahnel, *Socialism Today and Tomorrow*.

SOCIALISM AND THE MARKET
Michael Harrington

Having become a socialist at a time when every left Hegelian academic as well as would-be messiahs like Weitling had detailed blue prints for the good society, Karl Mark rightly refused to spend much time talking about the nature of the socialist future which he advocated. He outlined principles and general characteristics—from each according to his/her ability, to each according to his/her need; cooperative production; the radical increase in free time; and so on—but, profound democrat that he was, he then insisted that the victorious socialist workers would decide how they would be implemented.

Our situation is quite different from Marx's. Societies proclaiming themselves to be "socialist" rule over one third of the earth's surface. And there is a sixty year history of democratic socialist parties participating in the elaboration and administration of a more humane version of capitalism. Moreover, there is a ferment in the democratic socialist movement right now, a recognition that the Thirties' models of socialism (public property and democratic planning) as well as the Sixties' models (capitalist welfare states with socialist governments) are irrelevant. In Sweden the most radical proposal for a change in the structure of ownership ever made by a mainstream socialist party will be debated in the upcoming elections (it provides for "collective profit sharing" and decentralized social ownership).

So I agree very much with Michael Albert and Robin Hahnel: it is time to talk seriously, not simply of transition programs that go beyond the welfare state, but of socialism itself. Moreover, I think that their attempt to do so is stimulating, a contribution to the discussion. I will, of course, focus on my disagreements with it but that fact should not obscure my recognition of the value of their work. That said, let me focus on three questions: the nature of Communist (but not communist) societies in the world today; socialism and technology; consumption and production under socialism and, in particular, the use of the market as a socialist device.

To begin with, I have no substantial disagreement with Albert and Hahnel about the broad characteristics of Communist societies. They are class societies, politically totalitarian and therefore economically inefficient, which reproduce some of the worst aspects of capitalist alienation. When, however, Albert and Hahnel talk of "existing socialism," even in quotation marks, I have a disagreement which touches on more than semantic strategy. I know the use made of that term by Bahro in his fascinating analysis of—my phrase—bureaucratic collectivist societies. But I am against any vocabulary which obscures a radical fact: that there are two alternatives to capitalism not one. Thus, even though I often agree with those who see the Soviet Union and similar systems as "state capitalist," I think their name implies that the old categories are still on the track, that there is either capitalism or socialism.

In fact, as I have argued in a number of books, there are tendencies toward bureaucratic collectivism on both sides of the East-West dispute. Indeed some of the proposals for planned capitalism, like Felix Rohatyn's, move unwittingly in the direction of an authoritarian collectivism which could come to resemble a liberalized, but still totalitarian, Communism. Therefore I think it is politically important to choose labels which show that the fundamental choice is the one between the democratic communitarian and authoritarian collectivist successors to capitalism. When Albert and Hahnel write about the "coordinators" in late capitalism and Communism, they clearly recognize the substance of my point. I only propose that their language reflect that knowledge more precisely.

Second, and much more substantively, in their discussion of the problem of routine and boring work under socialism they make an error which Harry Braverman warned against in *Labor and Monopoly Capital*. Capitalist technology is *capitalist* technology, i.e. the design incarnates an attitude toward humans in general and workers in particular. In general—and Marx caught the trend as it was beginning in his magnificent analyses of the factory in Volume I of *Capital*—the guiding principle of capitalist technology has been the elimination of people from the production process or, where that is not possible, the expropriation of skill and decision-making, the routinization of work. Therefore, Braverman rightly argued, one cannot talk about the creation of socialist relationships of work within the context of an anti-socialist technology.

I am well aware that Marx himself, and many Marxists since, talked of the rotation of tasks as one of the ways in which boredom could be dealt with under socialism. But I think the other Marxist strand is, in the light of technological developments in the century since Marx's death, more important: to propose the wholesale elimination of such monotonous and unthinking jobs by means of a technology built upon socialist values. That requires new conceptual ways of defining efficiency and productivity, two of the most value-laden and bourgeois terms in the present economic debate. It is obviously visionary but, I think, also more realistic than the proposals made by Albert and Hahnel.

Third, and in some ways most important, there is the question of how to make production and consumption decisions in a socialist society.

To begin with, the capitalist model outlined early in the article is much too Smithian (or classically Marxist, for Smith and Marx analyzed the same type of capitalism). And more to the present point, they also simplify in their discussion of the market principle. Where the market operates within the framework of capitalist inequality (which, as Albert and Hahnel rightly insist, is a functional necessity of the system), there is corporate price fixing, rigged choices (between private cars and deteriorating or nonexistent public transit), institutionalized mendacity and pseudo-wants promoted by advertising as well as pervasive governmental intervention to subsidize the social costs of the system and thus to obscure the actual calculus of cost and benefit, and of course the outcomes are unacceptable to socialists. That is, so to speak, a tautology: capitalist markets are structured to yield capitalist outcomes.

But is that true of markets *per se*? I think not. Just as interest rates used to measure the yield of a given investment are different from interest rates which transfer wealth to an elite class, so markets under socialism would have a quite different impact than they do under capitalism. Let us assume that income and wealth are distributed in a roughly equal—"from each, to each"—fashion; that price and production decisions are made democratically in the full light of day; that the advertising industry is replaced, so to speak, by a socialized system of consumer reports; and that the government is democratized (more on that in a moment). Under such circumstances, consumers could, by free choice, provide decentralized, instant information on the details of private, discretionary spending.

This does *not* mean that the market dictates the production decisions (it doesn't even do that under capitalism any more). Obviously, the society will make investments which do not pass the test of capitalist efficiency but meet the different criteria of socialist efficiency. It does mean that, particularly in areas where taste is of importance (style, the color of clothes, etc.), the market could be a much less cumbersome device than the consumer councils envisioned by Albert and Hahnel.

Secondly, I would think that a good number of macro-economic choices in a socialist society would be made *politically* and would be an element in its pluralism (again, the genuine pluralism, not the capitalist pseudo-pluralism). For example, the question of how much increased wealth should be expended on material needs and how much in shortening the working day (Marx viewed the latter as the key to the leap from the kingdom of necessity to the kingdom of freedom) has to be made by the whole society. But a given industry or plant could then democratically determine how to organize the time for its tasks. There is, as the Yugoslavian experience demonstrates (and there is a limited, but real, relevance to that experience since it develops within an authoritarian political system and a relatively under-developed economy), egotism of the enterprise and of the region. That is resolved politically.

Thirdly, on the consumption side, socialist society would seek to take the necessities out of the sphere of commodity relations by making them free, i.e. socially financed. In, say, the health sector an individual's claim on resources would be determined by need. However, it is precisely in this free, public sector where the Albert-Hahnel proposal on consumer councils comes into its own. Hospitals and health systems in general should be, with regard to all non-technical decisions, controlled by both the providers *and* the consumers (a conception which was incorporated in Ron Dellums' bill for a national health service).

In the sphere of wants and tastes—as compared to the sphere of necessities—I can see another use for the market principle: the rationing of luxuries which are, by their nature, in limited supply, e.g. excellent wine.

Finally, I quite agree with Albert and Hahnel that *the* distinguishing mark of socialist production is the growth of non-material incentives and criteria for action. But given the experience of this century with enforced, compulsory "voluntarism," this is obviously at the end of a long process of cultural and psychological change and great care must be taken to avoid a subtly coerced "cooperation." Indeed, I would argue—and in this I think I am simply repeating Gramsci—that the growth of new forms of motivation will come spontaneously, as the indirect consequences of directly planned changes in the way decisions are made and wealth and time are allocated.

THE COUNCIL MODEL OF DECENTRALIZED PLANNING
A Critical Analysis
Carmen J. Sirianni

The ideal of a democratic and egalitarian alternative to capitalist society has inspired millions for nearly as long as capitalism itself has existed. And the values underlying that ideal—justice, freedom from exploitation, individual development, community, democracy—have formed the critical core of philosophical thought and popular culture throughout the ages. It is the distinctiveness of Marxism to have appropriated these values for a critique of economy and the division of labor. Yet, as powerful as the Marxist critique of capitalism has been, the *alternative* of a democratic, pluralistic, and egalitarian political economy has *never* been practically *or* intellectually compelling. In advanced capitalist societies that have enjoyed parliamentary democracy, a relatively wide variety of personal freedoms, life options, and consumer choices, this deficiency has represented a serious obstacle to an egalitarian politics that goes beyond social democracy. And social democracy, as valuable as its achievements have been, is unlikely to be able to see us through the profound economic and ecological crises before us, when the intolerably unequal distribution of the world's resources will demand a solution, when technological changes associated with microelectronics will dramatically transform divisions of labor and labor markets, and when the democratic demands of the world's population are not likely to be easily contained. Now more than ever, the challenge to make the socialist vision concrete and compelling must be taken up by activists and intellectuals alike.

Michael Albert and Robin Hahnel have taken this challenge more seriously than most in their writings over the past few years. Decisively breaking from authoritarian and economistic versions of Marxism, their work has helped legitimate the utopian dimensions of socialist theory and practice. This article and especially their recent book *Socialism Today and Tomorrow*, which develops some of their ideas in greater detail, represent a welcome contribution. Their attempt to outline the relevant issues and practical problems in a way that is understandable at the level of everyday activity is very appropriate, since theoretical discussions and technical models alone cannot yield systematic solutions or an appropriate politics. Although a much more technically based discussion than can be presented here of the political economy of a socialist alternative is warranted, let me indicate in this brief response what I see as some of the major problems in Albert and Hahnel's model.

Their basic assumption sets them apart from much of traditional Marxism: there should be no fixed division between conception and execution in the organization of work. There should be no permanent class of workers deprived of the opportunities to develop creative talents and to exercise initiative in the social division of labor. This is a basic tenet of democratic and egalitarian socialism today. But the model that Albert and Hahnel put forth is not adequate to the task of institutionalizing the equality and variety of outcomes that they intend. This model, which has emerged as the implicit basis of critique in most Marxist analyses of the labor process since Braverman, is a slightly modified version of what I have referred to elsewhere as the "productive integrity model."[1] It holds that all workers of each workplace share a broad range of both conceptual and executionary tasks of that unit, so that all have access to creative tasks and all can understand and control the entire production process. The entire society is composed of workplaces where *all* involved in *each* particular workplace perform both conception and execution, where none performs a disproportionate share of either, where all have an equal say over all fundamental decisions of that unit, and where all actually participate more or less equally. As appealing as this model sounds, it does not adequately allow for flexibility of work options. There is little room in it, for instance, for the possibility of individuals transferring their responsibilities for routine and less creative tasks to work units other than their primary work council. The institution of such flexibility (whether it be in response to shifting patterns of friendship, love or workmate relations, conflicts between the spatio-temporal requirements of certain jobs and family needs etc.) is absolutely essential for achieving variety of outcomes and broad options for individual growth and fulfillment. A pluralistic model of work opportunity must allow for more flexibility than simply the right to remove oneself completely from one council in order to assume a full range of tasks in another, despite what may very well be legitimate needs to engage in some of each. In short, the singular council as the locus of the individual's performance of a full range of conceptual and routine tasks is too narrow and rigid a basis for a societal division of labor that expands opportunities and options.

Related to this, and of no less importance, is the fact that it is not an adequate basis for achieving relative equality in the social division of labor. In a complex society, there will be many workplace units where the range of tasks therein is considerably less creative, challenging, and rewarding than in other units. Compare a university or medical complex, for instance, with a retail outlet or a restaurant. This is particularly true in view of the fact that alternatives must be created in the context of inherited technologies and divisions of labor, and opportunities for creative work for everyone will not necessarily be found within units whose preservation appears as necessary or relatively desirable under existing circumstances. Or at least not opportunities that everyone places a relatively high value on . . . and would be willing to train to do competently. Without cross-unit institutional mechanisms for distributing certain tasks on a relatively equitable basis, the productive integrity model could conceivably serve to legitimate significant and unacceptable inequalities among work units, and hence among different occupational groups and individuals. The institutionalization of more flexible options for the purposes of broader equalization and greater individual opportunities, even if this could occur only gradually, would significantly modify the assumptions of a council-based productive integrity model—more so than the minor modifications for which Albert and Hahnel do in fact allow.[2] Such modifications would have to permit in many workplaces less than holistic commitments in terms of both tasks and participation, and hence would have to institutionalize equitable forms of exercising power other than those of the completely egalitarian and radically democratic council. Such modifications would make things considerably more complex than the relatively homogeneous producer council infrastructure of Albert and Hahnel, and these would undoubtedly create certain tensions with democratic and communal values. Unfortunately, space does not permit a fuller discussion of these. Let it simply be said here that the absence of a very broad range of knowledge and control by each worker in each workplace unit would not necessarily disqualify such individuals from intelligent control over their lives or of global production, if adequate alternative opportunities were available for creative work and participation. Nor would the flexibility of options among less than holistic work roles necessarily undermine solidarity and community, if adequate supports for these were diffused throughout other institutional and informal spheres. And the council model elaborated by Albert and Hahnel does not pose as a problem an entire set of related issues that will continue to persist even in an egalitarian society: namely, "career" paths and steps within certain occupations, differential access to *some* of the conditions for further achievement, and meritocratic standards of evaluation.

Another issue that Albert and Hahnel's model does not adequately address is that of participation time. In fact, in both production and consumption there seems to be an enormous overload in the degree to which people must participate to make the model work. For example, they argue that "each council's final proposal must be accepted by all other work and consumption councils."[3] In a complex society with multifarious interconnections among a great array of production and consumption units, such a requirement could not possibly be met through open council meetings and fully participatory democracy—even if the information about other council proposals and their qualitative impacts were extremely summary. The days are simply not long enough, and people will invariably recognize the flaw of a model that requires that they spend much more time participating in decisions about work than actually working. This extraordinary escalation of time commitments is also implicit in Albert and Hahnel's model of consumption. True, "consumption is inherently a social process" in some sense, but there is no need to make it oppressively so. If, in a neighborhood council of up to 1000 people,[4] every consumption decision (on how much and what consumption items to request, and how to distribute individual items among all members) had to be filtered through a council meeting, people would spend 24 hours a day evaluating each other's relative needs. Would I really have to attend a council meeting just to order a bicycle?

This model appears particularly oppressive in view of their requirement that "the members of a consumption council can insist on a discussion of any individual's proposal."[5] Presumably, the individual would have to attend a meeting if anyone questioned his or her request for a particular item. Even in view of the individual right simply to assert equity and, hence, end the discussion, this procedure would undoubtedly be experienced as burdensome in the extreme, and thus as irremediably impractical. As a runner (who also happens to like group sports), I must say that the apparently self-evident lesson to be drawn from the comparison of the lone jogger to the experience available through communal sports facilities was particularly worrisome in this regard. If a friend were to question my running (with or without headphones), I would spend some time explaining how it can be a pleasurable or meditative experience. If someone insisted in a council meeting that I justify yet another order of running shoes instead of basketball sneakers (or even of headphones), I would tell that person to mind his or her own goddam business—and get on with the meeting.

But I wonder whether this entire idea of consumer councils, at least in the way presented, is not fatally flawed. It is rather difficult to imagine that, at this stage in the development of freedom of choice in the realm of consumption, and of urban civilization itself, all or even the vast majority of one's choices could be filtered through a single neighborhood unit. Albert and Hahnel insist that one would always have the right to leave a consumer council, but this is really beside the point. The ease with which one sets up a new organization of this sort, or relocates to another, is a lot more cumbersome in practice than in theory. And the smaller the unit, the lesser the range of goods one could choose from, or at least keep in stock. But these are minor problems in comparison to others. Can we really imagine people in cities or large towns having to acquire goods through only one outlet? Can we seriously propose to eliminate shopping and the spontaneity that often accompanies it? Would it really be practicable to have to discuss needs for all individual items and order them ahead of time in just the right proportions for each council?

Without belaboring this point, it seems to me that disposable income in the form of money that could be spent freely in retail outlets everywhere (and hence also on a great variety of services provided outside one's immediate locale) would be absolutely essential to a developed socialist society—and certainly one built on the foundations that we will inherit. Once we admit the right to a certain standard of living and individual choice, as Albert and Hahnel do, then the superstructure of consumer councils becomes unnecessarily restrictive, time-consuming, impractical, and potentially oppressive, if not obnoxiously imposing. But it is nonetheless true that consumption is a social activity, and important choices have to be made concerning investment in collective goods versus individual consumables, the environmental and social consequences of certain forms of consumption, etc. And organized discussion of the options faced by communities and the society (and world) at large are absolutely necessary in this regard. But these seem to be, for the most part, the kind of decisions that are best taken at the macro level, through taxation policy, planned distribution of resources, protective regulations, community development plans, and the like, and not at the micro level of everyday consumption decisions. This does not rule out cultural movements to reorient people's consumption habits, but it does not introduce the latter as a necessary part of the very infrastructure of personal choice mechanisms.

What the inadequacy of Albert and Hahnel's consumer council model implies, of course, is the necessity for markets of some sort. Markets have many problems to be sure, yet these have hardly gone totally unrecognized by market socialist theorists.[6] Markets institutionalize self-interest, often with serious negative effects; they cannot satisfy the needs for public goods; they can be dominated by monopolies; they can encourage a commercialization of consciousness; they generate inequalities; and, perhaps least seriously treated by market socialist theorists, they present systematic obstacles to the humanization of work and breaking down the division of labor.[7] However, in a complex industrial society with highly developed individual consumption needs, markets also seem to be quite necessary if we are to avoid the "terrorization of the consumer" by production units (as happens in centrally planned economies), even if this is unwitting; if the structure of supply is to adapt flexibly to the structure of demand; if we are to avoid the systematic waste of productive resources (admittedly not an unproblematic concept), the concealment of productive reserves, the overestimation of required supplies. These irrationalities are not simply the product of the centralized character of planning in Soviet-type societies. And in Albert and Hahnel's iterative mechanisms, there is no systematic check on them. In fact, there is no systematic check against the permanent bias of information (including all the estimates of the impact of economic decisions) in favor of each producer council providing it. In a complex society operating under conditions of relative scarcity, as well as anonymity of most producer-consumer interchanges, only mechanisms rewarding the optimization of producer self-interest could adequately deal with these problems. In such a society, one cannot assume an optimal harmonization of interests simply through repeated discussion and processing of unbiased qualitative and quantitative information. One cannot assume that collective behavior will come naturally as each recognizes that this is in his or her own self-interest. The problem of the "free rider" is far from being simply the result of capitalist structure and individualist culture.[8] An economic system cannot be built on the basis of the presumed honesty and good intentions of all the participants and freely interactive units.

Transparency in economic relations is certainly an important aspect of democratic socialism, but its achievement in a complex society could only be relative, partial, and, in many ways, ex post facto. It would be an absolutely impossible requirement for democratic planning to have to anticipate the full range of qualitative impacts of all economic decisions through the interactive exchange by each individual council of "vivid pictures" of "all their alternative possible material and human inputs and outputs."[9] If each individual council had to evaluate qualitatively and quantitatively each decision relative to each other council in terms of the "changes in individuals' personality traits, talents and skills, levels of understanding, attitudes and values, the changes in social relations within the group, and the degree to which different needs would be fulfilled or thwarted"[10]—paralysis would result. If every self-interested economic decision had to be fully calculated beforehand in terms of mutually agreeable and simultaneously achievable interactive effects, there would be no economic activity. Exchange relations based on asymmetries of power and information are inevitable in a complex society that is responsive to high levels of individual freedom and personal choice—and invariably spring up in the interstices of centrally planned economies to enhance responsiveness and choice.

The task before us, then, is not to reject markets out of hand as a generalization of the war of all against all, or as the totalization of commodity fetishism. Rather, it is to begin to theorize more clearly and concretely the various frameworks and boundaries within which the pursuit and optimization of individual and workplace self-interest can occur without sacrificing cooperative values, collective goods, the humanization of work, and relative equality. That is, we need to investigate the various ways that market exchanges can be articulated with planning, regulatory, corrective, and redistributive mechanisms. Albert and Hahnel never seriously analyze the possible combinations of markets and democratic planning, but merely assert that markets and central planning are each too "addictive." Developing the mechanisms for regulating the most noxious aspects of markets, without sacrificing their positive effects, represents an enormous challenge, to be sure, though we are hardly ignorant of some of the ways of mitigating environmental costs (a problem that the council model solves only by sleight of hand), or protecting labor from total subordination to the logic of markets. These, and many other mechanisms, need to be developed further, rather than being abandoned in the hope of discovering the institutional framework that will eliminate all competitive self-interest and "require" friendship, sharing, and love throughout.[11] Institutional imperatives of this sort are a pipedream even in the most developed utopian arrangements conceivable. But the belief that we could dismantle highly developed markets in the first generations of socialist construction is a far more dangerous illusion.

NOTES

1. Carmen Sirianni, "Production and Power in a Classless Society: A Critical Analysis of the Utopian Dimensions of Marxist Theory," *Socialist Review*, no. 59 (Sept.-Oct. 1981), 33-82, where these arguments are developed in greater detail, and the contours of a "global pluralist model" are indicated.

2. For example, *Socialism Today and Tomorrow* (Boston: South End Press, 1981), p. 296.

3. Ibid., p. 293.

4. Ibid., 289ff.

5. Ibid., p. 293.

6. See, for example, Wlodzimierz Brus, *The Market in a Socialist Economy* (London: Routledge, 1972); and *The Economics and Politics of Socialism* (London: Routledge, 1973).

7. See also in this regard Ellen Turkish Comisso, *Workers' Control Under Market and Plan* (New Haven: Yale Univ. Press, 1980).

8. Mancur Olson, *The Logic of Collective Action* (Cambridge: Harvard Univ. Press, 1965).

.9 Albert and Hahnel, *Marxism and Socialist Theory* (Boston: South End Press, 1981), p. 178.

10. *Socialism Today and Tomorrow*, p. 305.

11. Ibid., p. 288.

REJOINDER
Michael Albert & Robin Hahnel

We use the term "existing socialism" in deference to popular usage. But we argue that "existing socialist" economies are neither socialist nor capitalist, but "coordinator." Coordinators monopolize information and use it to maintain their own economic dominance. So, indeed, there is a third economic form little superior to capitalism and vastly inferior to true socialism. But despite these agreements with Harrington we additionally argue that, if corrupted by either central planning or markets, socialized ownership will lead to coordinator dominance rather than a people's economy. Further, we would rather not adopt the name chosen for those unfortunate societies by both their ruling elites and their capitalist enemies. "Communism," whether with large or small "c," is a label that deserves a better fate.

But we certainly agree with Harrington that technologies bear the imprint of surrounding social relations and that a socialist reconstruction of technologies will make work more rewarding, safe, and equitable. However, we feel this will occur only if technological reconstruction is implemented according to egalitarian democratic criteria. Socialist technologies will not materialize simply because socialist militants desire them. Nor, in our opinion, can they blossom in a setting defined by competitive markets or central planning. Therefore, while socialist technologies can certainly bring great improvements, it is unconvincing to argue like Harrington that they will appear without structural antecedents to then solve our most difficult problems. New technologies will spring from new social relations and aims, not vice versa. To successfully create the new technologies Harrington and all socialists desire, *as a prerequisite* we must have new socialist social relations and values largely in place. And while participatory planning can generate these values, competitive market structures and central planning cannot. To pin socialist hopes on socialist technologies instead of socialist social relations mixes up cause and effect.

Harrington argues that capitalist markets yield lousy results because they are "capitalist" not because they are "markets." We disagree and find this type thinking dangerously misleading. The question is not whether the combined effects of capitalist ownership and markets are worse than those of social ownership and markets. For socialists, the answer to that question is obvious but largely irrelevant. What really matters is whether competitive market relations have anti-socialist features even in the context of socialized ownership. We argue there is every logical reason to believe that markets—in and of themselves—tend to promote individualist competition, commodity fetishism, and anti-social decision-making; to isolate producers and consumers and impede social solidarity; to bias resource allocation in regard to production of public goods and externalities; and to promote technocratic norms and coordinator dominance. Perhaps we make this theoretical argument too briefly in this essay—we thought we should spend more time criticizing central planning—but in addition to the theoretical reasons for rejecting markets, there is overwhelming empirical evidence corroborating their faults. Indeed, Harrington's example of the Yugoslavian economy is also the one we use to substantiate our own more detailed presentation in *Marxism and Socialist Theory*. In Yugoslavia, not only is there commodity fetishism, privatized consumption and production, and economic inequality, but also a decentralized version of coordinator class dominance instead of real workers' self-management. Whereas Harrington would seemingly trace these, as well as all other ills in Yugoslavia, to their heritage of economic underdevelopment and non-democratic aspects of the political structure, we argue that despite their many ill consequences, these factors cannot be convincingly blamed for the particular ills listed above, whereas market dynamics can.

It doesn't help that Harrington offers a variety of political restraints to mitigate market faults. Saying he doesn't want market determination of production decisions doesn't tell us how we should make such decisions. Would the part of the economy saved from the logic of market allocation be run by central planning or by some form of participatory planning? And if it is to be the latter, would it look like what we have outlined or not? If what we have outlined is overly burdensome and unwieldy for the economy in general, then why would it be appropriate for the "free, public sector?" And, if participatory planning is acceptably superior for goods like health care, as Harrington suggests it might be, then why not for all goods? In our opinion Harrington gives away the debate by admitting our procedures may be best for "social goods" for, in fact, all goods are social and involve externalities—a major point of our analysis in the first place.

Sirianni's first criticism is that our model won't embody equality and variety to the extent we claim. He argues that our system would needlessly bar workers from doing manual or repetitive work other than where they have their creative jobs. He also says it would penalize workers in plants with few creative tasks since they would have little access to self-actualizing work.

On the latter point there is only a misunderstanding. Workers in a plant with too little conceptual work should all share equally in what's available, but if it isn't enough to provide a stimulating work experience, of course they should also work elsewhere. Likewise, other workers in relatively privileged production settings should do a stint in more backward environments. Whether this "sharing" is handled by splitting time between different production settings each day or week or during different seasons is a matter to be settled pragmatically. But wherever someone works he/she must be a full participant in the workers' council.

But as Sirianni fears, we do doubt the value of conceptual workers in plant 'a' doing all their repetitive work in plants 'b' or 'c'. For this would do nothing to demystify authority relations in plant 'a'. It is exactly like the Chinese having bureaucrats and managers work a month in the fields instead of in their own workplaces. No doubt it is better than Chinese bureaucrats doing no manual labor at all. But it misses the real point of what Sirianni himself calls "integrated work." Only a menu of balanced job offerings in each workplace ensures that all workers will command equal respect, have comparable knowledge and confidence and therefore participate equally in decision-making in their workplace. Having all the engineers operate lathes two days a month across town in their own little machine shops—with their friends—while production workers in each plant get two days off for conceptual work in the isolation of their homes may be nice, but it won't prevent class differentiation inside the future workplace. After all, production workers engage in a variety of creative conceptual activities in their leisure time now; and many engineers do manual work in their basements and garages. But this has little impact on contemporary class divisions in the capitalist workplace.

While it might make life less challenging for intellectuals to exempt them from rote tasks in their places of work, it would also undermine the social dynamics necessary to ensure social equality and collective self-management. Moreover, if workers do not win access to creative work in their familiar workplaces, they are not likely to get it in less familiar surroundings. Finally, the insights that come from each participant doing a variety of tasks in one work process are lost if workers do different tasks in different places. To be honest, for us the presumed discomfort of coordinator and intellectual workers performing executionary tasks in their usual workplaces isn't really a damning problem at all. Instead, it is part of the price paid to allow all workers a real say over their work lives. And a more serious problem, in any case, is the fact that many workers will only gain fully equitable roles after a period of adjustment, having to endure continuing disparities in "richness of worklife" in the meantime. Indeed, during this period of economic adjustment and restructuring, oversensitivity to temporary discomforts of intellectual workers—rather than the discomforts themselves—represents the more serious problem, one threatening to humanistically impose coordinator norms in place of socialist ones.

Sirianni also criticizes us for underestimating the time-consuming implications of our model. One response is that if participatory planning can save all the time wasted by market generated ecological disasters, mis-allocation of productive resources, production of useless goods, advertising, and packaging, etc.; then it would have to waste an incredible amount of time in meetings and negotiations indeed to come out a loser on balance. In the U.S., for example, it has been estimated that under 10 percent of labor time goes into productive, socially beneficial ends.

A second response is that it is disconcerting that Sirianni ignores our detailed treatment of these matters in *Socialism Today and Tomorrow* when criticizing the time-using implications of our system, after citing the larger study for other purposes. The planning procedure we outline does *not* entail meeting every day, or even every week or month, to discuss all economic consumption. It does not suggest that all goods will be gotten from a single place. Nor does it suggest that all consumption decisions will be reached in local councils. In *Socialism Today and Tomorrow* we go to considerable length to explain how a network of local, regional, and state councils can arrive at a plan in a collective, participatory manner with a relative minimum of hassle and waste. We describe a number of short-cutting devices for use whenever people find that continued meeting and/or haggling is not worth the time it occupies.

Moreover, Sirianni's related concern that people's private consumption patterns would be forcibly altered has little basis in anything we propose. There may be discussions about whether isolated people should jog in musical oblivion behind buses spewing pollution, or exercise in clean parks where social activities can also occur. But so long as any individual, or collective, is making requests whose total social costs are not excessive (and therefore oppressive to others), they will be free to persist against others' criticism. Sirianni makes it sound like each and every council's requests will have to be examined, item by item, by every other council before they are OK'd. This is *not* the case. Neighborhood and individual workers' councils' proposals do not ordinarily have to be reviewed by councils outside their regional and industry federations. And individual items and details need not be reviewed in any case. We consider it a prime advantage of our system that all parts of all proposals can be retrieved by any person or collectivity in the economy that wishes to do so. The information is collected, stored, and accessible to all—as are various aggregations, averages, and evaluations of all proposals. But this does not imply that everyone need avail him/herself of all these possibilities. To portray our system in this light is to criticize a caricature.

But our third response to criticism like Sirianni's is to ask what are the alternatives? Suppose we are grossly underestimating the time necessary to arrive at a plan through our procedures. We are not overestimating the time people now spend shopping for "best buys," and the extra time everyone must work to pay for useless packaging and rehabilitation from the ill effects of market-sponsored antisocial production techniques, pollution, and useless production. Nor are we wrong that markets promote coordinator/worker hierarchies within the workplace and antisocial economic interaction and personality development in the citizenry. Sirianni is apparently so worried that people would engage in time-consuming bickering under our system that he would forswear any attempt to develop a participatory, social approach to consumption and production, and instead search for ways to mitigate these ill effects of markets. And Sirianni is willing to suggest this route even though the structural failings of markets are inimicable to socialist development and can no more be wholly mitigated by government reform than the exploitative ills of private ownership can be wholly mitigated by welfare capitalism. Why doesn't Sirianni instead suggest ways of improving the participatory planning model to mitigate *its* weaknesses? After all, the faults Sirianni finds with our version of that model—he calls it time-consuming, inflexible, imposing—are much less endemic to the system's basic structures, and far less damning, than the faults he himself admits with markets—he agrees they are socially divisive and productive of class differences. Obviously focusing intellectual power on the problems of participatory planning has many fruits yet to bear. But continued efforts to rationalize the failings of markets will provide little sustenance for socialists, and will only serve the defense of particular capitalist or coordinator programs.

Part of the problem may be that Sirianni thinks the responsibility for creating solidarity and democratic impulses can be left to spheres other than the economy. For example, he suggests that choosing between less than holistic work roles needn't undermine solidarity if supports for solidarity are diffused through other social institutions. We agree on the need for other institutions to embody socialist norms, but we doubt such norms will prevail anywhere if they don't prevail pretty much everywhere, and certainly in the economy.

Perhaps the clearest indication of our differences with Sirianni lies in his view that "in a complex society operating under conditions of scarcity . . . mechanisms rewarding the optimization of producer self-interest" are necessary. And "an economic system cannot be built on the basis of the presumed honesty and good intentions of all the participants." The tone of these sentiments is 100 percent wrong. They are incapable of generating a socialist economics. A socialist economic system is a set of economic institutions that will move people toward collective self-management based on "honest" assessments of the effects of decisions in light of "good intentions" directed at all participants. To reject the possibility of such a goal is to deny the possibility of socialism. The idea that the socially isolated pursuit of self-interest—what we call greed—can be a basis for a socialist economy is more than a little hard to swallow. Sirianni thus inadvertently shows that those who propose markets for socialism are driven to more or less embrace this peculiar notion. No doubt not only Marx, but also Adam Smith would be amused.

This is not to deny the half-truths in Sirianni's concerns. "Under conditions of scarcity" indeed it cannot be presumed that *people with a long history of antagonistic relations* will automatically behave honestly and with good intentions toward one another. And, of course, "in a complex society" we cannot presume individuals will automatically or easily be able to deduce the full effects of their own and others' decisions. Moreover, socialism does require increasing complexity. And scarcity will remain with us always since every individual's time is limited. All this (and more) is true enough, and certainly poses powerful obstacles to building socialist economic forms. But it is precisely these obstacles that socialist economic institutions should be designed to overcome. We were not unmindful, for a moment, of any of these problems when we outlined the system Sirianni rejects. We specifically attempted to design an information system that would de-mystify a complex economy and promote honesty by making dishonesty impossible to conceal—rather than rejecting complexity or opting for a system that hides information about the workings of a complex economy from its inhabitants. We specifically tried to design an incentive system that would give people a self-interest in taking account of social interests in making their proposals—rather than relying solely on good intentions in an environment of irresistible temptations. Of course, it is possible that our proposals fail in these regards, that totally different mechanisms are required, or that improvements are needed in the ones we have suggested. But what is not possible, and what is, in fact, literally utopian, is to continue believing that markets (and incentives based on "optimization of individual producer self-interest") can overcome the historical obstacles to socialism. In the end Sirianni allows himself to be overwhelmed by the historical legacy that socialism must transform. He becomes convinced that real socialism is impossible, and so he becomes indistinguishable from the opponents of socialism who have long argued that scarcity, complexity, and human nature make capitalism (or some form of coordinator society) inevitable.

Finally, it is interesting that the history of workers' movements gives considerable evidence of the validity of our analysis. Not only do past revolutions illuminate the dangers of coordinator and bureaucratic rule, but when workers' movements become both militant and well organized they almost always form workers' and community councils. And in times of upheaval, if workers choose to maintain economic functions, they invariably begin planning their activities through social interchanges with other economic units rather than centrally or by technocratic calculations based on market prices.

Economists have not yet formulated a complete model that employs neither markets nor central planning, one that emphasizes participatory forms that workers gravitate toward when they express their desires most freely. And of course, no such allocation system has been adopted in any contemporary society. Instead, anti-capitalist economists have generally pledged allegiance either to markets or central planning models even though these systems have unequivocally demonstrated their incapacity to promote social well-being and collective self-management and the case against them is theoretically and empirically compelling. In this context we hope socialists will put their efforts into refining non-market, non-central planning alternatives instead of falling back on failed forms as if they were irrevocable facts of life rather than mutable, dispensable human creations.

SUGGESTED READINGS

Albert, Michael, and Hahnel, Robin. *Unorthodox Marxism*, Boston: South End Press, 1978.

Albert, Michael, and Hahnel, Robin. "Ticket to Ride: More Locations on the Class Map." In *Between Labor and Capital*, Pat Walker, ed. Boston: South End Press, 1980.

Albert, Michael, and Hahnel, Robin. *Marxism and Socialist Theory*. Boston: South End, 1981.

Albert, Michael, and Hahnel, Robin. *Socialism Today and Tomorrow*. Boston: South End, 1981.

Alderfer, Hannah et al. *Diary of a Conference on Sexuality*. 1982 (available from Beth Jaker, 299 Riverside Drive, Apt. 9B, New York, NY 10025).

Alperovitz, Gar, and Lynd, Staughton. *Strategy and Program: Two Essays Toward a New American Socialism*. Boston: Beacon, 1973.

Bahro, Rudolf. *The Alternative in Eastern Europe*. London: New Left Books, 1978.

Balbus, Isaac. *Marxism and Domination: A Neo-Hegelian, Feminist, Psychoanalytic Theory of Sexual, Political, and Technological Liberation*. Princeton: Princeton University Press, 1982.

Benello, C. George, and Roussopoulos, Dimitrios, eds. *The Case for Participatory Democracy: Some Prospects for a Radical Society*. New York: Grossman, 1971.

Berkman, Alexander. *What Is Communist Anarchism*. New York: Dover, 1972.

Bobbio, Norberto. "Are There Alternatives to Representative Democracy?" *Telos*. No. 35, Spring 1978.

Bobbio, Norberto. "Why Democracy?" *Telos*. No. 36, Summer 1978.

Boggs, James, and Boggs, Grace Lee. *Revolution and Evolution in the Twentieth Century*. New York: Monthly Review, 1973.

Bookchin, Murray. *Post-Scarcity Anarchism*. Berkeley: Ramparts, 1971.

Bookchin, Murray. *The Limits of the City*. New York: Harper Colophon, 1974.

Bookchin, Murray. *The Ecology of Freedom: The Emergence and Dissolution of Hierarchy*. Palo Alto: Cheshire Books, 1982.

Bowles, Samuel and Gintis, Herbert. "Education, Socialism, and Revolution." In *Schooling in Capitalist America*. New York: Basic Books, 1976.

Buber, Martin. *Paths in Utopia*. Boston: Beacon, 1958.

Burkes, John P., et al., eds. *Marxism and the Good Society*. New York: Cambridge University Press, 1981.

Cabral, Amilcar. *Unity and Struggle: Speeches and Writings.* New York: Monthly Review, 1979.

Callenbach, Ernest. *Ecotopia.* New York: Bantam, 1977.

Campen, Jim, ed. *Socialist Alternatives for America: A Bibliography.* New York: Union for Radical Political Economics, 1974.

Cardan, Paul. *Workers' Councils and the Economics of a Self-Managed Society.* London: Solidarity Pamphlet 40, 1972.

Carens, Joseph. *Equality, Moral Incentives and the Market.* Chicago: University of Chicago Press, 1981.

Coates, Ken, ed. *Can the Workers Run Industry?* London: Institute for Workers' Control, 1968.

Coates, Ken, and Singleton, Fred, eds. *The Just Society.* Nottingham: Spokesman, 1977.

Cohn-Bendit, Daniel, and Cohn-Bendit, Gabriel. *Obsolete Communism: The Left-Wing Alternative.* New York: McGraw Hill, 1968.

Corrigan, Philip; Ramsay, Harvie; and Sayer, Derek. *Socialist construction and Marxist Theory: Bolshevism and Its Critique.* New York: Monthly Review, 1978.

Coser, Lewis, and Howe, Irving. "Images of Socialism." In *The Radical Papers,* Irving Howe, ed. Garden City, NY: Anchor, 1966.

Crosland, R. A. *The Future of Socialism.* New York: Schocken, 1963.

Cross, Nigel, et al., eds. *Man-Made Futures.* Lawrence, MA: Hutchinson, 1974.

Dahl, Robert A. *After the Revolution? Authority in a Good Society.* New Haven: Yale University Press, 1970.

DeLeon, Daniel. *Two Pages From Roman History.* Palo Alto: New York Labor News, 1959.

DeLeon, Daniel. *Socialist Reconstruction of Society.* Palo Alto: New York Labor News, 1977.

Diquattro, Arthur. "Market Socialism and Socialist Values." *Review of Radical Political Economy.* Vol. 7, No. 4, Winter 1975.

Dofny, Jacques, and Arnaud, Nicole. *Nationalism and the National Question.* Montreal: Black Rose Books, 1977.

Dolgoff, Sam. *The Anarchist Collectives: Workers' Self-Management in the Spanish Revolution, 1936-39.* New York: Free Life Editions, 1974.

Draper, Hal. "The Two Souls of Socialism." *New Politics.* Vol. 5, No. 1, 1966.

DuBois, W. E. B. *The Education of Black People: Ten Critiques.* New York: Monthly Review, 1972.

Ehrenreich, Barbara. "Family Feud on the Left." *The Nation.* March 13, 1982.

Ehrenreich, Barbara; Hess, Elizabeth; and Jacobs, Gloria. "A Report on the Sex Crisis." *Ms.* March 1982.

Engels, Frederick. *Socialism: Utopian and Scientific.* New York: International Publishers, 1935.

English, Deidre; Hollibaugh, Amber; and Rubin, Gayle. "Talking Sex: A Conversation on Sexuality and Feminism." *Socialist Review*, No. 58, July-August 1981.

Erasmus, Charles J. *In Search of the Common Good: Utopian Experiments Past and Future*. New York: Free Press, 1977.

Feldberg, Roslyn. "Women, Self-Management, and Socialism." *Socialist Review*. No. 56, March-April 1981.

Freeman, Harold. *Toward Socialism in America*, 2nd edition. Cambridge, MA: Schenkman, 1982.

Friedland, William H., et al. *Revolutionary Theory*. Totowa, NJ: Allanheld, Osmun, 1982.

Friedmann, John. *The Good Society*. Cambridge, MA: MIT Press, 1979.

Goldman, Emma. *Anarchism and Other Essays*. New York: Dover, 1970.

Goldman, Emma. *The Traffic in Women and Other Essays on Feminism*. Alix K. Shulman, ed. San Rafael: Times Change, 1971.

Goodman, Paul. *Utopian Essays and Practical Proposals*. New York: Vintage, 1962.

Goodman, Percival, and Goodman, Paul. *Communitas: Means of Livelihood and Ways of Life*. New York: Vintage, 1960.

Goodman, Robert. *After the Planners*. New York. Simon & Schuster, 1973.

Gorz, Andre. *Socialism and Revolution*. New York: Anchor, 1973.

Gorz, Andre. *Ecology as Politics*. Boston: South End, 1980.

Gorz, Andre. "Nine Theses for a Future Left." *Telos*. No. 48, Summer 1981.

Guerin, Daniel. *Anarchism: From Theory to Practice*. New York: Monthly Review, 1970.

Harrington, Michael. *Socialism*. New York: Bantam, 1972.

Harrington, Michael. "What Socialists Would Do in America If They Could." *In Beyond the Welfare State*, Irving Howe, ed. New York: Schocken, 1982.

Hayden, Dolores. *Seven American Utopias: The Architecture of Communitarian Socialism, 1790-1975*. Cambridge, MA: MIT Press, 1976.

Hayden, Dolores. "What Would A Non-Sexist City Be Like? Speculations on Housing, Urban Design, and Human Work." *Signs*. Vol. 5, No. 3 suppl., 1980.

Hayden, Dolores. *The Grand Domestic Revolution: A History of Feminist Designs for American Homes, Neighborhoods, and Cities*. Cambridge, MA: MIT Press, 1982.

Hegedus, Andras, et al. *The Humanization of Socialism: Writings of the Budapest School*. New York: St. Martin's, 1977.

Heilbroner, Robert L. "What Is Socialism?" In *Beyond the Welfare State*, Irving Howe, ed. New York: Schocken, 1982.

Hochschild, Jennifer L. "Why There Is No Socialism in the United States." In *What's Fair: American Beliefs About Distributive Justice*. Cambridge, MA: Harvard University Press, 1981.

Horvat, Branko. *The Political Economy of Socialism: A Marxist Social Theory*. White Plains, NY: M.E. Sharpe, 1982.

Horvat, Branko; Markovic, Mihailo; and Supek, Rudi, eds. *Self-Governing Socialism: A Reader*. White Plains, NY: International Arts & Sciences, 1975. 2 Vols.

Huberman, Leo, and Sweezy, Paul. *Introduction to Socialism*. New York: Monthly Review, 1968.

Hunnius, Gerry; Garson, G. David; and Case, John, eds. *Workers' Control: A Reader on Labor and Social Change*. New York: Vintage, 1973.

Kolakowski, Leszek, and Hampshire, Stuart, eds. *The Socialist Idea: A Reappraisal*. New York: Basic Books, 1974.

Krimerman, Leonard I., and Perry, Lewis, eds. *Patterns of Anarchy: A Collection of Writings on the Anarchist Tradition*. Garden City, NY: Anchor, 1966.

Kropotkin, Peter. *The Conquest of Bread*. New York: New York University Press, 1972.

Lange, Oskar, and Taylor, Fred M. *On the Economic Theory of Socialism*. New York: McGraw Hill, 1964 (1938).

Layton, Lynne, and Papke, Mary. "Planning for a Non-Sexist Society." *Telos*. No. 45, Fall 1980. (Report on a Conference).

Le Guin, Ursula K. *The Dispossessed*. New York: Harper & Row, 1974.

Leiss, William. *The Limits to Satisfaction: An Essay on the Problems of Needs and Commodities*. Toronto: University of Toronto Press, 1976.

Lenin, V.I. *State and Revolution*. New York: International Publishers, 1943.

Lerner, Michael P. "After the Revolution." In *The New Socialist Revolution*. New York: Delta, 1973.

Lerner, Michael. "Recapturing the 'Family Issue'." *The Nation*. February 6, 1982.

Lichtheim, George, "What Socialism Is and Is Not." *Dissent*. Vol. 24, No. 1, Winter 1977.

London, Jack. *The Iron Heel*. New York: Hill & Wang, 1957.

Manuel, Frank E., and Manuel, Fritzie P. *Utopian Thought in the Western World*. Cambridge, MA: Harvard University Press, 1979.

Marable, Manning. *From the Grassroots*. Boston: South End, 1980.

Marable, Manning. *How Capitalism Underdeveloped Black America*. Boston: South End, 1983.

Marcovic, Mihailo. *From Affluence to Praxis*. Ann Arbor: University of Michigan Press, 1974.

Marcuse, Herbert. *An Essay on Liberation*. Boston: Beacon, 1969.

Marcuse, Herbert. *Five Lectures: Psychoanalysis, Politics and Utopia*. Boston: Beacon, 1970.

Marcuse, Herbert. *Counter-Revolution and Revolt*. Boston: Beacon, 1972.

Marcuse, Herbert. *The Aesthetic Dimension*. Boston: Beacon, 1979.

Margolies, Rick. "On Community Building." In *The New Left: A Collection of Essays*. Priscilla Long, ed. Boston: Porter Sargent, 1969.

Marx, Engels, Lenin on Communist Society: A Collection. Moscow: Progress Publishers, 1975.

Meszaros, Istvan. "Political Power and Dissent in Post-Revolutionary Societies." *New Left Review*. No. 108, March-April 1978.

Nove, Alec, and Nuti, D.M., eds. *Socialist Economics*. Harmondsworth, Middlesex, England: Penguin, 1972.

Ollman, Bertell. "Marx's Vision of Communism." In *Social and Sexual Revolution*. Boston: South End, 1980.

Pannekoek, Anton. "Workers' Councils." In *Root & Branch: The Rise of the Workers' Movements*, Root & Branch ed. New York: Fawcett Crest, 1975.

Pateman, Carole. *Participation and Democratic Theory*. New York: Cambridge University Press, 1970.

Piercy, Marge. *Woman on the Edge of Time*. New York: Fawcett, 1978.

Root and Branch. *Root and Branch: The Rise of the Workers' Movements*. New York: Fawcett Crest, 1975.

Russell, Bertrand. *Roads to Freedom: Socialism, Anarchism and Syndicalism*. London: George Allen & Unwin, 1966.

Sargent, Lydia, ed. *Women and Revolution*. Boston: South End, 1981.

Sargent, Lyman Tower. "An Anarchist Utopia," *Anarchy*. No. 104, October 1969.

Schweickart, David. "Worker Controlled Socialism: A Blueprint and a Defense." *Radical Philosophers' News Journal*. April 8, 1977.

"The Sex Issue." *Heresies*. #12, Vol. 3, No. 4, 1981.

Sirianni, Carmen J. "Production and Power in a Classless Society: A Critical Analysis of the Utopian Dimensions of Marxist Theory." *Socialist Review*. No. 59, Sept.-Oct. 1981.

Socialist Labor Party. *After the Revolution: Who Rules: A Socialist Critique of the "Marxist-Leninist" Left*. Palo Alto: New York Labor News, 1978.

Spiro, Melford E. *Kibbutz: Venture in Utopia*. New York: Schocken, 1963.

Sweezy, Paul M. *Post-Revolutionary Society: Essays*. New York: Monthly Review, 1980.

Taylor, Barbara. "Lords of Creation: Marxism, Feminism, and Utopian Socialism. *Radical America*. Vol. 14, No. 4, July-August 1980.

Thomas, Norman. *Democratic Socialism: A New Appraisal*. New York: Post War World Council, 1963.

Trotsky, Leon. *Literature and Revolution*. Ann Arbor: University of Michigan Press, 1960.

Trotsky, Leon. *Problems of Everyday: Life And Other Writings on Culture and Science*. New York: Monad, 1973.

Tucker, Scott. "Right Wing Lightening, Left Wing Thunder." *Gay Community News*. March 27, 1982.

Undercurrents Editors. *Radical Technology: Viable Ways to Live in Harmony with Man and Nature*. New York: Pantheon, 1976.

Vajda, Mihaly. *The State and Socialism*. London: Alison and Busby, 1981.

Walzer, Michael. "A Day In the Life of a Socialist Citizen." *Dissent*. May-June 1968.

Ward, Colin. *Anarchy in Action*. London: George Allen & Unwin, 1973.

Weinbaum, Batya. *The Curious Courtship of Women's Liberation and Socialism*. Boston: South End, 1979.

Weir, Stan. "Informal Work Groups: Invisible Power in the Workplace." *Against the Current*. Vol. 1, No. 4, Spring 1982.

Wilde, Oscar. "The Soul of Man Under Socialism." In *Complete Writings*. New York: Nottingham Society, 1905-09, vol. 4.

Willis, Ellen. *Beginning to See the Light: Pieces of a Decade*. New York: Wideview Books, 1982.

Wolfe, Alan. "Building a Nonrepressive Society." In *The Seamy Side of Democracy: Repression in America*. New York: David McKay, 1973.

Women's Work Study Group. "Loom, Broom, and Womb: Producers, Maintainers, and Reproducers." *Frontiers: A Journal of Women's Studies*. Vol. 1, No. 1, Fall 1975.

Wright, Gwendolyn. *Building the Dream: A Social History of Housing in America*. New York: Pantheon, 1981.

Wyatt, Michael David. *New Age Socialism: Integrating Emotional, Spiritual and Social Liberation*. Chicago: New Age Publishing Center, 1981.

Zukin, Sharon. *Beyond Marx and Tito*. New York: Cambridge University Press, 1975.